# Soviet Civilization

# Soviet Civilization
## A Cultural History

BY

ANDREI SINYAVSKY

TRANSLATED FROM THE RUSSIAN

BY JOANNE TURNBULL

WITH THE ASSISTANCE OF NIKOLAI FORMOZOV

*ARCADE PUBLISHING* · *New York*

LITTLE, BROWN AND COMPANY

First English-language Edition


Originally published in France in January 1989 by
Editions Albin Michel under the title *La Civilisation Soviétique*.

Excerpts from *The Twelve and Other Poems* by Alexander Blok, translated by
John Stallworthy and Peter France; © 1970; reprinted by permission of Eyre &
Spottiswoode Publishers. Excerpts from *Heart of a Dog* by Mikhail Bulgakov,
translated by Mirra Ginsburg; © 1968; reprinted by permission of Grove
Press. Excerpt from "A Cloud in Trousers" in *Mayakovsky* translated and
edited by Herbert Marshall; © 1965; reprinted by permission of Dobson
Books Ltd. Excerpts from *Mayakovsky* translated by Dorian Rottenberg;
© 1986; reprinted by permission of Raduga Publishers.

*Library of Congress Cataloging-in-Publication Data*

Siniavskiĭ, A. (Andreĭ), 1925–
    [Osnovy sovetskoĭ tsivilizatsii. English]
    Soviet civilization: A cultural history / by Andrei Sinyavsky ;
translated from the Russian by Joanne Turnbull with the assistance
of Nikolai Formozov.
        p.     cm.
    Translation of: Osnovy sovetskoĭ tsivilizatsii.
    Includes index.
    ISBN 1-55970-034-3
    1. Soviet Union — Civilization — 1917–     I. Title.
DK266.4.S5813   1990
947.084 — dc20

                                                    90-730

Published in the United States
by Arcade Publishing, Inc., New York,
a Little, Brown company


10  9  8  7  6  5  4  3  2  1
MV PA

*Published simultaneously in Canada
by Little, Brown & Company (Canada) Limited*

Printed in the United States of America

# Contents

# Translator's Note

All poetry and prose extracts have been translated from the Russian for this book except where a specific citation to another work is given. All titles of Russian-language works have been given in English. These titles are of already published English translations where they exist; elsewhere we have supplied our own translations.

# Author's Note

SINCE I WROTE THIS WORK, momentous events have occurred not only within the Soviet Union but throughout Eastern Europe, events almost unthinkable and certainly unpredictable only a year or two ago. Indeed, many Western periodicals have hailed the demise of communism as not only virtually certain but in fact already accomplished.

None of this changes my basic assumptions or assertions about Soviet civilization. Whether the recent wave of events is temporary or permanent, whether it heralds the end of communism or represents essentially a studied, carefully calculated strategy dictated by economic realities and political necessities, only time will tell. But already to sound the universal triumph of capitalism or free enterprise is, to my mind, to misunderstand the basic premise and stability of Soviet civilization, which, I strongly suspect, have not changed nearly as much as the print and television media of the West believe, or would have us believe.

— A.S.

# Preface

THIS BOOK was conceived and created as the result of my appearances before Western audiences where, as an émigré and a writer from Soviet Russia, I was asked many questions concerning my country's past and present. These discussions and debates forced me to scrutinize more closely the familiar features of my mother country, a face as magnetic as it is frightening and repellent.

Civilization as a concept presupposes a duration and stability of forms born long ago and refined by time. Soviet civilization is new. It does not have a long history, although even in a short time it has managed to show itself a very solid and expanding structure in the world arena.

Soviet civilization is a singular and formidable power of the twentieth century, the object of world interest and attention. Singular because it regards itself as the ideal and natural result of historical evolution; formidable because it claims to represent the future of all mankind and, after the Second World War, extended its domain by seizing new countries or spheres of influence. Soviet civilization is so novel and extraordinary that at times even those who grew up within it, who are its children, see it as a sort of monstrosity or alien environment — one, however, in which they belong. The complexity and difficulty of studying Soviet civilization, therefore, consists primarily of being too close to its history. We cannot be dispassionate since we are not historians but contemporaries and witnesses (sometimes even participants) in an ongoing process that will end no one knows when or where.

There are other difficulties too. Because everything about it is so permeated by contemporary life and pressing social problems,

Soviet civilization evokes extremely varied, and often opposing, views. There are no exhaustive or universal answers, nor can there be. Too much is arguable and unresolved.

This subject is vast, since civilization embraces the way of life, the psychology, the regime, the politics — and the literature on all these topics is enormous. I will therefore explore not so much the history of Soviet civilization as the theory and even what I might call the metaphysics. As theoretical aspects I will examine several features or cornerstones (call them what you will) of Soviet civilization, such as the revolution, the State, the "new man."

As part of my examination, I have elected to look at Soviet civilization through the eyes of Soviet literature. For literature, apart from its perspicacity, is composed of symbols. And here it is precisely the symbols, the Soviet epoch's majestic and enduring monuments, that interest us.

"If the symbol is a concentrated image," wrote Trotsky (still unsurpassed as historian of the Russian Revolution), "then the revolution is the supreme maker of symbols, since it presents all phenomena and relations in concentrated form." Literature offers this same concentrated, revolutionary perspective.

The epigraph for this book might be these lines by Aleksandr Radishchev from his ode "To the Eighteenth Century," written circa 1800, but equally applicable to our subject:

> No, you shan't be forgotten, century mad and wise,
> > Damned for ages to come, for ages a marvel to all.
> Blood in your cradle, hymns and the battle roar,
> > Ah, drenched in blood, you tumble into the grave.

# Soviet Civilization

# *1*

## The Revolution

"REVOLUTION" in the context of Soviet civilization refers not only to the watershed coup d'état of October 1917 but to a whole complex of events that provoked it, prepared it, and then prolonged it — from the revolution of 1905, which weakened the power of the tsar, to the hardships and military reversals of the First World War, the revolutions of 1917 and Russia's withdrawal from the world conflict, right up through the final victory of Soviet power in 1922 after five years of civil war. The revolutionary process claims to embrace the numerous aspects of the life of the country and of the world. At the same time, it presupposes the destruction — abrupt, violent, absolutely radical — and reconstruction of the society and its way of thinking, the destruction of all (or almost all) its institutions and historical traditions. Not only inside Russia but worldwide, since the October Revolution was regarded by its makers as only a prologue, the first link in a chain of revolutions that, in theory, would spark a world revolution, the most widespread and definitive in the history of mankind.

Even now, when the revolution in its original sense seems to have left no trace in the life of Soviet society, its energies and stimulants, which were fashioned to cut a universal, global swath, continue to function, albeit in other forms: hence the relentless expansion — ideological, military, political — of Soviet civilization in Europe and in Asia, in Africa and in America. Thus, in the end, and in the ideal, the entire globe would fly the red flag first raised by the October Revolution to signal the victory of a new social order. These same revolutionary propensities still persist, if in utterly distorted forms. Aleksandr Blok, in his poem "The Twelve"

(1918), conveyed these moods in a re-creation of the *chastushka*, or musical folk lyric:

> *To smoke the nobs out of their holes*
> *we'll light a fire through all the world,*
> *a bloody fire through all the world —*
> *Lord, bless our souls!*[1]

This desire to dominate the world matched the intensity and totality of the revolution in its break with all of world history. According to Marx, mankind's prerevolutionary development was only prehistory. Real history would begin with the proletarian socialist revolution, which the October coup d'état was considered to be. Hence these lines by Vladimir Mayakovsky (from his 1924 poem "Vladimir Ilyich Lenin"):

> *Long live*
> > *the Revolution*
> > > *with speedy victory,*
> *the greatest*
> > *and justest*
> > > *of all the wars*
> *ever*
> > *fought*
> > > *in history!*[2]

Incredible pretensions: the only great war and the last. The last aggression and last war, launched in order to obliterate all aggressions and all wars from the face of the earth (forever — imagine!), so that all mankind might finally be — forever — happy and free.

## THE RELIGIOUS ROOTS OF THE RUSSIAN REVOLUTION

How is the revolution viewed by its instigators, its true believers? Like the Apocalypse. As if history had ended and "a new heaven and a new earth" were beginning. The Kingdom of God, Heavenly Jerusalem descending, promising paradise on earth. Yet not by

1. Translation by Jon Stallworthy and Peter France in *The Twelve and Other Poems* by Alexander Blok (New York: Oxford University Press, 1970), p. 147.
2. Translation by Dorian Rottenberg in *Mayakovsky*, vol. 2 (Moscow: Raduga Publishers, 1986), p. 206.

God's will but by man's exertion. This isn't a dream, but a historical law, scientifically proven by Marx, an ineluctable law that will prevail, like it or not. There is only one thing to do: to bring this new world about by means of a joyful and swift revolution.

This logic is a marriage of the most exact historical science (Marxism, by its own definition) and man's religious strivings from time immemorial. This is why the revolution appears so like the Apocalypse, but an Apocalypse grounded in dialectical materialism, devoid of divine intervention, so that the idea of providence is transformed into a historical law ordained by Marx. And it is the Communist or the proletarian — as the ultimate link in the history of mankind, as the "purest man," having nothing to lose but his chains — who enforces this scientific law, who enacts this twentieth-century Apocalypse.

Given this interpretation, one understands the words on the flag of the October Revolution which captivated the masses, and which still fascinate and seduce, not Soviet people, of course, but people in other countries. "All Power to the Soviets!" "Land to the Peasants!" "Peace to the Peoples!" Scanning these truly great slogans, however, one can see that they are mostly biblical and evangelical formulas transposed into the revolutionary vernacular. Minus the name of God, but in the name of man who will become God.

In the Apocalypse, in biblical as well as other prophecies, it is announced that one day, in a single instant, everything will change and the entire human social order will be overturned, the "first shall be last and the last shall be first" (as it says in the Gospel). And in "The International," sung by Communists the world over, we seem to hear an echo of this biblical formula, which gives an impression of Divine Liturgy. This is the verse that corresponds best to the spirit of the revolution and the Apocalypse:

> No more tradition's chains shall bind us,
> Arise, ye slaves, no more in thrall!
> The earth shall rise on new foundations,
> We have been naught, we shall be all!

It is the end of the time and the dawn — via the revolution — of a new era: Soviet civilization.

Other revolutionary slogans also come from the Bible, but in such a way as to exclude the Bible and God while retaining the beautiful words: "Workers of the World, Unite!" or "The Proletarians Have No Native Land." These formulas are, in effect, the famous Christian rule: "There is neither Greek nor Jew" before God, before the new religion . . .

One could devote a whole book to the borrowings or coincidences between communism and the Bible, and this is possible, it seems to me, only because communism and the revolution attempted to fulfill some of the most noble aspirations in the human soul, fundamentally to remake the world, having repudiated everything that went before as wrong or unjust. In this sense communism enters history not only as a new sociopolitical order and economic system, but also as a new great religion denying all others. Dostoyevsky's Pyotr Verkhovensky predicts this in *The Possessed* when he says: "Here, my dear, a new religion is coming to replace the old. That's why there are so many soldiers about."

Marxism-Leninism constantly characterizes itself as the only scientific worldview, the only scientific philosophy, as if it were the most scientific science, in command of the laws of nature and society, the laws of history. But that specific claim on the part of communism does not preclude its religious aspect. Since the end of the eighteenth century, science has grown steadily more powerful, to become the only universal worldview. Modern man must rely more or less on science. He can't get by without it. Thus, even communism's religious appeals are shrouded in scientific forms and formulas.

The powers and the laws revealed by Marxism — productive forces and relations of production, determining economic base and class struggle — play the role of divine providence or ineluctable fate. Once history has attained an ideal state of communism, communism ceases to evolve qualitatively and does not envisage, even in the most distant future, this social system being replaced by another. Just as one doesn't ask what comes after eternity, the question of after communism never comes up: after communism, the ideal state, there will only be more communism, still bigger and better in its "communistness." Communism recognizes no other social or historical science: they are all either not sufficiently scientific or pseudoscientific. This exclusivity, this uniqueness, this claim to holiness are still other ties binding communism and religion. The judgments of the Marxist-Leninist classics are no more subject to doubt or criticism than are the texts of the Holy Scripture or the teachings of the church fathers.

The religion of communism is distinctive in that it applies its doctrine on the grandest scale, affecting all areas of life, all spheres of human endeavor. The sudden transition from dogma to its generalized application requires violence. And wholesale violence requires power. Therefore, en route to the realization of the most just society on earth, the moral and social ideals of communism undergo a sea change: their application is amoral and inhumane. But even here a religious undertone is present. The violence assumes the guise of an expiatory sacrifice, while the role of Almighty God demanding that sacrifice is played by Historical Necessity. With one innovation: here it is not just a matter of self-sacrifice — held sacred through the ages — but of offering up others, the so-called exploiter classes and much more. One might say that what was sacrificed was the past. This very closely resembles religious rituals dating back to primitive, prehistoric cults and involving the immolation and cremation of the past, to ancient rites celebrating the periodic renewal of the earth and of life.

This break with the past suggests a sacrificial rite accompanied by a revolutionary bacchanalia wherein the participants assume the roles of holy assassins or holy sinners (as in Blok's "The Twelve" or Isaak Babel's stories and other early descriptions of the Russian Revolution). The orchestrators of this drama — leaders and hangmen — acquire the traits of high priests and are not just political bosses. From here it is only a stone's throw to the deification of the revolutionary dictator who has seized supreme power and applies violence. The very idea of violence and power can imbue communism and the revolution with a sacred, even mystical aura. The break with the past, including religion, takes on a religious coloration.

The revolution's watchword was "everything anew." The denial of the past was so radical that destruction or the threat of destruction extended to indisputable human values. Incidentally, the Futurists' calls to throw the classics overboard "from the ship of contemporary life" came at the opportune time for the revolution.

Written in 1917 by the proletarian poet Vladimir Kirillov, these
famous verses entitled "We" sounded like the smashing of the idols:

> *We're drunk with a rebellious, brutal passion;*
> *Let them scream: "You are the hangmen of beauty,"*
> *In the name of our tomorrow, we'll burn Raphael,*
> *Destroy museums, crush the flowers of art underfoot.*

The past and the old were synonymous with evil, the new was
synonymous with beauty. It isn't surprising that the notion of
"vestiges of the past" persists to this day in Soviet civilization.
Everything bad is deemed either the work of the enemy (who also
embodies the past) or, at best, a hangover to be eradicated with
time. If one can't attribute drunkenness or thievery or rudeness to
the class enemy, one can call this a "vestige" or, as they often used
to say, "a legacy of the accursed past." The harshest attacks and
denial were reserved for Russia's past and national traditions: the
old estates (nobility, clergy, merchants), the autocracy, the church,
or the great names, heroes of the past such as Aleksandr Nevsky and
Aleksandr Suvorov, who were rehabilitated (partially) only much
later. "Let's have a crack at Holy Russia," goes Blok's "The
Twelve." Such was the pathos of the revolution. Even the words
"Russian" and "Russia" vanished from the scene. The revolution,
by its own definition, was not a Russian but an international phenomenon. According to this logic, the revolution occurred in Russia rather than elsewhere mainly because in the past Russia had been
worse off than other countries — the oppression was greater, the
power was more rotten, and Russia's backwardness had made it the
weakest link in the chain of world capitalism.

Consequently, the enemies of the revolution also tended to regard
it as a non-Russian phenomenon. Among the petite bourgeoisie
(and elsewhere) the consensus was that the revolution had been
instigated by the Jews and the Germans. In fact, the revolutionary
leadership and avant-garde did include a number of non-Russians:
Jews, Poles, Letts, and even Chinese. Though a tiny minority compared to the Russian forces, they stood out as nonnationals and
invited unkind attention. Hence the theory that the revolution was
imported and had nothing to do with the Russian people or Russian
soil — a theory that still exists and has even gathered new momen-

tum recently. Russia, this theory's adherents claim, is an occupied country. The occupiers came from the West, since Marxism was brought to us from there. Personally, I completely disagree with this theory and yet find it difficult to concede the opposite view, that the October Revolution and Soviet civilization are a strictly Russian, national product. The revolution, it seems to me, combined both elements: national and international, local and global. And the fact that it broke with the national past, with Russia's national physiognomy, does not divorce it from the soil, even if it far exceeds those bounds.

This religious aspect constituted one of the most distinctively national characteristics of the Russian Revolution. Fyodor Dostoyevsky was the first, with all his passion, to evoke this feature as it was manifested in the nineteenth-century revolutionaries; and at the beginning of the twentieth century he was followed by other Russian thinkers whose ideas were far removed from the revolution. Nikolai Berdyaev, for one. In his article "The Russian Gironde," written in 1906, at the height of the first Russian revolution, he compares the Kadets (liberals favoring a constitution and democracy) with the moderate Girondists of the French Revolution. The Kadets' political program — rational, progressive, and at the same time moderate, a middle ground between left-wing and right-wing extremes — very much appealed to Berdyaev personally. But he considered that it couldn't last in Russia precisely because it lacked religious pathos. In a polemic with Peter Struve, a supporter of this program, Berdyaev wrote:

> Social Democracy conveys a religious pathos which grips the heart of the masses, enthralls the youth. Politics is a religion for the Social Democrats, a religious act. How can the Constitutional Democrats [Kadets — A.S.] counter this? They have no ideas save the unassailable but limited notion that a constitution guaranteeing rights and freedoms is better than an autocratic and bureaucratic regime. Neither the youth nor the workers will support the Constitutional Democrats since they offer no spiritual nourishment and their desire to offer material nourishment is dubious.
>
> Struve underestimates the real significance of Social Democracy's religious rhetoric, which cannot be countered by the bare, formal

principles of liberalism alone; they won't draw anyone. As fate has it, Russia is given to the power of extremes, the black and the red are holding sway,[3] and what we need here is not pale, moderate, unemotional theories, but fiery new ideas.

These ideas can only be religious ones and no less radical than those of the Social Democrats or the Black Hundreds. So long as Struve fails to recognize this, all his abilities will amount to little. Being a skeptic, he doesn't know the secret of power over hearts — which the men of the red and the black do.

Berdyaev was right, though then it sounded paradoxical to suggest that the Social Democrats (from which would spring the future Bolsheviks) were religious in their politics.

Dmitry Merezhkovsky, another religious writer of the time, treated this subject in an analysis of the 1905 revolution:

> The Russian Revolution isn't just politics, it's religion — this is what is hardest to understand for Europe, for whom religion itself has long been politics. . . . The Russian Revolution is as absolute as the autocracy it rejects. . . . Bakunin [Mikhail Bakunin, a nineteenth-century revolutionary and anarchist — A.S.] already sensed that the final revolution would not be national but worldwide. The Russian Revolution is worldwide. When you Europeans have understood this, you will rush to douse the flames. But beware: it's not you who will smother us, but we who will incinerate you.

For Merezhkovsky, the greatest prophet of the Russian Revolution was Dostoyevsky who, he said,

> fears and loathes revolution but cannot imagine anything other than this fearful and loathsome revolution. The revolution for him is an absolute, if negative, measure of all things, a universal category of thought. It's all he thinks about, talks about; he's mad about the revolution. If anyone brought the revolution down on Russia, like a magician summoning a storm, it was Dostoyevsky. From Raskolnikov to Ivan Karamazov, all his favorite heroes are political and

---

3. *Translator's note:* Black refers to the Black Hundreds (League of the Russian People), a right-wing, antirevolutionary, anti-Jewish political group; red refers to the Social Democrats.

religious rebels, criminals before the laws of man and God and, at the same time, atheist-mystics, not simply negators of God but resisters of God.

This reasoning may seem odd. How can one be a religious atheist, or even an atheist-mystic? And what difference is there between an atheist who denies God and one who fights God? The fact is, Russian atheists who want to fight God often have a religious psychology; this is why they aren't simply negators, but resisters of God. The atheist of the rational, Western type who is content to deny God is unmoved by all these problems: if God doesn't exist, why worry and why wrestle with him? But the Russian atheist resister of God, in his innermost soul, in his subconscious, grants that God exists and begins to test him, to provoke him, or else to debate mentally with him in a contest to determine who is the better, the more just, or the stronger. This partly explains the Bolsheviks' extravagant acts against sacred objects, as when they did not just remove the icons from the churches but used them to make floors for the village bath without even sanding off the saints' faces. Or when they lined them up against a wall and shot at them, as if, for these atheist resisters of God, the icons were living beings.

In Dostoyevsky's novels we meet resisters of God of a high moral and intellectual level like Raskolnikov (*Crime and Punishment,* 1866), Ippolit (*The Idiot,* 1868), and Ivan Karamazov (*The Brothers Karamazov,* 1879–1880). Atheists, nihilists, and rebels, they are also good and sensitive souls — too good and too sensitive. Fatally wounded by the consciousness that they have of injustice and universal evil, they are filled with profound love and compassion for their fellow man. Hence their rejection of God as neither good nor merciful enough since he permits such suffering on earth. Ivan Karamazov's famous remark is a sort of formula for the Russian antagonism toward God: "It's not that I reject God . . . I'm just turning in my ticket to him, most respectfully" (the ticket to the Kingdom of Heaven). "I'm turning in my ticket" because evil reigns on earth, because it is impossible to accept this evil or to forgive God the tears of an innocent, martyred child.

Russian socialism, says Dostoyevsky, springs in part from this brand of atheism as a quarrel with God. According to this argument, if there is no God then I, a man, become God and, in my human capacity, I want to build an earthly paradise excluding evil and suffering. This is why the "Russian boys" sitting in the tavern talk endlessly about God or about socialism which, adds Dostoyevsky, is virtually the same thing. For this is all a search for God, a search for religion, despite the rejection of one and the other.

It's not difficult to find similar traits in the spiritual profile of the Russian revolutionary. Mayakovsky painted the finest portrait of this psychological type. Already a recognized Soviet poet, he proclaimed in "It" (1923):

> On the bridge of time,
>               abused and despised,
>     redeemer of earthly love,
>               I'll keep
>     my vigil here
>               and for all be chastised,
>     I'll pay for all
>               and for all I'll weep.[4]

The cross on which Mayakovsky crucifies himself as a bearer of the pain and love of all men became the enduring symbol of his life and art. And along with this crucifixion, other ideas and images, obsessions, recur throughout his work: the Nativity, thaumaturgy, the Resurrection of the dead, apocalyptic visions of the end of the world and of the advent of the Kingdom of God on earth. This is not a pseudo-Christian stylization; it is an assimilation, conscious or unconscious, of a religious idea, radically reinterpreted in the sense of the quarrel with God and the rejection of all earlier religions, which have not brought the world the renewal it hoped for.

In his earliest poems, Mayakovsky's messianism reaches its apogee in "A Cloud in Trousers" (1915), originally entitled "The Thirteenth Apostle." It is a brief self-portrait of the man and the poet, and of his extreme ambivalence toward the Gospel. The expression "thirteenth apostle" sounds almost like Antichrist: to call oneself an apostle and the bad and impure thirteenth to boot is

4. Translation by Rottenberg in *op. cit.*, p. 126.

sacrilege. At the same time, as depicted in his poem, this superfluous, additional, and unacknowledged apostle, Mayakovsky, aspires to work life's religious transfiguration more completely and more courageously than the twelve apostles, and in a way even more real that the Lord God himself imagined or was capable of. Religion transforms itself into revolution, which begins with the denial of God, but it remains nevertheless, for Mayakovsky, a religion of supreme love.

Boris Pasternak said that the young Mayakovsky reminded him more than anything of Dostoyevsky's "younger heroes," the nihilists and the rebels.

In "A Cloud in Trousers," the "thirteenth apostle," Mayakovsky, like Ivan Karamazov, returns to God his ticket to the Heavenly Kingdom — only he does so with extreme disrespect and rudeness, like a new-style nihilist. But behind his blasphemy, we hear the pain, the love, and the yearning for God — here, on earth, now, in his whole and real form. If not, look out! . . .

> *Almighty, a pair of hands you invented,*
> *arranged for everyone*
> *a head like this, —*
> *why didn't you conceive*
> *that without being pain-tormented*
> *one could*
> *kiss and kiss and kiss?!*[5]

With his fantastic passion and despair, with his determination to remake the world in an instant, his readiness to perform an unheard-of religious feat, to impinge on God himself, Mayakovsky embraced the revolution and became its master poet.

## THE ROLE OF THE POPULAR ELEMENTAL FORCES

Both supporters and opponents of the revolution likened it to a natural cataclysm: the Flood, a colossal earthquake, a fire, a storm, a cyclone.

And indeed, Russia during this period was in such an elemental,

---

5. Translation by Herbert Marshall in *Mayakovsky* (New York: Hill and Wang, 1965), p. 121.

confused, chaotic state that out of the chaos came a new, unknown civilization. What brought about the collapse is arguable — the fall of the monarchy during the February 1917 Revolution, or the unleashing of new elemental forces in October and later during the civil war? I myself tend to think the most devastating blows to the monarchy, the old civilization, were dealt by the First World War, at the front, during the last acts of the war with Germany. When Russian soldiers began deserting in droves or fraternizing with the Germans to signal an end to hostilities, when men began killing officers who tried to prevent them from returning home to divide the land. Old tsarist Russia was founded on the subordination of the highest and lowest officials, the highest and lowest estates. The military defeats and incipient revolutionary anarchy smashed the strongest link in the hierarchical chain: the army.

Given this, it has to be admitted that the Bolsheviks produced slogans that were tactically highly effective and timely: "Down with War!" "Peace to the Peoples!" "Bread to the Hungry!" Also: "Land to the Peasants!" "Factories to the Workers!" "Pillage the Pillagers!" or "Expropriation of the Expropriators!" This was socialist revolution.

The Bolsheviks won primarily because they unleashed elemental forces and, by breaking the hierarchy, kept the old society from mounting a real resistance. This came later, during the civil war, but by then it was too late.

In Russian literature the most sublime and satisfying expression of the revolution's primal forces is found in "The Twelve," Blok's poem about a detachment of Red Guards in the streets of Petrograd. It crackles with that furious energy he called "the music of the revolution." By this he meant not simply the music resounding in the streets but, as he put it, the strains of "the world orchestra" emanating from higher, unknown spheres. As if the revolution, in Blok's understanding, had begun in the heavens and only then on earth. But to him, both moments signified the unleashing of elemental forces, and such was the essential content of the day. Blok detected "the music of the revolution" even before it began — like a seismograph, recording the approach of this world catastrophe for which he also felt a kinship, as the source of his lyricism and of his own historical fate. But one must consider, too, Blok's original notion of the "elemental force" as opposed to "civilization." Whether or not we share his views, they are of particular interest and use to us here, not only because Blok was the greatest Russian poet of the early twentieth century, but also because today we are dealing with the same problem, with the correlation between the primal force and its antithesis, civilization. For Blok, that force is always a revitalizing, creative, musical principle, biding its time in nature's depths, in the popular and cosmic soul. It is the wild, unbridled spirit of music, where the cosmos and harmony are born, where, in the history of humanity, culture blossoms and thrives. The elemental force is irrational and organic. It may bring havoc and death, but it is also the measure of all things to come, which is why it is always right, even in the destruction with which it threatens the world. To try to resist it is as senseless as trying to battle the storm or the earthquake. The poet's role is to listen for the rumble and to echo it, even if it presages his own doom.

Civilization is the antithesis of the primal force and of culture. For it is the cold, dead crust that congeals on the surface of life and culture, stifling them. But underneath, as under the earth's crust, the elements are raging and rioting and will burst one day and sweep that civilization away to sow the still-warm soil with a new life and a new culture. In this sense, history is a series of elemental bursts and explosions, like volcanic eruptions, after which the outer crust again begins to congeal, to mold a lifeless civilization.

It is this huge role of the elemental force, overturning and transforming everything, which Blok conveys in "The Twelve." For the revolution — which he welcomed not so much politically as metaphysically and musically — was to him the highest expression of the elemental force, its apotheosis. "The Twelve" was such an apotheosis.

But when the explosion and storm of revolutionary elements abated, when the State system, organization, and order (in other words, civilization) began to take hold, Blok stopped hearing that music of the revolution, and the poet fell silent. He never disavowed "The Twelve," but without that primal force he could neither speak nor breathe. He died a few years later, as if he had wrung himself out — physically and creatively — in that poem so in harmony with the revolution.

Finally, one should note another vital aspect of Blok's evocation of the elemental force: its value in itself, its self-justification. Most remarkable of all is that while Blok justifies the revolution as an elemental force, he avoids the usual idealization, the hymns and eulogies. Instead, he alludes to the saddest, most sinister things he saw then, in early 1918: murder, stealing, the debauch of a crowd drunk with its own triumph, senseless shooting at an invisible enemy . . . And whirling all this around, piercing the pitch-black night with white snow and flashes of fire, Blok paints the revolution as the play of light and shadow, ultimately crowned, in a gleam of contrast, by Jesus Christ who, like an ambiguous phantom, looms ahead of the revolution.

> *Crack — crack — crack! But only the echo*
> *answers from among the eaves . . .*
> *The blizzard splits his seams, the snow*
> *laughs wildly up the whirlwind's sleeve . . .*
>
> *Crack — crack — crack!*
> *Crack — crack — crack!*
>
> *. . . So they march with sovereign tread . . .*
> *Behind them limps the hungry dog,*
> *and wrapped in wild snow at their head*
> *carrying a blood-red flag —*
> *soft-footed where the blizzard swirls,*
> *invulnerable where bullets crossed —*
> *crowned with a crown of snowflake pearls,*
> *a flowery diadem of frost,*
> *ahead of them goes Jesus Christ.* [6]

This substitution of devastating irony for absolute principles, of art or of carnival for reality, implies that the revolution, as an elemental force, has value in itself. It's not a question of being right or wrong. It is what it is.

The image of Christ at the end undoubtedly signifies a moral and emotional acceptance of the revolution. It is, I would say, the mysticism of an emotion which, beyond Blok and his "Twelve,"

6. Translation by Stallworthy and France in *op. cit.,* p. 160.

concerns the revolution as a whole, as a spontaneous phenomenon. After all, the spontaneous emotional outburst of even one individual, as long as it is significant, requires no proof or justification. Besides, this outburst is irrational and illogical.

To illustrate, I'll use the famous central chapter from *The Brothers Karamazov*, "Rebellion," in which Ivan Karamazov returns to God his ticket to the Heavenly Kingdom. This chapter is interesting not only for Ivan's arguments as an atheist resister of God but also for the response of his brother Alyosha, who is Dostoyevsky's moral ideal, a messenger of Christ and Christianity in the modern world. Ivan tells his brother a story, one about the sufferings of an innocent child: an old general, a landowner, sets his hounds on a young house-serf, who is torn to pieces before his mother's eyes. How, Ivan then asks Alyosha, should one have dealt with the general so as, he specifies, "to satisfy our sense of morality?"

" 'Shoot him!' Alyosha said softly, looking up at his brother with a pale, twisted smile.

" 'Bravo!' cried Ivan with a kind of delight. 'If you even said it, that means . . . Ah, the monk!' "

Then Alyosha, as a genuine Christian, corrects himself: " 'I said an absurdity, but . . .' "

Alyosha's answer is absurd from the standpoint of the Christian morals to which he has always adhered. But there is a spontaneous, emotional response in the man who says "Shoot him!" despite his own logical and even moral arguments. Such is the force of this spontaneous reaction.

If we shift Alyosha's response to the time of the revolution, we understand why the practice of executions and even the phrase "Shoot him!" suddenly acquired a noble, if not romantic sense. What else can be done with a general who sets his dogs on a child before its mother's eyes? Like Alyosha Karamazov, we will probably say: "Shoot him!"

This emotion is the soul of the elemental force vindicated by Blok in "The Twelve." And it is why the word "revolution" sounded to many like a kind of supreme justice.

But perhaps Blok was too carried away by the elemental force and overestimated it? No, it's more complicated than that. In *Doctor Zhivago* (1957), Pasternak also argued in favor of the elemental force, though at the time he was not in the revolution's thrall and found much about it to criticize (including its spontaneous energy). Nevertheless, Pasternak felt compelled to describe the revolution as the most sublime and inspiring moment in the creation of history and nature: "A staggering spectacle. . . . The stars have come out and are conversing with the trees, the night flowers are philosophizing, and the stone buildings are holding mass meetings. Somewhat evangelical, wouldn't you say?"

All this is reflected in *My Sister Life*, a book of poems that Pasternak wrote in the summer of 1917. But perhaps, we interject, the poems were inspired by only the February, not the October Revolution? Again, no: Pasternak, too, saw the October Revolution as an extension of that same elemental force. And in *Doctor Zhivago*, there is a landscape similar to the one in "The Twelve," only in a different, realistic key:

"Yury Andreyevich was turning out of one lane into another and had already lost count of how many turns he had taken when suddenly the snow began swirling down, whipping itself into a blizzard, the kind of blizzard which, in an open field, swishes across the land with a scream."

It is striking that, separated by nearly half a century and opposite points of view, Blok and Pasternak dovetail in this positive, emotional assessment of the elemental force, of its metaphysical as well as sensual image. The power and appeal of this force must have been great for two such different poets, independently of one another, to have surrendered in one voice.

## THE SPONTANEOUS ELEMENT IN ITS POPULAR INTERPRETATION

Let's now look at another social element in this same emotional, revolutionary ferment: the peasantry. The poet Sergei Esenin embraced the revolution with Blokian passion but in an earthier way, so to speak, closer to the soil, to the muzhik, the peasantry and its revolutionary brawn. For good reason: Russia was primarily a country of peasants for whom the revolution meant one immediate gain — land. During the revolutionary years, Esenin expanded more fully than others on this theme of the revolution's spontaneous, strictly peasant component.

But at the same time, it is also Esenin who evoked the clash between this primitive force and the new State system, the new civilization. Having produced the revolution, this force was cast aside, then crushed by the new order.

Very early on, by 1919, Esenin had detected the contradiction between the peasants' revolutionary spontaneity and the revolutionary power, symbolized by the "city" in his poems. Esenin's "city" signified something else as well — the onslaught of a new civilization:

> *City, city! in your cruel melee*
> *You christened us carrion and scum.*
> *The field congeals with ox-eyed longing,*
> *Smothered by the telegraph poles.*
>
> *Sinewy muscle in the diabolical neck,*
> *Cast-iron logs an easy load.*
> *And so what! We aren't the first*
> *To become rickety, to be lost.*

What is this about? The assault of the city on the country? Outwardly, yes. But in essence this is about the assault of a new, lifeless civilization on the revolutionary spontaneity which created that civilization, the struggle of the State against the elemental force that conspired unwittingly to build it.

In Esenin's 1920 poem "Sorokooust" (or "Prayers for the Dead"), there is a remarkable scene taken from nature: a foal is racing across the steppe, trying to overtake a train. This contest between the living horse and the iron one was enormously symbolic for Esenin. That same year, he described the episode in a letter (to Ye. Livshits):

> Here's a graphic example . . . We were on our way from Tikhoretskaya to Pyatigorsk . . . Suddenly we see a foal galloping with all its might behind the locomotive. Galloping so fast that it was obvious it had taken it into its head, for some reason, to try to overtake the train. It ran for a very long time but in the end began to tire, and at a station they caught him. An insignificant episode perhaps, but to me it speaks volumes. The iron horse beat the living horse. And this little foal was for me the actual, dear, dying image

of the countryside and of Makhno. In our revolution, both terribly resemble this foal, this living force pitted against the iron one.

This comparison of the foal to peasant leader Nestor Makhno is striking given that Makhno was the spontaneous, anarchic, peasant element in the revolution. The element for which Esenin felt an affinity. The element that helped the revolution triumph only to find itself at odds with the new State power by which it would ultimately be destroyed.

The fate of this spontaneous element, as seen by Esenin, is depicted in a 1923 poem from the cycle *Moscow of the Taverns*:

> They're drinking again here, brawling and crying,
> To the accordion's yellow melancholy strains,
> Cursing their misfortunes,
> Remembering Russia of old . . .
>
> They've all lost something forever.
> O, my dark blue May! Sky blue June!
> Is this why the rankness of death
> Hangs over this hopeless revelry? . . .
>
> There's evil in their wild eyes,
> And rebellion in their clangorous words.
> They're sorry for those foolish fellows
> Who threw their lives away
>
> They're sorry that cruel October
> In its snowy whirlwind deceived them.
> And already a new boldness is honing
> The knife hidden deep in their boot.
>
> No! They won't be crushed or scattered,
> They're reckless because they're rotten.
> You, my Russia . . . sacred . . . Rus . . . sia . . .
> My Asiatic land!

The drunkards in the tavern are mourning Muscovite Russia as the derelict, thieving element of the old empire. At the same time, they're mourning their recent revolutionary past. Like Esenin, they're all disillusioned with the revolution and ripe for a new, spontaneous movement, but this time in a delinquent, mercenary vein. Corrupt and rotten, they also remember the first, intoxicating rush of youth. If they're sorry for the boys who died for the revolution, they're actually sorry for themselves. As for those who "went far" (in the same poem), they are the Communists who have forgotten their old comrades, forgotten the spontaneous popular force on which they once relied.

As commentary on this view of the taverns as the spontaneous revolutionary element, though already rotten, here is a little-known letter of Esenin's (never published in the USSR) to his old Imagist comrade Aleksandr Kusikov dated February 7, 1923. Esenin was abroad when he wrote to Kusikov, who was about to emigrate. Esenin hadn't liked the West and was making his way home. Meanwhile, he knew that in Russia nothing good awaited him:

> Sandro, dear Sandro! the longing is deadly, unbearable. I feel a stranger here and superfluous, but when I think of Russia and what awaits me there, I don't want to go back. If I were alone, if it weren't for my sisters, I wouldn't give a damn and I'd go to Africa or somewhere else. It makes me sick that I, a *legitimate* Russian son, should be treated like a bastard in my own country. I'm fed up with this whorish condescension of the powers that be. And it's even more sickening to watch one's own brothers toadying to them. I can't stand it! By God, I can't! It's enough to make one scream or grab a knife and stand by the highway! [In other words, go out marauding — A.S.]
>
> . . . I'm in a foul depression. I can't understand to which revolution I belonged. I only know that apparently it wasn't to the February or the October Revolution. In us there hid and hides still some November . . .

November here refers to a third, future revolution, directed against the new model of the State; and it clarifies these lines: "And already a new boldness is honing / The knife hidden deep in their boot." The betting is on a new, Pugachev-style rebellion, which has retired to the taverns nursing the memory of its old abandon. This isn't a revolution anymore, of course, but its ragtag remains holed up with another broad, primitive, criminal or semicriminal element: bandits, thieves, hoods. But it's interesting that Esenin links this new milieu with the October Revolution which, after using this primitive element, would deceive or crush it, despite the poet's hopes that "reckless" people like us "won't be crushed or scattered."

## THE SPONTANEOUS ELEMENT AND POWER

Poetic images certainly can't convey the total complexity of real-life processes, insofar as they give us only a general, somewhat idealized picture. For a more accurate, historical account of the revolutionary instinct, I will use Dmitry Furmanov's *Chapaev* (1923). Though it is an inferior novel artistically, Furmanov's flaws as a writer are to our advantage here. *Chapaev* is a factual document of great importance in which events and people speak for themselves, often saying more than the author may have intended.

Our interest is in Chapaev himself, an extraordinarily colorful figure who seems to have been summoned from life's lower depths to bring about history.[7] From the humblest peasant origins, Chapaev rises to become a distinguished member of the revolutionary command. He hates the old system — the landowners, the merchants, the tsarist army — and is ready to die for the revolution. But he also detests and distrusts the Red officers who bridle him and even, in his view, prevent him from fighting in earnest. In the past, Chapaev knew anarchists who surely responded better to his spontaneous nature. Now a commander at the front, Chapaev, according to Furmanov's description, is a Bolshevik, but a primitive, uncouth, uneducated one. For instance, he crosses himself furtively before going into battle, something that wouldn't become a genuine Communist and which excites the author's censure and dismay.

In Chapaev's character, we find a visceral, atavistic connection to such historical figures as Stenka Razin and Emelyan Pugachev, leaders of peasant revolts in the seventeenth and eighteenth centuries. Furmanov's jottings on "Chapaev's Biography" include this quote: " 'Do you know who I am?' Chapaev asked me, a naive, secretive gleam in his eye. 'I was born to the daughter of the governor of Kazan and a Gypsy actor.' "

---

7. *Translator's note:* General Chapaev was a leader of Bolshevik guerrilla forces during the civil war. Furmanov was a political commissar with the Twenty-fifth Division of the Red Army under Chapaev. The novel is based on Furmanov's own diaries and notes.

Furmanov attaches little significance to this report, noted simply as an odd fact about the original and fantastic Chapaev. Chapaev saw himself as something like a Pretender to old Russia, a people's tsar with an inherent right to claim the power and the love of all. This detail links Chapaev once again with the Russian tradition of spontaneous revolts, with the Razins and the Pugachevs.

Against this background, we now meet Party envoy Fyodor Klychkov, in the role of supervisor and informer, easily recognizable as the author. Here a new theme begins of which, I think, Furmanov hardly has any inkling. I would call it *the theme of the struggle for power,* a struggle led by Klychkov-Furmanov at the Party and State's behest, and aimed to contain this partisan leader, Chapaev.

We are told from the start that Klychkov (Furmanov) has been sent to keep an eye on Chapaev, to report on him and — slowly, without letting on — to subjugate him. A commissar, a State spy, that is, has been dispatched to the popular revolution, since the new power now considers it dangerous, or at least unguided. Klychkov's object is not so much to admire Chapaev as to watch and tame him. Thus he truthfully and dutifully records all Chapaev's failings as well as merits that may yet be of use to the Red Army and the new State. This role of observer attached to Chapaev helps Furmanov the writer. He never embellishes but is consistently evenhanded, as if weighing Chapaev on the scales of Party and State.

Klychkov thinks almost exclusively about how to subject Chapaev. To do this, he must first gain authority. Therefore, as an intelligent man, he doesn't interfere in the battle plans, which he doesn't understand anyway, but tries instead to impress Chapaev with his erudition, with his knowledge of State policy. Klychkov writes frankly about himself and his concerns:

"How to gain authority? I must take Chapaev spiritual prisoner. Kindle his desire for knowledge, for education, for science, for broad horizons." . . . Here Fyodor knew his superiority and was convinced that as soon as he had sparked this desire, Chapaev the anarchist, the partisan, would sing another song. Little by little, with prudence but persistence, he would divert Chapaev, arouse his interest in other things. Fyodor had great faith in his own powers. True,

Chapaev was unusual, nothing like the others, it would be difficult to break him, like a wild steppe horse, but . . . even wild horses get broken. Only was this necessary? the question arose. Why not leave this handsome, colorful character to the mercy of fate, leave him untouched? Let him parade and sparkle like a precious stone! This idea did occur to Klychkov, but it struck him as absurd and childish against the backdrop of the gigantic fight.

This idea — of leaving Chapaev intact because he is so remarkable, so worthy of admiration — dawns on Furmanov but is instantly suppressed by his political common sense. Furmanov's primary concern is to remake Chapaev in the Party mold and to bridle him.

This story is interesting as a self-exposé revealing the Party's shrewd, totalitarian tactics with respect to the individual and to humanity. Despite a certain fondness for Chapaev, Furmanov sees him simply as the raw material from which he wants to create the best possible State servant. For him, Chapaev is a gifted child, but a child nevertheless, who must be properly brought up.

Power, however, also originates within primitive forces; it isn't always imposed on them from without. The complex processes of transition from one principle to another, of the formation of a civilization, are played out in the very heart of this primitive element.

Let's take Isaak Babel's story "The Life and Adventures of Matvei Pavlichenko" from the *Red Cavalry* collection (1926). This "life" is written in the style of a first-person account by Pavlichenko himself — or as he might have told his own story. But this biography is based on that of a perfectly real historical figure: Apanasenko.[8] Babel's story gives us a fairly objective idea of what kind of revolution it is that transforms the last into the first, the slaves into the masters. Pavlichenko, the story's hero, is not a plain soldier but a top military commander, a Red general. He sees himself as a role model for all oppressed people who now, with the revolution, are coming to power. Today he is a general, but yesterday he was a simple swineherd; Pavlichenko sees in his fate that of all workers.

8. *Translator's note:* Iosif Apanasenko (1890–1943) was a division commander in the First Cavalry during the civil war.

Incidentally, Chapaev, as a young boy, was also a herdsman. So Pavlichenko's trajectory — from swineherd to general — was typical for a revolutionary commander: child of nature turned member of the top brass. Babel alludes to this spontaneous element in an idiom somewhat reminiscent of "The Twelve." In the adventures of Pavlichenko, for one moment, the space of a paragraph, it's as if a verse from a popular epic has broken in, or a song in praise of the revolution. In a few musical phrases composed in an obviously folkloric style, Babel depicts the entire cataclysm that catapulted the poor peasant — only recently humiliated and down on his knees — to the top.

> And what d'you think, you Stavropol boys, comrades, fellow-countrymen, my own dear brethren. . . . Five lost years I went to pieces, till at last the year eighteen came along to visit me, lost fellow that I was. It came along on lively stallions, on its Kabardin horses, bringing along a big train of sledges behind it and all sorts of songs. Eh you, little year eighteen, my sweetheart! Can it be that we shan't be walking out with you anymore, my own little drop of blood, my year eighteen?[9]

From these few lines, one senses how the revolution seduced thousands upon thousands of people. Not only by proclaiming new ideas. And not only by promising miracles. For many who joined the revolution, it was an end in itself. It was the same celebration we saw in "The Twelve." Here the revolution is presented as a fairy-tale feast of life — a feast fit for kings.

So, Pavlichenko appears before his old master, Barin Nikitinsky, and announces that he has brought him a letter from Lenin.[10] The barin is surprised:

> "A letter to me — to Nikitinsky?"
> "To you," I says and takes out my book of orders, opens it at a blank page, and reads, though I can't read to save my life. " 'In the name of the nation,' " I reads, " 'and for the foundation of a nobler

---

9. Translation by Nadia Helstein in *Red Cavalry* by I. Babel (New York: Alfred A. Knopf, 1929), pp. 86–88.
10. *Translator's note:* A barin was a member of the landowning gentry.

life in the future, I order Pavlichenko, Matvei Rodionich, to deprive certain people of life, according to his discretion.'

"There," I says, "that's Lenin's letter to you."

Why was this mythical order from Lenin necessary? Couldn't Pavlichenko deal with the barin without orders from on high? Indeed he could. But what we have here is a situation akin to the Last Judgment, and for this one must have supreme, quasi-divine instructions emanating from Lenin himself. Simple revenge isn't enough for our hero, he needs to feel like the supreme master, brandishing Lenin's highest sanction.

On the other hand, these fantastic, fabulous powers received directly from Lenin to administer justice and mete out punishment conform with the facts of the day, with judicial practice in those years. Because then they judged not according to the law but "according to the voice and duty of revolutionary conscience." Pavlichenko wasn't in any way violating the judicial norms of the revolutionary period. His conscience, his class intuition told him that Barin Nikitinsky must be liquidated. So that was the law, the order received from Lenin himself.

Babel puts Pavlichenko's punishment of the barin in a kind of double perspective. On the one hand, the former herdsman has some moral justification. This isn't baseless spite, but a desire for personal and class retribution for injuries suffered — for his wife Nastya, for his cheek, which burns, he says, and will go on burning at the Last Judgment, for the years of subjection.

On the other hand, Pavlichenko in his moment of triumph does not arouse our sympathy. Moral and emotional justifications notwithstanding, his behavior is despicable and frightening. The price the barin must pay is truly monstrous: he is trampled to death by Pavlichenko, who luxuriates physically and morally in this slow torture.

> Then I stamped on my Barin Nikitinsky, and trampled him for an hour or more. And in that time I got to know life through and through. With shooting — I'll put it that way — with shooting you only get rid of a chap. Shooting's letting him off and too damned easy for yourself. With shooting you'll never get at the soul, to where it is in a fellow and how it goes and shows itself. But I don't

spare myself, and I've more than once trampled an enemy for over an hour. You see, I want to get to know what life really is and how it is inside us —

This isn't sadism or a mental aberration. Pavlichenko tramples the barin because this method of execution corresponds with his class sense of himself, the former swineherd and future general. Pavlichenko used to be on the bottom, in the mud, on the ground, "lower than any earthly depth," as he says, remembering how he got down on his knees before the barin. Now it's the barin's turn to be in that same "low place" and for as long as possible. This is why Pavlichenko says that while trampling the barin he got to know life through and through, that he was beyond bliss. He was born again in that moment, feeling himself, in the fullest sense, master of the situation. The idea of power here is vital. For power is the principal product of the revolution and the class struggle. To Pavlichenko, this idea of power is so great, so universal, and so precious in itself that simply to kill the barin would be letting him off. One can't just destroy the enemy, one must trample him underfoot so as to achieve the desired sense of power.

The last sentence of Babel's story is truly terrifying. It turns out that Pavlichenko has made a habit of trampling enemies. His sense of the fullness of life comes from this sense of power, bloody power over another human being.

The revolution creates unprecedented power, which knows no compassion, no mercy, and no bounds. Compassion would be to the detriment of power. And besides, this is the eternal judgment, Judgment Day.

Babel evidently realized what an awful truth his tale told. Entries in his journal addressed to Apanasenko, Pavlichenko's prototype, read: "A new generation — of the petits bourgeois" and "A new breed — of the petits bourgeois." He obviously meant this thirst for power and triumph which the military and political leaders of the new victorious class possessed. Terrible was the power of the barin over the disfranchised herdsman, but more terrible still was the power of the conquering swineherd over the barin.

## 2

# Utopia Found

### THE POWER OF THE IDEA

THUS FAR we have considered the revolution mainly as the manifestation of elemental forces. Now let's approach it from the point of view of the idea: an idea that was put into practice in a State system that sees itself as the best, most advanced model in the history of the world. Here we have a real-life utopia with claims to world hegemony.

This utopia is in an ambiguous situation vis-à-vis the world (in space) and history (in time). On the one hand, it proposes itself and imposes itself on the rest of humanity, as if with open arms, beckoning it into the embrace of the great, victorious idea. On the other hand, it divorces itself in every way possible from the outside world as from an alien and dangerous environment. The idea of capitalist encirclement, even if no such thing exists any longer, plays the part of the sea to this island utopia. Though the island already encompasses an enormous, ever-expanding continent, it continues to feel itself an island in the middle of an ocean. Extreme expansionism goes hand-in-hand with extreme isolationism. Given the nature of this ideal State or the victorious idea, this is understandable. For the real-life utopia conceives of itself as a universal system and doctrine; at the same time, it is singular and unique and will brook no other idea.

The relationship to history is similarly equivocal. On the one hand, the history of humanity is viewed as the slow and necessary preparation for this supreme, crowning stage. Thus, we are the heirs of world history and its last word; all humanity's greatest and most progressive minds foresaw and foretold us. Thus, the evolution of human thought has culminated in this greatest utopia, which finally materialized in victorious socialism. On the other hand, since no one has ever achieved this before, the entire history of the human race is imperfect as compared with the perfection of life in the era of this idea put into practice. This explains why the word "utopia" in Soviet usage can have a pejorative meaning. Utopians only fantasize about the radiant future, having no idea how to get there in fact, whereas we already know and are getting there. This sense of superiority causes the real-life utopia to be sharply critical of the past. Before Marx, humanity's great intellects, close to us in mind and spirit, were victims of their own class or historical parochialism: they were mistaken or not fully versed or didn't understand. The best-case excuse for this is that they hadn't lived to the era of mature and victorious socialism. And again this inspires a sense of superiority — historical, social, intellectual, whatever. So much so that on the one hand, in space, as Mayakovsky wrote:

> The Soviets have their pride:
> at the bourgeois,
> one looks
> down one's nose.

On the other hand — in time, in history — as Mayakovsky declared:

> . . . Revolutionary battles
> more earnest than "Poltava,"[1]
> And love
> more grandiose
> than Onegin's
> love.

This sense of superiority is invariably associated with the notion of the "Soviet man." As a rule, this is not a personal quality of the man, who must be modest, but a function of his affiliation with the best, most advanced world — Soviet civilization — with a real-life

---

1. *Translator's note:* "Poltava" is a poem by Pushkin (1828) evoking Peter the Great's victory over Charles XII of Sweden in 1709 and the primacy of national sentiment.

utopia. Much has been written about the good fortune of living in the Soviet land in the Soviet era. Yury Olesha may have expressed this attitude best. In 1935 he wrote:

> We young poets didn't understand what a frightening world we were living in [before the revolution — A.S.]. This world hadn't been explained as a world. This was before the great explanation of the world. Now I live in an explained world. I understand the causes. I am filled with a feeling of enormous gratitude, expressible only in music, when I think of those who died to make the world explained, to explain it and reconstruct it.

This intellectual rhetoric is connected with the famous Marxist thesis according to which earlier philosophers tried to explain the world, whereas the object was not only to explain the world but to reconstruct it. Marxism, and especially Leninism, shift the emphasis from theory to practice, from utopia to its realization. For the man who finds himself in this world for the first time, this practice and this realization make it suddenly explained, harmonious, comprehensible. As if he had come from a dark, dense forest into a bright, spacious barracks: the barracks of Soviet civilization. This isn't just a dream come true. It's a scientifically constructed and scientifically organized utopia. It's a world that is finally rational and that, in turn, imparts rationality to all that preceded it and all that is going on around it now. Man doesn't merely experience rapture in this utopia, he adheres to this strict plan in which he finds a definite place for himself and for everything.

Therefore, in considering this real-life utopia, we must add to the elemental processes a patent intellectual and ideological aspect, which should be analyzed through real events and situated in the course of history.

The twentieth century is generally the century of utopias found or being found, utopias that most often take the shape of ideological or ideocratic states, of societies based on one doctrine or another. It isn't the peoples or the doctrines that institute these states: it is largely the ideology which, as it is translated into reality, is grounded more or less in science. This phenomenon is apparent everywhere, from Hitler's Germany to the regime of the Khmer Rouge. We won't dwell on its various forms, our subject being the

Soviet version of the real-life utopia. What's more, Soviet Russia pioneered this utopia and set the example. The process of forming new states of an all-new ideological type is accomplished in the shortest possible time and accompanied by seismic social shocks. The triumphant idea patterns the life of the entire society after itself and remakes the world in its own image.

This supremacy of the idea is conspicuous even when the idea, by its own logic, is assigned a secondary role. It is conspicuous in Marxism, which took hold in Soviet Russia in the form of a guiding idea. Marxism materialized there despite its own teaching that the socialist revolution would occur first in industrially developed countries where the proletariat was a majority and where the economy was ready for the transition, and despite its own fundamental premise that existence determines consciousness and thus the idea, not the other way round. In practice, the idea transforms everything, dominates everything.

In Boris Pilnyak's 1920 novel *The Naked Year* there is a curious discussion between two Bolsheviks. A rare and special breed, they are attempting to overcome reality with the idea, to turn poor, backward, frightening Russia into the radiant world of socialist utopia:

> That evening, in the hostel, after taking off his boots and kneading his toes with sweet pleasure and then clambering into bed on all fours, Yegor Sobachkin pored over the pamphlet by the light for a long while. Then he turned to his neighbor, buried in *Izvestia:*
>
> "What do you think, Comrade Makarov, does existence determine life, or does the idea? Because if you think about it, there's existence in the idea."

Pilnyak didn't invent this. The history of Soviet civilization is full of examples in which the idea thinks of itself as existence and as even more important than existence; and if existence cannot or will not conform to the idea, so much the worse for existence . . . A well-known Marxist-Leninist notion has it that Marx put Hegel's dialectic back on its feet. But what's remarkable is that Marxism, en route to its realization, stood itself on its head and on this head the new society was built. Henceforth, consciousness determined existence. Ideology determined policy. And policy determined the economy. The scientific Marxist utopia materialized, but wrong side up, with its feet in the air.

It's no surprise that contemporary literature has witnessed an antiutopian wave. While utopian works continue to be written, as part of a long tradition, the antiutopian novel is fundamentally new, beginning with Yevgeny Zamyatin's *We* (1929) and continuing through the works of Aldous Huxley and George Orwell. Again the forerunner of this genre in Russian literature was Dostoyevsky — with his "Legend of the Grand Inquisitor" and the schemes of Shigalyov and Verkhovensky in *The Possessed* (1871–1872). When Dostoyevsky wrote these antiutopias, few believed him. We believe him because we have experienced the twentieth century. This attests, as does the antiutopian wave, to the fact that the Soviet people live in a real-life utopia and know the cost. The antiutopian novel isn't simply a rejection or contradiction of the utopia, it depicts utopia found, the real-life absolute. True, this utopia may not have turned out as originally intended. But that's another matter: why the ideal, in becoming real, changes in appearance, sometimes to the point of unrecognizability.

Add to this the fact that in the twentieth century the earth's crust started to move, and history saw an appreciable shift from idea to deed, to action on a large scale involving brutal change. From that perspective, the nineteenth century looks peaceful, moderate and relatively uneventful.

To simplify the comparison, I will take the liberty of summarizing from some reputable Russian journals published circa 1899 that I had occasion to peruse. These were New Year's issues containing detailed surveys devoted to the new, twentieth century. What we would call futuristic surveys accompanied by the usual well-wishing. These were, I remember, thick, liberal journals like *Russian Riches* and *The European Herald,* with articles by venerable scholars, professors, historians, and sociologists describing their ideas and expectations of the coming century.

Such predictions, based on objective, scientific analysis, rarely come true. Probably because obvious, stable trends of the present moment are projected into the future, making the future look like a continuation of the present, only consolidated and improved. Indeed, these predictions for the twentieth century were full of starry-eyed, ultraoptimistic constructs based on progressive nineteenth-century ideas and norms. These included the firm conviction that in the twentieth century war would end forever — at least among civilized nations. Given their extreme unprofitability, the logic went, wars were already on the decline. And they were becoming increasingly limited and local affairs, like the then-current Boer War. Even the Franco-Prussian War (1870–1871) had been fairly contained. Meanwhile, the last truly big war — the Napoleonic invasion at the beginning of the nineteenth century — seemed like a distant and unreal reflection of antiquity, a romantic and unsuccessful attempt to imitate Julius Caesar. The possibility of this kind of war in the future was completely excluded on the grounds that the development of European civilization — of industry, science, and technology — made it impossible. Economically, wars benefited neither side. Instead they promised the ruin of the common economy, since the market, production, and trade were internationalizing. In the future it would be more convenient, natural, and logical to resolve international conflicts not by means of war but by means of commercial negotiations and diplomatic parleys . . .

I must admit that such prognoses seduce one at first with their scientific persuasiveness — their logic, their facts, their statistics, their arguments. They seem irrefutable. It seems as if history can only unfold this way as it passes from one century into the next. Only by remembering that we are deep in the twentieth century — having lived through world crises and cataclysms that were wildly unprofitable contradictions of logic and common sense — do we come to and dismiss this scientific illusion fostered by the comparatively sanguine nineteenth century: pacifistic, progressive, and positivistic.

The predominant sense of life and self in the nineteenth century was expressed not by Dostoyevsky but by the far more serene and optimistic Jules Verne. His marvelous novels radiate scientific complacency. From a cannon to the moon. *Nautilus* . . . Everything seems peaceful, promising, and, with time and evolution, perfectly accessible. The solution of all crucial problems depends on progress, which is steadily edging humanity toward its cherished goal. In this sense, even Marxism is only a variation, a more resolute variation, on the theme of progress, which promises man scientific prosperity willy-nilly. Indeed, the thinking goes, science is making progress with each passing year and inching toward complete dominion over nature. Simultaneously, the humanization of man and society is making great strides. So, irrespective of how it comes about — through evolution or revolution — the radiant future is well provided for.

Then suddenly, after all this progress, after all these New Year's wishes, we land not in the hypothetical but in the real twentieth century, the century of real-life utopias. Nothing is what the experts predicted. The most unnatural wars and revolutions shake the world. Trade and diplomatic relations go ignored. Civilized nations sink into the barbarity of mass executions and deportations. Beloved Germany introduces the gas chamber. The leap from the kingdom of necessity to that of freedom gives way to slavery such as mankind never imagined. Physics loses dimension and mass and becomes relative, having reached the pinnacle of scientific and technological progress — the possibility of total, universal annihilation. The bomb makes us wonder if perhaps the ultimate goal of world evolution isn't that life, as we know it, disappear altogether, that life in general not exist: this is man's purpose and mission. In short, history and progress have come to nothing . . .

## The Loss of Meaning in History

The great utopia or antiutopia, call it what you will, would not have materialized in Russia had it not been for the World War. Again, I am referring not to social and political change brought on by the war but to the war's intellectual and semantic aspect. The war made no sense; it wasn't driven by any serious, substantial, or intelligent arguments. Compared to the First, the Second World War and even the civil war were far more sensible and understandable. The First World War was like a madman's nightmare or delirium — as illogical as it was inexpedient. Question: Why did the civilized nations of Europe, with their relatively liberal governments and material prosperity, their humanism and enlightenment, suddenly hurl themselves into this slaughterhouse and start massacring each other in such appalling ways and numbers? There was and is no answer. The absurdity of this war killed and demoralized as much perhaps as the physical horror. In his 1918 article "The

Intelligentsia and the Revolution," Blok evoked this world war
from which Russia had just emerged:

> Europe has gone mad: the flower of humanity, the flower of the
> intelligentsia has been sitting in a bog, sitting with conviction (isn't
> this a symbol) along a thin, thousand-verst strip called the "front."
> . . . It's difficult to say which is more sickening: the bloodshed or
> the sitting idle, the tedium, the banality; they're both called the
> "great war," the "patriotic war," the "war for the liberation of
> oppressed peoples" or what else? No, under these auspices you won't
> liberate anybody.

How to disengage from this absurdity? The Bolsheviks' answer
echoed a logical and popular demand: better a horrible end than this
horror without end! Better a revolution! And a necessary revolution, since for European civilization to have crowned itself with
such a nightmare, the old world was obviously rotten. If the world
war was the fruit of this civilization then the latter was intrinsically,
fundamentally depraved.

Given this assumption, world revolution seemed the only way
out of the impasse into which human history had propelled itself. A
risky venture, but what could one do? This was the last chance to
break out of the trap and find a meaning. Or as Mayakovsky wrote
then about the revolution: "It's the world's last stake in this gam-
bling-hell." The logic of a gambler? The logic of despair, perhaps?
It's interesting that Lenin himself resorted to this logic when trying
to explain why, despite the laws of Marxism, it was decided to
undertake something as risky as a socialist revolution in backward,
peasant Russia. Polemicizing with classical Marxists shortly before
his death, Lenin sounded as if he were justifying himself:

> The triteness of their argument [of traditional Marxists — A.S.],
> learned by heart during the heyday of West European social democ-
> racy, knows no bounds. It consists in the claim that we haven't
> developed to the point of socialism, that we lack, as various
> "learned" gentlemen among them express it, the objective economic
> prerequisites for socialism. It never occurs to anyone to ask himself if
> the people, faced with the revolutionary situation that took shape
> during the first imperialistic war, if the people, faced with the

hopelessness of their own situation, might not have thrown themselves into this struggle which offered them at least some chance of bringing about conditions, however unconventional, that would promote the further development of civilization.

That Lenin mentions at least some chance to escape the hopeless situation created by the First World War is striking. This chance was afforded by the revolution — a desperate attempt to conquer civilization by replacing it with another, a new, sensible, Soviet civilization.

And that substitution took place. Here one should note that the victory of the revolution for many of its supporters in Russia and in the West brought a rediscovery of meaning. History assumed a grandiose and universal significance, the more compelling and inspiring for being contraposed against the darkness and catastrophic absurdity of the First World War, which were now superseded. Lunacy gave way to a sensible world order. Humanity had found a purpose and a way to achieve that purpose. For many people, for many years, this was undoubtedly the attraction of the revolution and the civilization it forged. The attraction in spite of all the horror and loss it entailed. The logic here, conscious or unconscious, was roughly this: Things are bad, so be it; this real-life utopia is not what we anticipated or hoped for in many respects, but it exists and is an answer to the question, What is there to live for?

If man is inclined to ask himself about the meaning of life, the purpose of existence, a Russian is perhaps especially so. Berdyaev wrote in 1904: "The Russian longing for meaning in life — this is the principal motif in our literature and what constitutes the innermost essence of the Russian intelligentsia." Incidentally, Berdyaev explains, this thirst for purpose and yearning for meaning in life fueled the Russian intelligentsia's radicalism and revolutionary spirit, its desire to serve the people and its passion for socialist ideals.

The revolution introduced this meaningful purpose, offered it to the course of history and to the life of society. True, it deprived the individual of his freedom and in so doing alienated many Russian intellectuals. But there were plenty of others, like Blok, who accepted the revolution with its consequences, who embraced it as the consciousness of a new existence, of a new historical stage. In "The Intelligentsia and the Revolution," Blok is not only ecstatic over the elemental force but also exultant over the rediscovery of meaning in history, which had been lost in the absurdity of the world war. Blok asks about the revolution's aims: "What's been planned?" And answers:

> To redo everything. To organize things so that everything will be new; so that our lying, dirty, dull, ugly life will be just, pure, merry, and beautiful.
>
> When such designs, hidden for long ages in the human soul, the people's soul, burst the chains that had bound them and come rushing in a stormy torrent . . . this is called a revolution. [Further on comes a warning to intellectuals — A.S.] . . . Sorrow upon those who think they will find in the revolution only their dreams come true, however lofty or noble they may be. Like a thunderstorm, like a blizzard, revolution always brings the new and unforeseen; it cruelly deceives many; it easily cripples the worthy person in its maelstrom; it often ferries unworthy people to dry land unharmed; but these are details and do not change the essential direction of the torrent or its terrible, devastating rumble. This rumble, all the same, always speaks of something great.

What is implied here is a grand design, a wonderful world order.

From this vantage of great historical meaning, Blok berates the intelligentsia, which has dreamed of the people's liberation for nearly a hundred years while eroding the foundations of the old society with its radicalism. But now that this old world has come crashing down and the people have shown their real face, the intelligentsia is flinging itself in the opposite direction and trying to smother the fire it started. The intelligentsia's dashes to and fro revealed much that was indeed inconsistent and even ludicrous. Such as when Konstantin Balmont, who had once sung the revolution's praises, wrote about himself:

> *You were utterly mistaken: your beloved people*
> *Are not at all the people you dreamed, not at all.*

But beyond all this lay the manifest inconsistency of history itself, which had brought about a utopia completely other than the one dreamed of by Russian intellectuals. This inconsistency was eventually detected by Blok, who sensed himself suffocating in the airless confines of this wonderful world opening up before him.

Speaking generally, it is safe to say that during the revolution and for many years thereafter the intelligentsia was in the throes of a profound internal crisis, the consequences of which are still being felt today. By this I do not mean the physical extermination of intellectuals or their forced exodus abroad. This internal crisis had to do with the meaning of life. For the enormous meaning offered by the new era involved conditions that were hardly comprehensible to the free and honest thinking man. Hence all these oscillations between the Reds and the Whites.

The year of Blok's death, 1921, saw the emergence in White émigré circles of the *smenovekhovstvo* (changing landmarks) movement, united by a common "intuition about the greatness of the Russian Revolution." This was the intuition Blok displayed at the revolution's outset (the revolution's "rumble . . . always speaks of something great") and which others were discovering post factum, having struggled against the revolution and been defeated. I don't intend to digress into an analysis of the changing landmarks ideology, but I would like to quote a curious observation by its intellectual leader, Nikolai Ustryalov. In a 1921 article entitled "The Intelligentsia and the People in the Russian Revolution," Ustryalov evokes the terrifying crisis of faith (or, in our terms, crisis of meaning) that seized the intelligentsia during the revolution.

> The Day of Judgment has taken place [the revolution — A.S.] — the judgment of the body and soul of the Russian intelligentsia. The intelligentsia has seen its dreams incarnated [the real-life utopia — A.S.] in their most extreme forms, in their most logical and precise expression. . . . The intelligentsia has reaped the fruits of its thoughts and deeds. Its most resolute and fearlessly loyal elements [the Bolsheviks — A.S.] fought with storm and thunder to transform its past into the present [its dreams into reality — A.S.]. "Monks of the church militant that is the revolution," they feared no inquisition for faith in their "golden dream." But the masses, the "army" of the intellectuals, shuddered. These real images of life seemed terrifying and senseless to them and they recoiled in horror.

They were seized by a visceral sensation of the abyss, the spiritual void where they had once seen the supreme law of wisdom [the ideals of the revolutionary, atheistic intelligentsia — A.S.]. And when these traditional "torches" that had been blinding them went out in their consciousnesses, the darkness that enveloped them was pierced by the lights of real and profound values that before had seemed alien and remote [these genuine values, to Ustryalov, are concepts of nation, Motherland, the traditional State system, religion, and so forth — A.S.].

But this past-now-present [the real-life utopia — A.S.] did not forgive the intelligentsia its defection. Brought to life and to power in an original alliance with the popular forces roused from their sleep, it called the intelligentsia to account. A tragic battle ensued in which the army of the Russian intelligentsia, having risen up against itself, against its own history, was routed.

The point here isn't so much the armed struggle between the Reds and the Whites as the spiritual and intellectual struggle, the struggle of ideas. Though the great intellectual forces didn't accept the revolution and resisted it, they (let's call them White) couldn't pride themselves in an idea as advanced or universal as that of the Reds. The old revolutionary and democratic traditions had been smashed or stained by their encounter with the reality of the revolution. But the rediscovered values — religion, morality, national sentiment — were vague and without prospect, without, I would say, great historical meaning.

In another article Ustryalov recalls his thoughts and conversations in early 1919, when he was in league with the Whites. Here he shares his impressions of that time with a comrade:

> I couldn't keep from expressing one feeling that was torturing me and that I couldn't seem to get over:
> — Of course, God willing, Kolchak[2] will win and one wants to believe in this victory. But you know, even so, in spite of everything, Moscow is so much more impressive, so much more interesting than what we have here. . . . The pathos of history is

---

2. *Translator's note:* Admiral Aleksandr Kolchak (1873–1920) was commander of White forces in Siberia, 1918–1920.

there. . . . Whereas here . . . here it's enough to go to "Russia" to be
gripped with doubt. . . . This isn't the new Russia, this isn't the
future. . . . Has-beens . . .

Morally, the ideals of the Whites were probably no less lofty than
those of the Reds. But as a rule these were the ideals of Russia's
past, while the future seemed uncertain, fragmented, and contradictory. So the "pathos of history" for Ustryalov, fighting for the
White flag, turned out to be in Red Moscow.

## The Fantastic and the Rational

The injection of meaning and purpose into history and the reorgani-
zation of life according to revolutionary or socialist principles
strictly limited the possibilities for human initiative, for displays of
individual or group will that did not coincide with the will of the
State and the Party. At the same time, this new world wasn't yet
habitable. The incipient State was physically incapable of regulat-
ing everything, reducing everything to a common standard. And in
many spheres the standards themselves hadn't yet been determined.
Meanwhile, the old norms and rules were either in ruins or in
question, since everything in the new society should be new. As a
result there were gaps that the State needed filled with fresh energy
and ideas. If the State used the old cadres, or "specialists," only in
controlled situations, it welcomed the masses more warmly, invit-
ing them to collaborate in this enterprise and giving them much
wider authority. The State truly wanted to be for the workers and
the peasants, and counted on the goodwill of these millions of
people. The equality, even primacy, accorded the lower classes
ignited in them a revolutionary zeal and the keen desire to bask in
the new light, to breathe the new air. In short, the expectation was
one of mutual satisfaction from a shared creation.

There were, of course, exceptions, since the living conditions of
ordinary people had barely improved or had changed for the worse.
But the Party still counted on love in return. In her reminiscences
about Lenin, his wife, Nadezhda Krupskaya, tells this story:

> One day, soon after the revolution, Lenin was walking up the
> staircase in the Smolny when he saw a woman washing the stairs.
> Tired, she stood up and leaned against the banister. Lenin started to

talk to her. She didn't know who he was. He said: "Well, comrade, what do you think of life now? Is it better under Soviet power than under the old government?" And she answered: "Doesn't bother me, I just wish they'd pay me for my work."

Not everyone displayed such a lack of class awareness. For many people, life under Soviet power was, if not better, at least brighter. In part because existence now had a greater meaning. New avenues were opening up, leading to the administration, to knowledge, to creation. And these feelings were encouraged and promoted from on high so long as they didn't conflict with Party policy. It was on this basis of rediscovered purpose, personal and historical, that the new democracy emerged. Democracy in the absence of democratic freedoms. Democracy subordinated to a dictatorship of the State or the Party watching over these humble classes. Initially there was a wholesale awakening of people's creative energy, the various manifestations of which made up the panorama of the real-life utopia. Yesterday a herdsman, today the commander of a regiment or an army: in some sense this too was an actual utopia. Yesterday a tailor, today a commissar. Yesterday illiterate, today a halting reader of *Pravda* who understands everything: who understands that he is a person, that he is the master, and who therefore reads aloud so that everyone will hear.

In the communal apartment in Moscow where I lived as a child at the end of the twenties, we had a neighbor from the country who read the paper aloud to himself every evening — so loud that no one else could hear himself think. But if one asked him to read more quietly, he would fly into a rage or even hit the person, thinking that again his class dignity had been attacked. Later he would listen to the radio turned up full blast. Ridiculous or sublime, touching or frightening, all this attests to the awakening of people's creative energy, to a purposeful existence in an explained and meaningful world.

Understandably, this milieu — mainly at the start of this phase of revolutionary initiative — generated all sorts of utopias. This was the spirit of the times. If the one, principal utopia had materialized, why not invent others so as to pave the revolutionary way to communism?

"Proletkults" were such a utopia. Mass organizations to school workers in how to create the highest and purest Proletarian Culture, they were only partially launched before being scrapped by the State that had instituted them. In scientific and technical circles, mass inventiveness seized self-taught workers and just plain ingenious people. Such people had always existed in Russia, but now it was as if they had been woken from their sleep. They began bombarding the top scientific authorities with all kinds of projects, some astounding, others ludicrous and farfetched.

But not only the lower classes were swept up in this utopian whirlwind. The left wing of the creative intelligentsia, notably the Futurists, took active part. Their romanticism as former rebels, their inventive genius, and their desire to turn art into life and life into art (what they called life-construction or life-creation) dovetailed with the spirit of the revolution and with this new field for the fantastic with practical applications. Though the State soon severed relations with the Futurists and labeled them holdovers from the bourgeois past, the Futurists initially had a distinct influence on the epoch of the real-life utopia. The State simply had no other creative elite willing to collaborate so wholeheartedly and so actively. And as for what the art of the victorious proletariat should be, the State still hadn't decided.

Not to digress into the fate of the Futurists, I would like to stress the romanticism of their revolutionary utopian construct, of their fantasy, of their originality, their striving to vault from aesthetics into life, into the streets, to merge with the revolution itself. This is what allowed the Futurists to color this period in the best sense. Artistically, their utopia was relatively harmless. But in terms of sheer size, their projects were grandiose, as if to match the vast historical horizons that were unfolding. Take Mayakovsky's "Open Letter to the Workers," written in early 1918, in which the fantastic allegories speak for themselves:

> No one is allowed to know what immense suns will illuminate the life of the future. Perhaps the artists will turn the gray dust of the cities into hundred-color rainbows; perhaps the mountains will resound endlessly with the thunderous strains of volcanos transformed into flutes; perhaps we'll force the ocean waves to run their fingers

over the strings that stretch from Europe to America. One thing we do know: the first page of the newest history of the arts will have been written by us.

The most colorful of the Russian Futurists, Velimir Khlebnikov, was also the most brilliant and inspiring of the utopian architects. Though he was shaped as a poet and thinker by earlier times, it wasn't until after the revolution that he deployed his grandest and most forceful designs. Khlebnikov considered that his poem-projects were the best response to the new universal civilization. He wanted to improve this new house, this real-life utopia, to enlarge it and equip it with his own discoveries. Confined to a small circle of Futurist friends, Khlebnikov was hardly a mainstream poet. But his utopias reveal the intellectual defiance which, it seemed at the start, was to be that of the new era and the new society. They represent the era's unrealized potential, so to speak, the utopian spirit that the revolution partly adopted and encouraged and then destroyed.

Khlebnikov himself viewed his designs not as utopias or fantasies but as meriting the utmost scientific seriousness; he saw them as revelations of the supreme laws ordering the world. These discoveries, he thought, would allow people of the future to alter radically their concept of the world and way of life. Khlebnikov epitomized our century — with his emphasis on science, his utopianism, his focus on the future.

## Revolutionary Utilitarianism

It's time we considered this process from another angle, that of utilitarianism, which reduced the utopia to real terms and made it possible to switch from high-flown rhetoric and ideas to the actual construction of the new world. This utilitarian zeal afforded the utopian fantasy a real, rational foundation; at the same time it checked it and corrected it, forcing it down to earth, not to dream but to do useful things.

Soon after the revolution, left-wing artists and intellectuals veered sharply again, this time in the direction of material application, of utilitarian tasks, even to the complete exclusion of aesthetics. This swerve was especially striking in that before the revolution Russian Futurism had been essentially a pure art form, art for art's sake. But evidently Futurism also contained a certain dynamism and will to act sufficient to have propelled itself from the "word per se" — pure aesthetics — to pure function, exchanging its aesthetic catchwords for superutilitarian banners. Futurists, just after the revolution, didn't stop fantasizing; on the contrary, they threw themselves into utopian schemes, most of which never got off the drawing board. But these new designs were distinguished by a rationalistic and utilitarian element. Even Khlebnikov regarded his fantastic plans — to conquer time and language — not as a game of poetic form or intellect but as a highly rational endeavor. The Russian Futurists' militant and ultrarevolutionary core, led by Mayakovsky, swung even more violently from theory to practice, from aesthetics to action. Mayakovsky evokes this passion for the utilitarian and the fantastic combined in his poem "150,000,000" (1920). Not to be taken literally, of course, it is a rejection of the old romanticism, of sentimental idealism. While fantasizing wildly, Mayakovsky also expresses an intense desire for useful action and classifies all things according to their utility:

> *Let's march!*
>> *Let's fly!*
>>> *Let's sail!*
>>>> *Let's roll!*
> *checking the list of all creation.*
> *That thing is necessary —*
>> *Fine, keep it.*
> *Unnecessary?*
>> *To the devil!*
>>> *A black cross.*
> *We'll destroy you,*
>> *old romantic world!*
> *In place of faith*
>> *in our soul we have*
>>> *electricity*
>>>> *and steam.*
> *In place of misery,*
>> *pocket the riches of all worlds!*
> *The old men? Kill them.*
>> *And use the skulls for ashtrays!*

Lenin, who didn't understand poetry, much less poetic hyperbole and metaphor, called these lines hooliganism and was indignant that a State publishing house had printed them. But Mayakovsky wasn't being a hooligan, he was voicing the spirit of the revolution in this combination of noble ideas and concrete actions, of utopianism and the crudest materialism (thus the soul possessed by a religious idea is composed of electricity and steam). Mayakovsky was lending the Leninist slogan "Pillage the Pillagers" (or "Expropriation of the Expropriators") a romantic harmony. Thus he proposes "pocketing" not the money of others but the riches of all the worlds in the universe. At the same time, he puts this romanticism and this fantasy on a utilitarian track, separating the things the revolution can use from those it cannot. And since old things are obsolete and of no use to Mayakovsky, the Futurist, he proposes — not literally, but in his usual hyperbolic style — that the skulls of old people be used to produce ashtrays. An ashtray is a useful thing . . .

Here Mayakovsky has obviously gone too far. But then Lenin, no kin to the Futurists, had a utilitarian approach to the problem of life and death: he proposed that life be reserved principally for useful people. Lenin was extremely solicitous about the health of his comrades and collaborators. But when he asked or even ordered them to take care of themselves, he always added, half joking, half serious, that by neglecting their health they were squandering "State property" and thus guilty of official misconduct. A person and even a person's life were "State property" and of no intrinsic value except in conjunction with the useful work of Party and State. Lenin related to himself and to all people from this practical point of view.

Years before the revolution, in 1911, in France, the Lafargues committed suicide. As two old people they had decided they could no longer be of service to society. These were eminent Marxists: Laura Lafargue was Karl Marx's daughter and Paul Lafargue had been a member of the Paris Commune. They were Lenin's ideological allies and dear friends besides. In her reminiscences, Krupskaya recalls Lenin's reaction to the news of the Lafargues' suicide: "If you can't work for the Party anymore, you should be able to face the truth and die the way the Lafargues did."

For Lenin, the value of human life was purely a function of its use to the Party cause. And Mayakovsky, in his exaggerated, Futuristic manner, said the same thing.

The revolution had furnished Futurism with a purpose that conformed to its new focus on dynamism and the creation of useful things as opposed to form pure and simple. This purpose expressed itself in a rather interesting movement dominated by the slogans "Art to Production!" and "From Painting to Chintz!" (in other words, from easel painting to textile production). Nonrepresentational artists abandoned abstract art for perfectly concrete objects: tables, chairs, cars, cotton prints, architectural plans, and so on. This movement of left-wing abstract artists dedicated to production was dubbed "design" in the West. But Russian "design" of this period distinguished itself in that it was not confined to the aesthetics of contemporary industrial and technological culture. It was art sacrificed to production, to a socialist production that encompassed all of life in its march toward the future. Art's enormous new task was constructivist. Everything was suffused with the idea of purpose and usefulness introduced by the real-life utopia.

This reconstruction of Futurism on a rational, utilitarian basis echoed a typically Russian tradition. While the Futurists rejected all traditions, they unwittingly embraced this one in their revolutionary fervor. In the nineteenth century the Russian intelligentsia had been similarly struck by the idea of the social good — not its own, individual, or limited good but the universal good, that of all people and even the entire world. Many Russian intellectuals lived not for themselves but for the good of the cause and judged everything in terms of the universal good. This undoubtedly is what led them to revolution and socialism at the appointed hour in history.

This propensity for the ultra-utilitarian recurs periodically in Russian social thought, regardless of its champion, of his social origins, his ideological, religious, or historical affiliation. What Mayakovsky did by going to work as a propagandist for the *Windows of the Russian Telegraph Agency,* by going from word to deed, Gogol did long before him by writing, in place of a work of fiction, his practical *Selected Passages from Correspondence with Friends* (1846). Lev Tolstoy, too, did something in this vein by anathematizing aesthetics in the name of the moral good. Similar tendencies, if somewhat diluted, appear in Pasternak's later works and, on another basis entirely, in the contemporary Solzhenitsyn. In short, this conflict between art and usefulness, between the intrinsic value of an object (any object) and its higher purpose, crops up repeatedly and in various contexts. It is the eternal Russian dilemma, the age-old question: What is more important, "beauty" or the "universal good," the Apollo Belvedere or a baking dish, an artist or a shoemaker? This conflict arises independent of the author's welt-anschauung — be he an Orthodox Christian or a Marxist, a Futurist or a Populist. The general bent is toward usefulness, toward the greater purpose, at the expense of aesthetics and at the expense of a person's independence.

In the nineteenth century this utilitarianism burst forward in the intellectual and literary movement of the *shestidesyatniki,* or nihilists of the 1860s, headed by Nikolai Chernyshevsky and Dmitry Pisarev and epitomized by the fictional Bazarov, hero of Ivan Turgenev's *Fathers and Sons* (1862). Bazarov was convinced that "a shoemaker is necessary, a tailor is necessary, but a Raphael isn't worth a brass farthing," that "a decent chemist is twenty times more useful than any poet." Bazarov takes this belief right up to its logical conclusion, up to the necessity of sacrificing one's own life: "If one's decided to mow everything down, one shouldn't spare one's own legs."

The Russian Futurists took a little after Bazarov, beginning as they did with the idea of form's inherent value, of art for art's sake, and ending with the call to smash aesthetics. Of their own accord, they reiterated the logic of Bazarov the *shestidesyatnik.* Here I will quote from an article by Osip Brik, eminent theorist of Futurism in its new, revolutionary incarnation, author of the slogans "From Painting to Chintz!" and "Art to Production!" and Mayakovsky's closest friend and associate. Written in 1919, at the revolution's height, the article was entitled "The Artist and the Commune":

"The cobbler makes boots. The joiner makes tables. And what does the artist do? He doesn't do anything; he 'creates.' This is vague and suspect. . . . The Commune doesn't need priests or parasites. Only workers will find a place in it. If artists don't want to wind up like the parasitic elements, they'd better prove their right to existence."

Further on, Brik recalls several definitions of art only to sweep them aside, one by one, as utterly unsuited and useless to the revolution, to the proletariat, to the future. The first definition echoes the spirit of the old realism:

> The artist reflects life.
>
> Who needs it? What use is a reflection if one has all of life at one's disposal? Who'd prefer a copy to the original?
>
> The artist reflects life as he sees it.
>
> So much the worse! That means he distorts it.
>
> The artist serves beauty.
>
> Here the monks are the perfect analogue. Somewhere over there, in monasteries, they serve God. There's no place for monks in the Commune.

Thus, in Brik's view, art in the old sense must disappear.

"Their bourgeois art will perish. Artists who know only how to 'create' and 'serve beauty' will perish. But there are other artists. They do socially useful work. That labor gives the artist the right to stand alongside other labor groups in the Commune: the cobblers, the joiners, the tailors."

All these arguments resemble Bazarov's rationalistic logic. The cobbler is more useful than the artist. Consequently the artist must either disappear or turn into a cobbler, into a useful member of society involved in production. But this extreme utilitarianism and rationalism would never have prevailed in Futurist circles had it not been for the revolution. The traditional Russian readiness to sacrifice art for the sake of life and the people, beauty for the sake of usefulness, was fired by the grand revolutionary design applied to man's every thought and deed. The revolution introduced a spirit of cruel expediency that went as far as ascetic intolerance of anything that seemed useless in the moment. And this single-minded, utilitarian spirit consumed Futurism, ready to sacrifice itself for the good of the cause.

Not long before his death in 1930, at one of his last public appearances, Mayakovsky was handed a note from the audience which read: "Mayakovsky, if for the good of the proletarian revolution you were required to write in iambic verse, would you?"

Though a staunch opponent of iambic verse as an antiquated and useless form, Mayakovsky was compelled to answer: "Yes." Naturally, he was thinking not simply of a Party order from above to write in iambic verse but of some genuine necessity, as it was stated in the note, *for the good of the revolution.* Mayakovsky couldn't have responded otherwise, since he himself regarded the good of the revolution as the greatest criterion and requirement of contemporary art, to which all poetry, including his, must submit. History's irony, the bitter irony of the fate of Mayakovsky and other revolutionary artists, lies in the fact that "for the good of the revolution" iambic verse was later required . . .

But the pressure of utilitarianism went far beyond artistic problems and permeated all aspects of life in the new society. With the revolution, humanity had entered an era of the most brutal expediency. Man's every move was now judged by the good or harm it did vis-à-vis communism's supreme goal. Given these conditions, it's understandable that initially the greatest champions of the idea and practice of utilitarianism were the Bolsheviks. They played the principal role in translating the utopia into reality, in turning the ideal into a real and universal edifice. Superutilitarianism became perhaps the essence of the Bolshevik psychology, a wonderful illustration of which appears in Pilnyak's *The Naked Year.* At issue here are not the highest but the lowest Party workers, charged with bringing revolution and socialism to the grass roots, to the provinces. Children of the people, they have retained the democratic traits of their social and national Russian nature. At the same time they are a new breed. Their energy and toughness have been harnessed to the laws of cruel regimentation and expediency. They work all the time, or rather carry out orders: anyone can work in a factory or a field, but Bolsheviks are supposed to carry out orders according to Party instructions. In Pilnyak's novel this military-bureaucratic style of Party organization is conveyed instantly by the Bolsheviks' dress. As the commanding caste, the Bolsheviks all wear leather jackets (these would become as much their symbol as their uniform). Pilnyak calls them simply "leather jackets." This costume makes them stand out in the crowd while advertising their toughness, discipline, efficiency, single-mindedness, and revolutionary asceticism. One of these leather jackets is called Arkhip Arkhipov, a name that immediately betrays him as a common bumpkin.

Men in leather jackets, Bolsheviks, were assembling upstairs at
the Executive Committee. And what men these were in their leather
jackets, every one the model of a leather Adonis, every one strap-
ping and curly-haired under his peaked cap pushed back, every one
with razor-sharp cheekbones, creases at the corners of his mouth,
and perfectly pressed gestures. From the gnarled, podgy Russian
people, this was the cream of the crop. And in their leather jackets,
they wouldn't get wet. One knows, one wants, one decides — and
that's enough. . . . Arkhip Arkhipov spent the days at the Executive Committee signing papers, knitting his brows . . . he held his
pen like an axe. When he spoke at meetings, he mispronounced the
foreign words. He said: "askertain," "enegretically," "litephono-
gram," "frunction," "bodget," and the Russian word *mogoot* came
out *magoot*. . . . Arkhip Arkhipov was always up at dawn, cram-
ming books on the sly: Kiselev's Algebra, Kistyakovsky's Economic
Geography, Nineteenth Century Russian History (Granat edition),
Marx's *Capital,* Ozerov's Financial Science, Weitzman's Account-
ing, a Teach Yourself German primer, and Gavkin's glossary of
foreign words absorbed into the Russian language.

It's a curious list of books that Arkhip Arkhipov pores and
sweats over; it smacks of parody, this collection of volumes meant
to be a crash course in the world, in the principal sciences. This is
more than the elimination of illiteracy or a kind of specialization,
this is a syllabus for Party leaders in all spheres of life and the
economy. All the sciences are examined from the standpoint of their
practical application. And the foreign words, which Arkhip Arkhipov hastily memorizes and then mangles, make up the workaday
and newspaper jargon of the new civilization, the new utopia rising
from the ruins of the old Russia. One solid formula, culled from
these foreign words, acquires special emphasis in Arkhip Arkhipov's lexicon and in Pilnyak's novel: "function energetically," or
"frunction enegretically." It is the symbol of the Bolshevik faith
with its tough, energetic utilitarianism. In the novel it sounds
slightly ludicrous, since one must "frunction" amidst general devastation and hunger and there isn't anything much to "frunction"
with. This exposes the utopianism of the whole enterprise, albeit
utopianism with a distinctly practical bent and designed with the
iron will of this new type of man in mind. The novel has this to say:

" 'Frunction enegretically!' that's what the Bolsheviks are all about. And the hell with you and everyone else — you hear — lemonade is bitter-sweet!"

"Bitter-sweet lemonade" is obviously a reference to the old liberal intelligentsia, which babbled and sighed but didn't do anything, which indulged in lovely dreams and lofty sentimentality. But the leather jackets don't dream or babble: they're building the new society.

Pilnyak's "function energetically" epitomizes the spirit and style of Bolshevism and, more broadly, the style of the new revolutionary era. In this connection I would like to quote a remarkable historical document produced by Aleksei Gastev. This picturesque if not atypical figure inspired great hopes in his capacity as a proletarian poet. A veteran of serious revolutionary work and an ardent Bolshevik, he bore the nickname Iron Gastev. He dropped poetry to pursue practical activities, life-construction and life-creation. As director of the Central Labor Institute, Gastev took charge of scientific organization in modern industrial production, social education, and what was known as cultural construction or the cultural revolution. In 1923 he gave a paper (later published) entitled "The Equipment of Contemporary Culture," addressed to Soviet youth leaders or "the agents of culture":

The true agent of culture must have a good disposition. This alone will give him the capacity for hard work he needs to shake people awake who have been asleep for three centuries. Let three hundred people commit suicide, but when the whistle blows, let the machines whirr!

You must become masters of the attack and pressure. You must know everything there is to know about how knife and hammer are made and love them both damnably. . . . And the synthesis of these two instruments, the handsome axe?! It should function like the ball in a game. We must bring it to perfection. Then we'll reach a capacity we've never dreamed of.

It is essential to learn how to sleep. . . . When you want to rest, you should be able to collapse onto a bed and momentarily reach the maximum passivity in all your muscles, as if you had vanished into thin air. . . . You must take stock of everything around you. In the ravine where we are, there is rotten wood: take stock of this, and if there's a stone take stock of that too! Finally, if there isn't anything, take stock of your own hands, which are always dreaming of an instrument. This is what's called making revolution.

If we create any other kind of philosophy, it will kill us, but it won't teach us how to win.

It's difficult for us to call this philosophy, even if it does teach one how to win. And it's difficult to call it culture, given that all culture and philosophy here sink into utilitarianism, that of the poor and uneducated, from whom only one thing is required: that they "frunction enegretically." But this was Soviet civilization in the days before it had a culture, with its taste for the technical, for sports, for stock-taking and for control. Control over the rotten wood, over the hammer, and over one's own mental and physical state.

This too is a sort of utopia, though it flies in the face of all utopianism and insists on useful and rational action. In the real-life utopia, there are always two sides of the coin. On the one hand, for the utopia to materialize, it ceases to be a utopia and instead adopts the language of practical benefit and action. In this sense, its rationalism contradicts its utopianism and ultimately precludes it. On the other hand, even this rationalism and utilitarianism can have a utopian quality, though often turned inside out: twisted into a malicious parody of human good and an intelligent world order.

To illustrate how all this got mixed up and one thing turned into the other, I will quote one more document, a project which fortunately never materialized and which was frankly idiotic. Published privately in 1919, it concerned a reform of the language, literary and vernacular. This project reveals how far the revolution had gone in people's minds and how extreme rationalism and extreme utilitarianism could take on incredibly utopian proportions. The draft's author (a certain Kiselev) was advocating that the Russian language be reconstructed as quickly as possible to conform with revolutionary reality and advanced Marxist science. Kiselev's complaint was the language's myriad unscientific-sounding metaphors, overt and covert vestiges of religious, mythological, and anthropomorphic notions. Expressions like "Spring arrived" or "The sun hid behind the cold peaks." And similarly unscientific imagery in contemporary literature and the classics — Pushkin, Lermontov, Turgenev, Lev Tolstoy — which, Kiselev claimed, needed correcting. For example, in *War and Peace* Tolstoy writes: "The clouds go scudding along this high, endless sky." But to be accurate and scientific, he should have written: "The clouds move in the atmosphere of our planet." Kiselev's reform contained the following perfectly rational and utilitarian argument:

> Russia is going through a period of radical reorganization of social relations. The foundations of the capitalist system have been reduced to ruins and on these ruins a new socialist system is being built. This system can and must have a strictly scientific basis. From this it follows that the structure of this system's language must strictly correspond to its scientific basis.
>
> Proceeding from a scientific understanding of a day and a year, we have found that expressions to the effect that they come, arrive, or approach are incorrect and constitute blots, hangovers, and reactionary occurrences. The same can be said of certain words used to depict the life of the individual or the masses such as: hunger set in; the revolution came, approached; death came, set in, etc. Given a scientific understanding of the life of the individual and of society — and in a socialist system such an understanding is compulsory — all these phenomena are nothing other than . . . natural processes. . . . Therefore all these expressions must be reconstructed."

Now imagine the monstrous antiutopia we would have found ourselves in had such a reform been instituted. We would have found ourselves in a world where people speak in a dead, scientifically rectified language, where *War and Peace* and all world literature had been reissued in new, revised, rational editions.

This project was exceptional, of course, for its stupidity. But it does reflect, to some extent, the spirit of the real-life utopia, which sees itself as a scientifically stipulated and rationally constructed society. From this point of view, the most frightening phenomena and processes that shaped Soviet civilization were based on strictly scientific and utilitarian rationales, be it the mass terror or the dispossession of the kulaks, the camps or censorship.

# 3

## Lenin: The State of Scholars

IF THE PARTY'S RANK AND FILE was busy functioning energetically and cementing the utopia to utilitarian practice, who was giving the orders? Who could prove all this, explain it, and impose it? After the revolution, Soviet Russia was run by a State of scholars. Other interpretations of this dictatorship are certainly possible, but here it is this scholarly twist that strikes me as especially compelling and significant.

By its own definition, Marxism is not only a science but the quintessential science vis-à-vis the history of man and society. Leninism boasts the same absolute scientific authority, which it complements with a practice based, in principle, on a rigorous analysis of the concrete historical situation that itself constitutes a new scientific argument. This State of scholars, alias the victorious Bolsheviks, should be compared not to liberal scholars past or present but to other ruling Russian regimes: the tsarist autocracy and the Provisional Government. Such a comparison makes it clear that after October, and perhaps for the first time ever, the State was headed not by tsars or generals, lawyers, or heroes, but by wise men and scholars who proclaimed their government to be a dictatorship of the proletariat. Here I'm thinking of the comparatively small but cohesive core of top Bolshevik intellectuals united around Lenin. Far from being amateurs, these were what you might call scientific experts in political struggle and social relations of whom the chief expert was Vladimir Ilyich Lenin.

## THE PRIMACY OF SCIENCE AND REASON IN LENIN'S PSYCHOLOGY

Opinions of Lenin vary tremendously and even conflict. But again this scholarly aspect is the one I would stress. The most striking thing about Lenin's psychophysiology is his disproportionately large head, working away like some outsize calculating machine. In this light, certain minor facts and details about Lenin speak volumes. For instance the anecdote that, as a child, Lenin was forever falling down and hitting his head because it threw him off balance. Or the fact that Lenin died from sclerosis of the blood vessels in his brain, an incredibly widespread sclerosis, as if this fossilization had been the result of some colossal mental labor. Despite a modest, even unprepossessing appearance, Lenin captivated audiences with this head of his, with the logic that dominated his oratory and his vision of the world. Many memoirists, scholars, and poets have depicted Lenin with this hyperbolic cranium, which seems to be either crushing the whole of humanity or saving it. As Mayakovsky wrote:

> *Then over the world loomed*
> *Lenin of the enormous head.*
>
> *In his skull he juggled*
> > *hundreds of provinces,*
> *He carried*
> > *men*
> > > *up to billions and a half,*
> *He weighed*
> > *the world*
> > > *overnight,*
> *and in the morning . . .*

And in the morning, he drew the proper, scientific conclusions. Undoubtedly, this was the only way to bring about the real-life utopia — not by brute strength alone, but by painstaking mental computation.

This primacy of intellect, however, stamps Lenin as a kind of inhuman improbability — as if some huge-headed Martian had turned up on earth with a brain so developed it outstripped ours by several thousand years. But such was the scientific spirit of the twentieth century in the ideal. Even Stalin with his passions, his cruelty, and his religious personality cult seems more understandable than Lenin. The incomprehensibility of Lenin is precisely this all-consuming intellectuality — the fact that from his calculations, from his neat pen, flowed seas of blood, whereas by nature this was not an evil person. On the contrary, Vladimir Ilyich was a rather kind person whose cruelty was stipulated by science and incontrovertible historical laws. As were his love of power and his political intolerance. It is said that Lenin loved power. This is entirely possible. But his love of power (if it was that) was devoid of any intoxication with power, just as it was devoid of vanity, pride, or arrogance. Lenin craved power as if it were a scientific prerequisite for the correct formulation of the sociohistorical experiment. As if the experiment had required that a head take power, and since Lenin didn't see another worthy of his own, he — not for his sake but for that of a scientifically exact operation — assumed the leadership. For all his political and ideological bias and intolerance, Lenin was neither vindictive nor out to settle scores with rivals. His intolerance and bias may simply have been a function of the fact that, as a scholar, he had arranged all those Mensheviks and Socialist Revolutionaries, Kadets, and Western Social Democrats according to strict, scientific classifications from which he could not and would not deviate. Reading Lenin's works, often built on internal Party polemics, one is reminded of the systems of Linnaeus or Darwin applied to sociohistorical classification and to the political struggle of the twentieth century. As if Lenin, cursing his opponents, were trying to pin them like butterflies into the boxes of his Marxist table. His concern is to establish a rigorous and rational order, to establish control by determining who's who — not according to the ordinary traits of a "scoundrel" or a "rascal," but according to specific, generic, or class affiliation.

But Lenin's almost complete lack of the human foibles so typical in dictators makes him a doubly eerie figure. For it implies an equal lack of a natural human quality, whether we call this quality heart, soul, freedom, or something else. Lenin evidently lacked the irrationality that is natural in any person. And since he had only his brain, his rationalism assumed irrational proportions.

To illustrate I will use a few perfectly prosaic examples. Shortly before the October 1917 uprising, Lenin was living clandestinely in a Petrograd apartment. The landlady, a Bolshevik sympathizer but a simple soul, later described how Lenin had stayed with her and this evocation was, as it should be, unaffected and touching. Lenin lived out of sight in a back room without windows opening onto the interior courtyard. He worked all the time. He was writing something. Occasionally an Italian girl wandered into the yard singing; stranded by the war in our Palmyra of the North, she went from yard to yard begging. Lenin's landlady knew this girl, who had tuberculosis, and felt terribly sorry for her. She told Lenin all this. From his back room, he listened to the songs with pleasure since they reminded him of Italy and émigré life. But the day Lenin saw his landlady lowering a small packet of change into the yard on a string for the Italian girl, he was shocked. "Why are you doing that?" he asked. The landlady tried to explain that she was doing this out of compassion. "All the same, those half-kopecks won't do her any good." Lenin was sincerely indignant at the illogicality and uselessness of any philanthropy. He said that after the socialist revolution that was being prepared, there would be no more of these unfortunate women and beggars. The new State would give them work. As for those who didn't want to work and went on sponging, they would be forced physically to do something useful.

Lenin's surprise at this simple gesture of charity speaks not so much of a cruelty as of a rationalism precluding emotional acts and other illogical impulses.

His brain worked nonstop in only one direction: that of the scientifically effected utopia.

This impression is confirmed by a very different episode dating from 1904, when Lenin was in Switzerland. There he was visited by a Party colleague, Maria Essen. She tells of a walk they took in the mountains which ended in their scrambling up to a peak from where the view was breathtakingly beautiful. Essen describes the romantic landscape below and adds: "I'm filled with inspiration — ready to recite Shakespeare, Byron . . . I look over at Lenin. He is sitting lost in thought. Suddenly he blurts out: 'Those Mensheviks really know how to play dirty! . . .' "

From this distance it's difficult to know what prompted Lenin's remark which, against the Swiss scenery, sounds comical. Possibly he wanted to deflate Essen's rapture, to anchor it to practical, Party concerns. But more likely Lenin simply couldn't and wouldn't be distracted from his then principal intellectual preoccupation: fighting the Mensheviks.[1] No manner of magical landscape could compete. Like the mathematician out for a stroll who can't stop deducing and proving a certain theorem. Touching in its own way, this episode is treated by Essen with gentle humor. But if one recalls how consistently this trait surfaces in Lenin, then one senses that something in him was atrophied, thus allowing his specialized, scholarly intellect to burgeon.

Just after the revolution Maksim Gorky asked Lenin to intervene on behalf of a liberal, intellectual family that had just been arrested. Before the revolution, this family had saved a number of Bolsheviks from the tsarist secret police by hiding them in their home. Gorky hoped that Lenin, as a sign of gratitude, would show this family mercy. But Lenin burst out laughing. He said the Cheka — the first in a long line of secret police organs in the Soviet era — needed to pay particular attention to these intellectuals, whose kindness and compassion would always make them bleed for the less fortunate and the persecuted. Before, they were saving Bolsheviks, now it's Socialist Revolutionaries. Consequently, they deserved special sur-veillance and punishment. Lenin's reasoning was correct and strictly scientific: a sense of gratitude did not figure in his objective logic.

Yet, Lenin came from this same intellectual milieu and had adopted many of its habits, including personal disinterestedness, humility toward one's inferiors, and a careless style of dress, since the true Russian intellectual didn't think or care too much about his appearance. In the middle of his militarized dictatorship, amidst the leather jackets, Lenin remained the inveterate civilian. But the day after coming to power, this civilian drew up a detailed list itemizing the "duties of the guard attached to the president of the Council of People's Commissars." Then he tackled the Cheka's organization and activities right down to the minutiae. He didn't just give orders to shoot at the slightest provocation, he issued special instructions indicating whom to place under surveillance

---

1. *Translator's note:* The Mensheviks (unlike the Bolsheviks) thought that Russia wasn't yet ready for socialism, that society must first evolve for a time under capitalism.

and how; where and into what Chekists should change to facilitate surveillance and sudden searches. Lenin also worked out what he called (in a 1921 letter-directive) "systems of double and triple sudden checks according to all the rules of police investigation."

These messages to the Cheka crammed with all kinds of instructions (published in Moscow in 1975) suggest that Lenin not only created and inspired the Cheka but also had a flair and penchant for police investigation. In fact, Lenin simply wanted to give the police and punitive organs a solid scientific and technical base. He approached any task with this same zeal — the economy or the military, foreign policy or the collection of reusable raw materials — always focusing on the utilitarian and the rational, trying to inject science wherever possible. Lenin's correspondence with Feliks Dzerzhinsky, the Cheka's head, in 1919 contains an amusing episode on this score. An inventor (evidently they were plentiful then) had suggested using a magnet in weapons searches. So Lenin ordered a magnet to be used as the latest innovation in police investigation. The magnet was not a success, Dzerzhinsky wrote back to Lenin. But, he added: "We plan to use it so that people will give up their weapons voluntarily for fear that the magnet will find everything."

This is like Gastev's advice to take stock and control of any rotten wood, like Pilnyak's formula to "frunction enegretically" no matter what. If the magnet doesn't work, use it to frighten people — maybe that will help. But the interesting thing here is that even after being told the magnet is a failure, Lenin insists:

"Instruct the Cheka to find two comrades sufficiently intelligent and appropriate for purposes of using a magnetic device to detect concealed weapons, and offer them a substantial reward for the successful use of said device."

Such was Lenin's veneration for all-powerful science and technology. This "scientificness" was in him from the beginning, like a formative personality trait. In her memoirs, Krupskaya gives us a picture of Lenin in Geneva in 1905, diligently studying the science of insurrection, devouring mountains of books (including works on military affairs, on the strategy and tactics of armed struggle). Who would have suspected what this very civilian-looking man, personally incapable of killing anyone, this typical intellectual, was about? Krupskaya writes, as if from a distance:

An employee of the Reading Society witnessed the arrival early every morning of a Russian revolutionary in cheap trousers which he rolled up out of the mud in the Swiss fashion and forgot to unroll. Having collected his book from the day before on barricade fighting or the technology of attack, he would take his usual place at the table by the window, smooth his thinning hair back over his bald pate, and plunge into his reading. Sometimes he wouldn't get up except to take a big dictionary down from the shelf and look up an unfamiliar term, after which he would pace and then sit back down and start furiously filling squares of paper with a fine script.

Here you have the image of a scholar, even if this scholar writes on squares of paper about how one must, before any insurrection, attack the police and the cossacks, shoot and throw bombs, and not worry about hurting innocent bystanders: their blood will be compensated by the great purpose en route to which we will practice and ultimately master the science of armed struggle, and we will learn, learn, learn . . .

### LENIN: PRACTITIONER AND UTOPIAN

Lenin was an eminent scientific expert in the field of political struggle. The soul of Marxism, he said, was concrete scientific analysis of the concrete historical situation; in other words, the fusing of scientific theory with actual practice which, refined by this theory, turns into a new reality. But then, one may ask, given Lenin's logic and scientific bent, his penchant for solving actual problems based on analysis of the actual situation, was he a utopian? Yes and no. It was precisely this combination of qualities that allowed Lenin to launch his utopia, to put it on a practical track.

To Lenin, the word "utopia" had essentially a negative meaning since it suggested a fantasy for the more or less distant future. Utopia is a place that doesn't exist on earth and may never exist. But Lenin wanted to build his utopia in the here and now. For this reason he could not stand "utopians," a word he often used to curse Socialist Revolutionaries and other dreamy, overexcited socialists. Lenin's forte was not in abstract theory or starry-eyed intellectual constructs but in the ability to scientifically evaluate the evidence and draw rational conclusions on that basis. Here I will mention four of Lenin's findings; these were perhaps the key ones in bringing about the Bolsheviks' success.

The first was Lenin's recognition of the exact moment and political opening for the October coup d'état, at a time when most of the Party leadership was undecided about whether to take this step. Leon Trotsky later wrote in his journal that if Lenin hadn't been in Petrograd at that point, there wouldn't have been any October Revolution. One man, Lenin, changed the course of history: on the strength of his neat, businesslike calculations and over the objections of numerous Party comrades, he insisted on an armed uprising at precisely that moment.

The second finding was Lenin's push for immediate peace with Germany and the Treaty of Brest-Litovsk when Russia, again at his insistence, suddenly withdrew from the World War. As a result, the Bolsheviks gained the support of huge numbers of soldiers, thus securing their victory in the civil war. From Lenin's point of view, continuing the war with Germany after seizing power would have been to pursue a patent utopia, one that would have led to the loss of the October conquests.

The third finding was Lenin's New Economic Policy which, as a concession to the peasants and a sharp turn after the civil war, saved Russia from hunger and ruin, from a wave of peasant revolts. Interestingly, with the introduction of NEP in 1921, Lenin came to regard the previous period of "war communism" as a somewhat utopian one — utopian in that the Bolsheviks, even before consolidating power, had considered that they could instantly establish communism by confiscating all "surplus" grain from the peasants and distributing it to the workers. In a 1921 speech (at the Second Congress of Political Educators), Lenin called this utopianism a mistaken approach to building society that could not have lasted long. "We had decided that the peasants would apportion the necessary quantity of grain to us," said Lenin, referring to the war communism period, "and that we would apportion this grain to the factories, and that then we would have communist production and distribution."

Even Lenin had to admit that this policy of requisitioning grain hadn't been simply a compulsory, emergency measure under war communism, but a utopian attempt to make Russia Communist once and for all by abolishing private trade and introducing the forcible socialization of all production, including agriculture. This utopia was then amended to include the more realistic NEP — reviving limited free enterprise and allowing the sale of surpluses by the peasants — thus postponing the war with the peasantry until the forced collectivization instituted by Stalin.

Finally, Lenin's fourth finding — grounded in science and applied in practice — consisted in his rejection of all freedom and democracy, outside as well as inside the Party. To maintain democracy would have been utopian and the Bolsheviks' downfall. As a scholar, Lenin gave us a concise definition of the term "dictatorship" and, by extension, of Soviet State power: "The scientific concept of a dictatorship signifies nothing other than a power which, unrestricted by any laws, uninhibited by any absolute rules, resorts freely to the use of violence."

There is no denying the honesty of this formula or its scientific basis. That it sounds frightening to all liberals, democrats, and humanists, to you and to me, is another matter. It sounds equally frightening to all utopians of the Marxist or generally socialist persuasion, since it deprives them of any hope that socialism will bring democracy and freedom, that the revolution will be that leap from the kingdom of necessity to the kingdom of freedom described by Marx. On the contrary, as Lenin says and proves, the revolution is a leap into the kingdom of unlimited violence sponsored by the State power on behalf of the proletariat. The power is this violence, which extends in principle to the entire population and without which this utopia could not exist.

Certain Western historians, Marxists or European Communists who idealize Lenin, now claim that this Leninist conception of the dictatorship and of State power as blanket violence was a necessary but temporary measure connected with the first phase of the revolution and the civil war, with war communism. This necessity then fell away, while the blame for the later terror lies with Stalin and his disciples. But let's take the year 1922: with NEP in full swing, it was the height of freedom, the height of Soviet democracy. Investigations, mass executions without trial, and revolutionary tribunals are giving way to Soviet legal procedure. Soviet legislation is being refined. On this score, Lenin's first concern in peaceful 1922 is that

Soviet legislation contain a justification for terror, that it give terror a scientific and juridical framework. In a letter to People's Commissar of Justice Kursky, Lenin insists: "Jurisprudence must not eliminate terror; to promise this would be to deceive oneself or to deceive others. It must vindicate and legalize it."

Not that Lenin was cruel, but he scientifically foresaw that socialism would require total violence. He therefore legalized terror as a condition for the existence of Soviet civilization. Now, when Soviet leaders assert that after the Stalin era we have finally returned to the Leninist norms of socialist legality, this means that we have returned to legalized terror.

Thus Lenin was not a utopian; he approached political struggle scientifically and rationally, in a businesslike way, having analyzed the concrete situation. But at the same time, these well-thought-out decisions usually hinged on utopias that were necessary for their implementation. Lenin timed the October coup d'état and the Brest-Litovsk treaty perfectly, but he was relying on the utopian notion of a world revolution that would come to the aid of the revolution in Russia and carry the center of world socialism to developed Europe with its evolved proletariat and its advanced economy. If Lenin hadn't been under the influence of this utopia, he might not have decided to take such a risk. When the utopia didn't materialize, he had no choice but to tackle socialism by purely Russian means, by turning the screws as tight as they would go and instituting violence as the basis of socialism in Russia while continuing to hope for revolutions abroad, in developed capitalist countries.

NEP, another example of Lenin's pragmatism, was a necessary and sensible step, a protracted respite allowing Russia to recover and the State to set the government and economy on socialist foundations. There was nothing obviously utopian here: if anything, as we saw, this was a rejection of the utopia. But there is still a utopian element. For what is the Leninist conception of socialism? It is political power in the hands of the Party and a technologically advanced economy. Lenin thought a lot about this and even came up with a kind of mathematical formula: "Socialism equals Soviet power plus the electrification of the whole country." He had several of these formulas. But they all boil down to this "plus," to this addition of unequal values: "Soviet power plus the Prussian railway system, plus American technology and the organization of trusts, plus American public education, etc., etc., equals socialism."

These formulas have an obviously artificial, utopian ring. Lenin takes what he likes about the West (he was astounded by the exactitude of German trains and by American technology) and mechanically transposes it to Russia. Even today this wouldn't be possible, much less then, with Russia in ruins. It sounds like the logic of the exacting bride in Gogol's comedy *Marriage,* which Lenin liked to quote when ridiculing the utopian Populists who said: If one were to take the Russian patriarchal peasant community and add the English Parliament and Swiss egalitarianism, that would be the ideal system. Or as Agafya Tikhonovna says in *Marriage:* "If one could just attach Nikanor Ivanovich's lips to Ivan Kuzmich's nose, then take a touch of Balthazar Balthazarovich's unbuttoned manner and perhaps add to this Ivan Pavlovich's portliness, then I would make up my mind in an instant."

Lenin, with his formulas for socialism, resembles this bride somehow, despite his extremely practical and rational discourse. He retains nothing from Russia except Soviet power, to which Western order and technology are added. But even under Lenin, Soviet power as originally conceived had become a fiction, since it wasn't the soviets — the elected councils — that were running the country but the Party apparatus, gone the way of unlimited violence. So far, in fact, that Lenin's socialism was nothing other than a dictatorship plus technology.

## VIOLENCE AS THE BASIS OF THE NEW STATE SYSTEM

Let's take the problem of violence, the problem of the State as soberly conceived by Lenin, as not promising any freedom or democracy. Lenin arrived at this conception only after some time and having passed through a utopian phase himself. If not for this preliminary utopian vision, the revolution would not have triumphed: the workers and the peasants would not have backed it, and even the Party, one suspects, would not have thrown itself into this venture had it known what lay ahead. But the Party didn't know what kind of dictatorship this would be and neither did Lenin, still in thrall to the utopia, on the eve of the revolution.

This utopia embraced two essential elements in which Lenin sincerely believed and which he constantly stressed — until he came to power and rejected the utopia, based on his own experience of the State. First, on the eve of the October Revolution, it was held that violence would be necessary for only a brief period while seizing power; this done, the new State would immediately begin to wither away since, as Lenin wrote, "in a society without class conflicts a State is unneeded and impossible." Second, it was thought that this new State power (or "dictatorship of the proletariat") would be implemented by the masses themselves and even by all people in turns, without detaching a special bureaucratic apparatus. Moreover, the most senior officials would not benefit from any material privileges, and the salary of a top functionary would not exceed the average wage of a worker. Lenin insisted on this last point, which he considered to be a law of the proletarian State that distinguished it from all others. This new State, Lenin thought, would be the most inexpensive and the most democratic in the world, without estrangement from the people, without any authoritarianism or red tape. Lenin set all of this down on the eve of October 1917 in his famous book *The State and Revolution*.

Lenin's most striking work in several respects, this is a manual on seizing power intended for Communists of all countries: a model of rigorous logic and utopianism combined. Lenin contends that the only way to achieve socialism is to seize power by violent means and smash the old State machinery, even if it happens to be a democratic parliament. Simultaneously, he depicts a State idyll, with the abolition of the State just around the corner. Finally, this book is remarkable as a source of the sedition that would come later, in the Stalin era and in ours. Nowhere is the breach between Communist theory and practice more conspicuous.

But this doesn't at all mean that Lenin was hostile to the bureaucratic monstrosity that he ended by creating. After October, even if he didn't say so publicly, Lenin revised his concept of the State. The actual revolution compelled him to act, think, and write in ways other than he had supposed on its eve. If Lenin hadn't given up his original utopia then, the revolution would have foundered and Soviet civilization as we know it would not exist. Still, this utopia was necessary to the Bolsheviks as a springboard, since it promised that the terrible dictatorship would be temporary and perfectly democratic.

It is interesting to note, however, that at the outset this dictatorship had a somewhat utopian demeanor, which it shed only gradually. Even after the coup d'état the utopia continued to affect the words and consciousness of the new State. Taking the cruelest and most brutal measures at the beginning of the revolution, Lenin said these were necessary interim steps and not the essence of the new power. Thus, two days after the October coup, a decree signed by Lenin outlawed all "bourgeois" newspapers accused of engaging in counterrevolutionary propaganda. Freedom of the word and press was quashed. But quashed with this mollifying proviso (to quote the decree of the Soviet of People's Commissars, signed by its chairman, Lenin): "Imposing restrictions on the press, even at critical moments, is permissible only within the confines of absolute necessity. . . . The current arrangement is of a temporary nature and will be countermanded by special order as soon as life returns to normal."

What's implied here is that we are now going through the most critical period of the revolution, but even so we are taking only the minimum measures with respect to restricting the press. And when the critical period has passed and life returns to normal, we will restore the freedom of the press and lift the restrictions. Need one add that the special countermand was never issued? Apparently, Soviet life has never returned to normal: in most official press and television reports, the heavy-handed influence of the Party is felt to this day, as if society were still going through that critical period. And this is true despite the so-called liberalization of the Gorbachev era.

Or take the question of capital punishment, of the use of violence, the use of terror. In early 1920 Lenin said: "The use of violence is demanded by the task of eliminating the exploiters, of eliminating the landowners and capitalists; when this is done we will rescind all extraordinary measures."

But the rescindment of these extraordinary measures was forever being postponed. First the critical period had to pass, then civil war had to be over with, then world revolution had to triumph. Meanwhile, the theory and practice of unrestrained and uninhibited violence gathered momentum, buttressed by an increasingly strict and forthright rationale. At the start of 1918 Lenin declared: "The dictatorship supposes and signifies a state of contained war." In the middle of 1921, when the civil war was virtually over, Lenin expressed the same idea more exactly and mercilessly: "The dictatorship is a state of exacerbated war [after contained war comes exacerbated war — A.S.]. . . . So long as there is no definitive global result, this state of horrible war will continue. And we say: 'In war we act in a warlike way: we do not promise any freedom or democracy.' "

Since the civil war never produced a definitive global result (the world bourgeoisie and world imperialism are always there, ready to attack), we may extend Lenin's scenario to all of Soviet civilization, whose entire history is one of this state of horrible, endless war. The war changes shape — sometimes contained, other times newly exacerbated by the legalized terror which is Soviet law and justice — but it is always war. Consequently, the State as a system of violence does not wither away, but only grows stronger and more tenacious at the expense of human rights. The State turns from a temporary means of Communist development into an end in itself.

This too is a utopia, but already implemented and inverted: an antiutopian world without end. Even Lenin admits the horror of this protracted state of war. But this is also the pinnacle of world history. Soviet civilization is full of these paradoxes: violence is freedom (freedom from exploiters, from capitalists, and from landowners); and the absence of democracy is the most total democracy. Lenin declares that "we do not promise any freedom or democracy"; but at the same time, in 1919, at the Seventh Congress of the Soviets, he contends that our democracy is superior to all others: "Never before in the history of civilized peoples has there been a country where proletarian democracy was applied so broadly as it is here, in Russia." Lenin was referring to the State soviets, which he saw as the highest form of democracy. In theory, the soviets were (and still are) considered the supreme legislative organs. But in practice, and Lenin knew this, the soviets merely rubber-stamped laws and decrees drawn up by the Party elite.

The democratic role of the soviets was reduced to their class composition: the lower classes, worker and peasant representatives, were permitted to attend the discussions of these laws. But these representatives were also handpicked and supervised by the Party. And recalcitrant soviets were regarded as enemies of the revolution and abettors of the bourgeoisie. When the brightest workers began to realize that in this proletarian State, in the soviets, they were in fact being excluded from power and the actual government, they coined the slogan "Soviets Without Communists!" which caught on in some places. To the contemporary Soviet ear this sounds ridiculous, since the concepts of "Soviet power" and "Communist power" have long been synonymous, the Communists having substituted their own diktat for the soviets. But initially, the soviets were meant to be independent organs of power, elected by the workers and the peasants.

The demagogy consisted (and still consists) in the fact that the Communist Party billed itself as the vanguard of the working class, the greatest exponent of proletarian ideology. In other words, the Party knew better than the masses, better than the workers and peasants themselves, where their real class interests lay. Armed with Marxist-Leninist theory, the Party saw further and more profoundly than the class on behalf of which it acted. Naturally, this left the soviets with only a nominal piece of the supreme power which, in fact, belonged to the Party. The soviets played a supporting role, executing orders from on high and serving as a kind of bridge between the Party and the people. The trade unions were relegated to a similarly subsidiary role, deprived of all independence. Unilateral management became the rule, while self-government among factory workers was prohibited. Even the Proletkults, independent organizations for Proletarian Culture, were subordinated to a State organ, the People's Commissariat for Education. The logic was the same everywhere: Our power is proletarian! And the best, the greatest champion of the proletariat's interests is the Party! So the Party should guide us all! It already was guiding them not just ideologically, but physically as well. The economy, transportation, the press, the gigantic levers of violence — the army, the Cheka, and so on — were all in the Party's hands. And this was considered a dictatorship of the proletariat.

Lenin had an interesting view of the Cheka, the political police organ, whose role he defined scientifically: "The Cheka directly implements the dictatorship of the proletariat."

## THE AUTOCRACY

Thus there looms over the proletariat (and even more so over the peasantry) a colossal State superstructure, inclined not to wither away but to multiply, given its vast reserves of unlimited violence. The upper hand is retained by the Party: the ruling caste, whose members occupy the highest posts and are bound by the strictest Party discipline. For them, the Party is paramount, its command compulsory. The slightest conflict with the Party is grounds for expulsion. And to have been expelled from the Party is worse than never to have joined, since one is then politically suspect. Under Stalin, expulsion from the Party was almost invariably followed by arrest.

But the Party is also heterogeneous; it does not pretend to be a collective organ of power. The Party is constructed hierarchically, with the lower Party cadres subordinated to the higher ones. When they say "by order of the Party," they mean by order of the senior Party bosses, over whom there are still higher organs. And so on up to the Central Committee and higher, up to the Politburo, and higher still, up to the supreme leader. In this case, up to Lenin who, leaning on the Party elite, manages the dictatorship of the proletariat single-handedly. The essence and evolution of this dictatorship can be expressed in a phrase: "from popular uprising to autocracy." From the first day or, rather, first night of the uprising, the power was concentrated in Lenin's hands.

Lenin was not ambitious. But he realized that the revolution, incited by a minority in a country plunged into chaos, could not be saved except by an extraordinary centralization of power. He took this power upon himself insofar as he considered there was no alternative. And he used violence freely because only violence and the centralization of power could save his socialism, his real-life utopia. This was admittedly the right deduction given the political situation. And it forced Lenin to revise his utopia of the proletarian State, the one that was to have begun withering away as soon as power had been seized, the one where all workers were to govern in turn, the one he wrote about in *The State and Revolution*. Two years later, in 1919, Lenin expressed a very different idea in his lecture "On the State":

"It [the State — A.S.] has always been an apparatus distinct from society, composed of a group of people occupied exclusively or principally with governing. People divide themselves into those who are governed and those who are experts in governing, those who rise above society and who are called rulers."

This revealing passage suggests three conclusions. First: it isn't society that governs, nor the proletariat; rather, society detaches from itself a State or bureaucratic apparatus or, as Lenin says, "a group of people." In other words, of the entire dictatorship of the proletariat there remains just this small circle that dictates, headed by a dictator: Lenin. Second: people divide themselves into the governed and the governors. The old class division still applies: there are slaves and there are masters, and it's a much more radical division than before, since all other social links have been severed. There are only people who govern (masters) and people who obey (slaves). This is the "classless" Soviet civilization, constructed strictly according to the principles and mechanism described by Lenin. Third: the governing is done by scientific "experts." In other words, the State is governed by scholars, state-of-the-art specialists in the application of Marxism to present-day policy. And the head of this symposium, this scientific group charged with governing society, will of course be the most scholarly and meticulous of them all: Lenin himself. This is why I have called the first, Leninist, stage of Soviet civilization the State of scholars.

Lenin considered this graduated State formation, culminating in his own intellect, "proletarian democracy." This wasn't hypocrisy on his part, it was his sense of himself and the world. If the Party is the mind of the proletariat, and Lenin is the mind of the Party, then Lenin and his dictatorship embody the entire democracy of this new type, or the dictatorship of the proletariat. Moreover, Lenin, as a genuine Marxist, presumed that any person (himself included) was simply an expression of class interests. In this context, naturally, he was the expression of "the proletariat's interests," while those who differed with him politically were the expression of "the bourgeoisie's interests." It wasn't for the sake of his personal aggrandizement that Lenin ruled the country, but for the sake of this proletarian democracy for which he substituted himself.

In principle, one could also say that the Russian tsar (regardless of which), with his authoritarian power, embodied the interests and the will of all Russian people. This has been said — and is said still. But to Lenin, this view of the tsar was pure mysticism, since both the individual and society are ruled, as Marxist science proves, by class interests. The tsar was the exponent of the exploiter classes, landowners and capitalists. But he, Lenin, personified the dictatorship of the proletariat, and his autocracy was that of the toiling masses.

Indeed, Lenin was an unusual tsar, a tsar who wanted nothing for himself and worked sixteen-hour days, tending to every detail of the enormous State organism he had set in motion. Reading the last volumes of Lenin's complete works, one is struck with how, as the central brain of this sprawling apparatus, he managed to keep track of everything. Nothing happened without Lenin's personal say-so in Soviet Russia, which meanwhile pretended to first place in the international revolutionary movement. One can only marvel at the performance of this brain.

But at the same time, given the endless telegrams, corrections, and decrees on every question (including who should be arrested and who should be released from prison), all issued personally by Lenin, one is astounded at the unwieldiness and absurdity of this State apparatus. If everything is so incredibly centralized and tied to Lenin and a handful of his comrades, then the entire mechanism is devoid of initiative and in perennial need of prompting from above. People won't decide anything on their own: they are afraid to decide in anticipation of what the principal expert, Lenin, will say. So they barrage him with requests for instructions on anything and everything while he floods them with directives on the same. Everything depends on the tsar, but then the tsar must personally check and see to everything. And Lenin did check and did see to everything, even when he was close to death.

Toward the end of his life, Lenin evidently began to realize what a slow-moving, bureaucratic State he had created. But to eliminate the bureaucracy, he had to create new bureaucratic commissions, committees, and systems to control the bureaucrats who were functioning poorly. And since society was extraordinarily centralized, without openness or democratic autonomy, these new control mechanisms had little effect. They came too late: Soviet civilization was a fait accompli and society was already suffering from State sclerosis, from the same sclerosis that had attacked the blood vessels in Lenin's brain.

The State survived despite the death of its leader in 1924, periodically resorting to violence as its driving force. The State needs the knout and a tsar to run it. It needs Stalin. The phenomenon of Stalin is a new avatar of the Leninist utopia, where the dictatorship is the democracy, where the personal power of the Party or the dictator is the expression of the people's will. This could only lead to the profound antiutopia of Stalinism.

But before turning to this new stage of Soviet civilization, let's sum up, in a preliminary way, the State and society built by Lenin. What we have here is a socialist State that differs radically from all other formations. Even if NEP allowed a revival of the private economy with concessions to the peasants and the petite bourgeoisie, the basic means of production were still nationalized and in the hands of the State, which governed every aspect of Soviet life. Meanwhile, this private sector was strictly regimented by the State, which tolerated it only out of necessity and only for a time. In essence, socialism was already in place.

Some historians claim that what exists in the USSR is not socialism, or not "real" socialism, but what they call State capitalism. This is a semantic argument, however, since no one has ever seen another socialism or "real" socialism full-blown. What was done in the USSR was done in a definitive way, and the other socialist countries, with minor variations, followed suit. Like it or not, Soviet civilization can be considered the classic model of socialism where, in a word, everything belongs to the State: property, land, life itself, and the consciousness of the citizens. This State presents itself overtly (we know this from Lenin) as one of unlimited violence or legalized terror which at any moment may do to a person — to the individual or to society — whatever it likes, since it is not responsible to anyone but itself. Covertly, hypocritically, it claims to embody the will of the people, to whom everything ostensibly belongs. But insofar as the people own nothing and the champion of their supreme will is the State, the latter remains the sole lord and master.

I will illustrate this with an anecdote: In a certain village they were about to elect a chairman of the collective farm. In theory, the peasant farmers were supposed to do the electing. In practice, the candidate was imposed from above, by the Party district committee, in other words by the State. But at this particular collective farm the men had decided to choose their own chairman — a Party member and entirely reliable, but their own man. I was told about this by a farmer from the village, also a Party member. "When the instructor from the district committee arrived," he said, "we asked him at the general meeting: 'How shall we do this? Shall we vote for the person we want or for the person chosen "by the will of the people"?' He said: 'For the person you want, of course.' Then he took the village's Communists aside (there were just a few of them) and said: 'If you nominate your own candidate, you'll have only yourselves to blame! We'll kick you out of the Party and take measures against your collective farm.' So all the same," the farmer ended bitterly, "we had to elect the person chosen 'by the will of the people' rather than the person we wanted."

I should add that the formula "by the will of the people" is a dead formula, an official locution that means nothing other than by order of the authorities, by the will of the State. Hence the farmer's irony in this alternative: by the will of the people or like we want it.

In fact, "like we want it" was something the masses could say only during the first days or months of the revolution, as the voice of the elemental force that had brought the coup about or backed it. But no sooner had the new State power consolidated itself than it began giving orders on behalf of the people, substituting itself for the people; everything that disagreed with this power was written off as the "bourgeoisie" or "bourgeois manifestations" and subject to liquidation.

The intellectuals were naturally among the first to be written off as enemies of the State. More than others, they felt themselves to be suffocating without freedom of speech and tended to doubt the necessity of such a total dictatorship. Therefore, the intellectuals, regardless of their political leanings, were silenced. The frightened petty bourgeois was less dangerous for the government than the revolutionary intellectual who dared to argue and to criticize. Hence the fantastic control over thoughts and ideology imposed by Soviet civilization. There's more than a grain of truth in the old expression that so-and-so was arrested or shot because he "smiled counterrevolutionarily." The merest hint of skepticism, of doubt, of irony, of humor, had become a crime. To the members of the intelligentsia, it seemed as if they were entering a new ice age, both grandiose and horrible in its heavy progress.

## METAPHYSICS AND MYSTICISM OF THE SOVIET STATE

At the beginning of the 1920s, already sensing the heaviness and longevity of this new historical cycle, Osip Mandelshtam wrote (in his article "The Nineteenth Century"): "Our century is beginning under the sign of a superb intolerance, an exclusivity and a deliberate incomprehension of other worlds. In the veins of our century flows the heavy blood of terribly distant, monumental cultures, possibly Egyptian and Assyrian."

At first this sounds strange. What relation is there between Russia (or rather postrevolutionary Russia) and ancient Egypt or Assyria? At issue here, however, is a State power of a magnitude, of a despotic force, and of an intolerance never known to European civilization. The very existence of this colossal organism seems somehow irrational and monstrous. Hence Mandelshtam's association of the Assyrians and ancient Egypt.

Let's take just a few aspects of the life of this State: for example, its military style, which originated under Lenin but became what it is today under Stalin. As if this State, forged in the fire of an armed uprising and tempered by the civil war, had never let go its martial spirit. Lenin himself, if one recalls, described his dictatorship as a state of permanent and all-out war. Not that the USSR is eternally at war or that it is by nature bellicose and always poised for attack; nevertheless, it lives in a state of sustained military tension. Even when the danger of capitalist encirclement or Hitler's offensive is past, this military fever persists. There are logical explanations for this, as well as mysterious, irrational, quasi-mystical motives. One logical explanation has it that past acts of aggression (e.g., the usurping of Eastern Europe) now compel the Soviet State to retain these conquests to prevent its own collapse. Its position is thus one of active defense, so to speak. Though it doesn't want war and no immediate threat of war exists, it is perpetually preparing for war. The State believes that someone always wants to attack it and retake the conquered territories. Hence the lack of freedom in the Soviet Union, as if it were forever in a wartime situation. All this has its logic.

Apropos of this is a conversation I had in the relatively relaxed post-Stalin era with a colleague at the Institute of World Literature in Moscow. He wasn't a Party member, he was honest and somewhat liberal, and so I could be frank with him. One day I told him how hard I found it to live without freedom and what a bad effect the lack of freedom had on Russian and even Soviet culture. I argued that the Soviet State wouldn't necessarily collapse if it lifted certain restrictions in the cultural sphere. If it allowed abstract art, if it published Pasternak's *Doctor Zhivago* and Anna Akhmatova's *Requiem,* and so on. If anything, a slight thaw would benefit Russian culture and the Soviet State!

"Of course, the State won't founder because of such trifles," said my colleague. "But you're forgetting the effect all this would have on Poland."

"What does Poland have to do with it," I asked, perplexed, "when the point is they should publish Pasternak in Moscow?"

"If we ourselves, at the center, allow a relaxation in the cultural sphere, then in Poland, where it's freer than here, there will be an even greater drift toward freedom. If a thaw starts in Moscow, Poland will secede from the East bloc, from the Soviet Union."

"So let Poland secede!" I said flippantly. "Let it live the way it wants!"

"But after Poland, Czechoslovakia would secede, and after Czechoslovakia, the entire East bloc would break up."

"So let it break up," I said. "Russia would only be better off."

But my interlocutor saw further: "After the East bloc, the Baltics would go — Latvia, Lithuania, and Estonia!"

"So let them!" I repeated stubbornly. "What do we need these forcible annexations for?"

"But after the Baltics, the Ukraine and the Caucasus would go!

What do you want? An end to Russian power? For your Pasternak, you would let all of Russia crumble, Russia, which is now the greatest empire in the world!"

This was the whole conversation. Neither anecdote nor joke really, but logic, the iron logic of the empire and the State. Here the rational prevails.[2]

One can also understand, even if it is more difficult, the idea of world socialist domination on which all of this State's gigantic military-economic might is bent. If the USSR intervenes in Africa, in Asia, and in America, this should be taken as a belated effect of the "world revolution." Though people have long since stopped believing in the world revolution, it plows steadily on, sometimes in the shape of military actions in various points on the globe, always by means of terror and violence exercised by a minority over the majority. Here there is no grand idea, only a tradition, that of seizing power by violent means. Even if this leads to new conflicts in one's own socialist camp — such as those between Russia and China, Vietnam and Cambodia. All the same, conquest is essential. Because the world must be unified.

A more irrational element in this armed system is, to my mind, "enemy mania." Yesterday capitalists and landowners were the enemy, a real enough enemy, whom the Party annihilated and liquidated as a class and even physically. Then it was the Mensheviks and Socialist Revolutionaries, in other words, socialists, but of a more liberal stripe. They too would be annihilated. The next enemy to wake was the kulaks, the well-to-do peasantry. They would be liquidated by means of dekulakization in the countryside and complete collectivization. In the melee, "Trotskyism" would be liquidated as the principal enemy. But then came the "wrecking" — or disorder in the economy. The "wreckers" would be shot. But then the "cosmopolitans" appeared, and so on . . .

In reality there is no enemy, but one is necessary as a justification for this system of violence, which cannot exist without an enemy. Anyone you please — from Japanese spies to Social Democrats — may be an "enemy of the people." A frantic search is on for enemies

2. This exchange, which occurred many years before the momentous events of 1990, seems in retrospect less humorous than prescient. — A. S.

in any form. First Trotskyites, then Zionists. And it's no use pointing out that the number of Trotskyites or Zionists is infinitessimal as against the State's tens of millions of people, as against its tanks and rockets.

From the West, these hysterical cries into the void sound like a complete bluff. But it's not just bluffing, it's a persecution complex which, as any psychiatrist can tell you, often accompanies megalomania. Let's suppose that today the Soviet Union is being persecuted by Zionists, while before it was the kulaks, capitalists, and landowners, not to mention its perennial tormentors, the "warmongers" and the "imperialists," even if the supreme imperialist is the USSR. This is, in effect, a complete worldview. Sometimes this State seems like a paranoiac threatened from all sides. It's hard to explain this rationally: nobody is threatening, but it always seems as if someone is. Enter enemy mania, the linchpin of this paranoid reality.

Aleksandr Blok was the first to notice this mania in his poem "The Twelve," which depicts, in early 1918, a dozen Red Guards prowling the snowswept streets of Petrograd in search of the enemy. And there is no enemy.

> *Look — the flying*
> *Red flag greet!*
> *Hear undying*
> *Tramp of feet*
> *Foes wake, vying*
> *In their heat . . .*[3]

But the enemy doesn't wake. And for lack of anything better, for lack of an enemy, the guards fire at Christ and also at their own sick consciences.

This may have been all mysticism for Blok, but the "invisible enemy" materialized in Soviet history, studded with Decrees and Bulletins about who was to be shot. Executions became an accepted part of life. It is only natural that atop this mountain of bodies should tower Stalin, who shot so many "dangerous" Leninists.

---

3. Translation by Sir Cecil Kisch in *Alexander Blok: Prophet of the Revolution* (New York: Roy Publishers, 1961), p. 145.

But let's return to this idea that the enemy is everywhere and nowhere. The vying foe, as Blok says, is just waking. He is invisible. But communism cannot exist without him. The system, as absolute violence, must have someone to crush. Without an enemy it won't function. And if all its enemies have been destroyed, it invents new ones. To have someone to fight and thus to survive!

Metaphysically, this translates: if violence is wrought, then someone must resist it. An enemy is essential. Without him, the system will atrophy.

This is why one cannot understand everything about the Soviet State rationally. It is rational but, at the same time, it inhabits a world of paranoid and nightmare phantasms. The State persecutes everyone, while imagining that others are persecuting it. After all, if there is no one to kill, if there is no enemy, then the violence is senseless.

Hence this state of "active defense" and this military might to which Soviet power clings as if it were the only possible model of existence. Which brings us to the comic side of Soviet life: the "struggle for the potato," the "ideological front," "heroic labor."

Everything is put on a military footing. But this is also linked to the fact that society, lacking all individual initiative, must constantly be commanded and exhorted to work. Hence this enormous bureaucratic machine that cannot be dismantled. Otherwise work will come to a standstill or be run wretchedly. Slaves, after all, have little incentive to do good work.

Now let's go down the ranks to the people who are being governed by this gigantic State. Can it really be that this society is held together by bayonets alone, by the fear the State instills? The answer is no. Strange as it may seem, this society, though stripped of all democratic rights and freedoms, also holds together through democracy. Yet another mystery of Soviet power. On the one hand, it deprives society of freedom and democracy. On the other hand, it creates the illusion of democracy, thanks to which the Soviet people support it. Here we are again entering the realm of the irrational, though on the solid ground of "Soviet democracy."

What is "Soviet democracy"? It is equality for all, in the name of which freedom is suppressed. The people, as it turned out, were thirsting not for freedom but for equality. These two notions can be mutually exclusive: in a society where all men are equal, freedom isn't possible. Because freedom elevates certain people over others and allows for differences between them. But equality without freedom makes everyone the same.

This thirst for equality has always been inherent to Russia — and all the more when inequality reigned and the prerevolutionary class barriers were still firmly entrenched. Until serfdom was abolished in Russia (in 1861), the peasants were slaves. For centuries, in other words, an overwhelming majority of the population endured this state of inequality. The "class struggle" boiled down to the fact that the slaves wanted to be equal with their masters. The revolution not only brought about this equality, it placed the slaves over their former masters. The highest estates — the nobility, the bourgeoisie, the clergy, the intelligentsia — were reduced to ashes while the moral upper hand was accorded to the toiling masses, to those engaged in physical labor. Naturally, they experienced this new equality and even primacy as a state of freedom. Thus the revolution, though it deprived the individual of all rights, was nevertheless positively interpreted by the masses as newfound freedom. Or, more precisely, as newfound equality, which in the minds of the masses became freedom and a sense of self-worth. To explain this oddity, I will cite the Russian religious philosopher and historian Georgy Fedotov, who could never be accused of being a Communist sympathizer. He emigrated slightly after the first wave and so experienced Soviet Russia through the revolution and into the 1920s. Hostile toward this new power, Fedotov nevertheless wrote (in *It Is and It Will Be. Reflections on Russia and the Revolution*, 1932):

> It's astounding: in hungry, ravaged Russia, under a regime of absolute lawlessness, the worker and even the peasant have felt themselves the victors, citizens of the world's most progressive country. Only in Russia are the worker and the peasant masters of the land, purged of parasites and exploiters. They may be poor, but they are free (in the social sense — in other words equal or, rather, the first).

Thus the lower strata of society saw equality as freedom. In reality, there was no freedom. But there was equality of the governed, subjected to a higher State that was terribly repressive but composed largely of the masses. Consequently, there was a sense of social solidarity with this State that guided you and deprived you of all your rights, except the right to consider this State your own. This is the essence of Soviet democracy. To go back to Fedotov:

> One can always "collar" the passing commissar at the soviet. And in the district's chief town, the muzhik isn't shy of his boss: he is "his brother." Hatred for Communists has no class character. It is mollified by the consciousness that those in the new ruling stratum are all our own people. . . . It's hard to imagine a peasant family today that doesn't have a relative in the city in a prominent position: a commander in the Red Army or a judge, an agent of the GPU or, at the very least, a student.

Besides, anyone could try climbing the State ladder. All one needed was proof of social origin plus an aptitude for demagogy. Hence the stability of Soviet society.

# *4*

## Stalin: The State-Church

FROM THE FIRST, Leninist stage of Soviet civilization, let's turn to the succeeding, Stalinist stage. Stalin alone, of course, does not define this era, but he characterizes it just as, in the first years of Soviet power, Lenin epitomized the State of scholars. If Lenin was the State's chief scholar, Stalin was the self-anointed god of the State, which thus acquired a religious aura.

The first question is: In what ways did Stalin differ from his predecessor, and to what extent did Lenin pave the way for him?

### LENIN AND STALIN COMPARED

Outwardly, these were two wildly disparate leaders. Lenin was a scholar, Joseph Stalin barely educated. In his *Conversations with Stalin* (1962), Milovan Djilas reveals that Stalin didn't know, for instance, that Holland and the Netherlands were the same country and that no one in his entourage, the foreign minister included, dared enlighten him.

Lenin, by nature and by appearance, was a civilian. Stalin was a military man, or at any rate pretended to be. During the Second World War and after, he consummated his passion for the military style, titles, and trappings, the height of which was the magnificent title of generalissimo that he conferred upon himself. But even in the early revolutionary years, Stalin wore boots, a greatcoat, and his trademark moustache — a sign not just of his Caucasian origins but of his belonging to the military caste of Russian bolshevism. Meanwhile, Lenin's civilian affiliation was pointed up by his equally famous waistcoat. When speaking, he had a habit of tucking his thumbs into the armholes. This looked a little comical, but it also implied Lenin's Russian intellectual contempt for poses, for his appearance, and for his suit, even if it was an old-fashioned, three-piece affair.

Lenin's exterior matched his scholarly nature: a small, bald man with a guttural pronunciation and a huge forehead. Stalin, too, was not very tall, but he had a low forehead. One doesn't notice this, however, in the enormous statues — statues in boots, greatcoat, and moustache — which he erected in his honor. In place of the scientific discussions and caustic Party altercations to which Lenin was inclined, the military parade had begun.

Filling out a form after coming to power, Lenin stated his profession as "man of letters." But Stalin was, as he was celebrated daily, the "leader of all progressive mankind." Even their pseudonyms are dissonant. "Lenin," derived from a woman's name (Lena), is somehow indefinite. It's now that the word "Lenin" resounds, but at first there was nothing imposing or solemn about it. In power, Lenin continued to sign his name Ulyanov, to which he appended his pseudonym, Lenin; the combination sounded even more understated. Stalin, however, did not want to be reminded of his real name, Dzhugashvili, and immediately instituted the sonorous "Stalin" — from the word "steel" (*stal'*) — a one-word précis of the new steel era.

Fighter pilots were called "Stalin's falcons," which also meant "steel falcons." Steelworkers were honored — by analogy with Stalin. Nikolai Ostrovsky wrote his novel *How the Steel Was Tempered* (1932–1934), the title of which, like a steel string, resonated with Stalin's name. At Stalin's side there suddenly appeared one Suleiman Stalsky, a Dagestani folk poet who celebrated the leader in his odes and whom Gorky called "the Homer of the twentieth century."

The effect of this one name, "Stalin," was to give everything Soviet a new, Stalinist ring, a new style. Stalin called this style Socialist Realism . . .

Lenin lived very modestly, he was undemanding, almost ascetic. A product of the old Russian revolutionary and intellectual tradition, he subscribed to its unwritten rules: that a person should give himself to the cause of the people and the revolution; that he should not set himself apart (outwardly) from simpler people or look down on them; that he should struggle and live in a disinterested way, not seeking his own glory. Lenin didn't play at democracy: despite his being a dictator, he remained truly democratic in his habits, in his relations with people. We don't know that Lenin became intoxicated with his absolute power, or that he settled personal scores, or that he displayed the despotic behavior typical of dictators. Yes, Lenin showed incredible cruelty, but this was not in his nature, rather it was the result of his scientific approach to the class struggle and politics. Personally kind, Lenin was politically indifferent to the question of good and evil. For him, good was whatever served the proletariat and his policy of expressing the proletariat's interests; evil was anything that jeopardized those interests. Thus, while exhibiting monstrous cruelty and autocratic habits, Lenin shunned the glory and honors lavished on him.

One example: In 1920, Lenin was about to turn fifty and the Ninth Party Congress, then in session, wanted to mark the occasion. But as soon as the eulogies and ovations in his honor began, Lenin repaired to his study alone. From there, he sent a stream of messages to the congress and telephoned urging that the celebrations be cut short in favor of the useful business at hand. This was the sincere reaction of a revolutionary, an intellectual, and a democrat.

By way of comparison, one has only to recall the thunderous applause that erupted at the mere mention of Stalin's name, a response that Stalin himself clearly encouraged, occasionally shooting those who clapped too little. Stalin was drunk with his own power and displayed all the evil that only power can inspire. Vindictive, rancorous, and sadistic, he ignored class interests and even acted against them, revealing an extraordinary personal cruelty, insidiousness, and thirst for power.

Consequently, Stalin's slogan "Stalin Is the Lenin of Today," accepted as axiomatic during his tenure, sounded blasphemous to those who had known Lenin well. This is one of the many reasons why Stalin liquidated the old Lenin guard. He had no use for these witnesses. Having launched his personal, Stalinist reign and substituted himself for Lenin, Stalin loathed anyone who still remembered the former leader and could contrast the two.

But the Lenin-versus-Stalin debate is still going on. Any devoted

Communist who criticizes or rejects Stalin will generally allude to Lenin and say: If Lenin had lived everything would have been different and there wouldn't have been Stalin. Thus, Lenin came to embody the good communism that would have been had it not been for Stalin.

Indeed, it's hard to imagine Lenin in the role of Stalin. Not long before his death, Lenin cautioned the Party about the future chief's rude and willful character. But he didn't propose anyone else to take his place, obviously counting on a collective leadership.

In spite of himself, Lenin paved Stalin's way to power by excluding all democracy, even within the Party. Though a democratic intellectual by nature, Lenin had, in fact, prohibited all discussion, outside as well as inside the Party ranks. He had tied the entire State administration to himself, not troubling about the fact that tomorrow Stalin would take his place. Lenin's terror and centralization led perfectly naturally to Stalin.

In 1921, a prominent Party member, Adolf Ioffe, wrote to Lenin complaining that the Central Committee had been reduced to Lenin's autocratic "I." Lenin was terribly surprised. He told Ioffe that this notion was the result of nervous exhaustion and that he should take care of himself: "Why worry yourself to the point of writing something *completely impossible, completely impossible,* as if I were the Central Committee. You are overwrought."

In fact, by 1921 Lenin could not only say "I am the Central Committee" but "I am the State." By his own logic, the Party was meant to exercise absolute power over the State, while he, Lenin, who understood and decided everything, exercised absolute power over the Party. If Lenin didn't say "I am the State," his methods left no doubt. So that Stalin had only to change the plaque and oust potential rivals. This he did, having supplanted Lenin as "leader of the world proletariat," partly in Leninist style, with violence and State centralization.

Stalin, in my opinion, did not distort Lenin, he simply assumed his position as head of the government. It was only later that he let himself be run by his own psychology, by his own understanding of what was good or evil for the interests of the world proletariat. In this sense, Stalin was not a usurper but Lenin's legitimate heir. And if, in coming to power, he had to squeeze out the Leninist command, this is just a detail. In fact, Stalin was a faithful Leninist, but one who applied the idea of absolute dictatorship in his own, Stalin-like way.

## STALIN'S IRRATIONALISM

The year 1937 marks Stalin's zenith when, having liquidated all his real and imagined adversaries, he reigned supreme. This process, of course, had begun earlier and would continue for years after, but 1937 will forever remain a mystical date in Russian history, on a par, possibly, with the also quasi-sacred year of 1917. Nineteen thirty-seven was a response to 1917, if an irrational one. One could say that to Lenin's reason and exceeding rationality in 1917, Stalin responded in 1937, twenty years later, in an irrational way.

Stalin's irrationality consisted in imprisoning and assassinating the heroes of the revolution, in killing his own, the Party faithful, many of whom died pledging their allegiance to him. These purges consumed virtually the entire Central Committee, countless captains of industry, and the Red Army's high command (all this on the eve of war with Hitler). Then came the mass executions of the Party's lower echelons, of the regional and district committees, and finally of the population at large, including Chekists and militiamen involved in the actual purging. According to the operative slogan, "enemies of the people" had infiltrated everywhere.

This seems insane. And there are those who claim that Stalin was quite simply mad to have acted as he did, against his own interests and those of the Party. In reality, Stalin was far from mad: his actions were perfectly logical from his point of view and even somewhat in keeping with Leninist policy. And if one considers that a crazy man was able to run the State for decades, unchecked and unopposed, then this means that the State created by Lenin possessed this potential.

But Stalin, as I've said, was not mad and acted, from his point of view, with perfect reason. For all their psychological dissimilarities, Stalin was Lenin's student, as he hailed himself and others later chorused. But the student surpassed his master.

Lenin, as we know, destroyed the opposition in other parties primarily, including socialist parties: the Mensheviks and the Socialist Revolutionaries. But Stalin, once in power, immediately found himself faced with internal opposition from the Trotskyites; he liquidated them and then went on to destroy most of the Leninist guard, whom he saw as a threat. Many of these makers of the revolution were brighter, more experienced, and better educated than Stalin, in addition to having joined the Party before he did. The elimination of the Trotskyites meant there could be no more real opposition to Stalin, but he was painfully sensitive to the faintest suggestion of dissent, to the slightest show of independence. And since the old Party cadres had only recently occupied positions equal or superior to his, he wrote them all off as suspect. The only way to dislodge them was to destroy them, having accused them before the country and the people of heinous crimes, of treason. Hence the necessity of the show trials in the thirties, when preeminent leaders of Party and State confessed publicly to being secret agents in the employ of foreign services, their ostensible dream having been to resurrect capitalism in Russia.

One has to admit that these spectacles were superbly staged and produced. I will quote just one eyewitness, the German writer Lion Feuchtwanger, who, as a distinguished foreigner and friend of the Soviet Union, was invited to attend a court trial in Moscow in 1937. In his book *Moscow 1937* Feuchtwanger reports:

> One could never call these men standing trial tortured, despairing beings, cringing before their executioner. It would also be a mistake to think there was anything artificial or even solemn and bombastic about these proceedings.
>
> The premises were not large, seating about 350 people. The accused were well groomed and neatly dressed, their manner natural and relaxed. They drank tea, newspapers poking out of their pockets, and often looked out at the audience. In general, it seemed more like an informal discussion among cultivated people trying to get at the truth, to establish exactly what happened and why. One had the impression that the accused, the prosecutor, and the judges were all caught up with the same, I almost want to say sportsmanlike interest in elucidating everything with the maximum precision. If this trial was staged, then the director would have to have had several years and numerous rehearsals to get such a seamless performance from the accused: so conscientiously and painstakingly did they pick

up the least inconsistency in each other's testimony, so restrained was their emotion. . . .

They all confessed, but each in his own way: one in a cynical tone, another in a crisp, soldierlike style, a third resisting inwardly, running for cover, a fourth like a repentent schoolboy, a fifth sermonizing. But their inflections, facial expressions, and gestures all rang true.

Meanwhile, Stalin, as chief choreographer, scrutinized every detail of these productions, allegedly instructing one assistant to "make sure that at the trial all the defendants are served tea with lemon and cakes."

Ultimately, everything connected with Stalin is so involved and obscure that it's often impossible to know how to interpret the facts. For a long time one could only guess as to why Stalin's victims confessed and repented of the most implausible sins. We still don't know the whole truth behind Stalin's assassination of Politburo member Sergei Kirov in December 1934, which marked the beginning of the purges. Nor do we know which version of Gorky's death to believe. Did Stalin, as Trotsky suspected, make an attempt on Lenin's life? Was Stalin himself murdered (as some claim)? And what about the two versions of how his wife died?

In short, the figure of Stalin, given the opacity of his machinations, becomes lost in the murk.

But all of this smacks of Lenin's logic, if taken to absurd lengths by Stalin. For Lenin, all opposition to bolshevism, to his power, or to his point of view was an expression of bourgeois class or political interests. As a Marxist, Lenin did not recognize any individual ideology: everything was an expression of someone's class interests. Therefore, he lumped all his political opponents in the bourgeois camp which, he said, was bent on crushing the Bolshevik party and then Soviet power. Lenin salted all his articles and speeches with terms like "agents of the bourgeoisie," "agents of international imperialism," "social traitors," "traitors to the working class," and so on. A person's subjective honesty, his sense that he was neither bourgeois agent nor traitor, changed nothing in Lenin's view. Because what a person thinks of himself is not important, rather it's whose positions he expresses *objectively*, involuntarily. History's only laws are the objective laws of class struggle.

Stalin embraced this Leninist "objectivity," but on a grand scale, applying it even to Party members and veterans of the revolution who struck him as suspect.

Lenin, of course, was speaking metaphorically when he used the term "agents of the bourgeoisie" to describe Mensheviks or Western Social Democrats; or when he accused them of "selling" the interests of the working class. Lenin didn't think that they were literally in the pay of the world bourgeoisie or acting at the behest of a foreign secret service. But Stalin took everything literally: an "agent of the bourgeoisie" equalled an actual spy. In this sense, the trials and executions of the thirties were nothing other than literal translations of Leninist metaphors. On Stalin's orders, the Soviet Chekists and investigators began torturing people arrested as agents of the bourgeoisie so that they would confess to spying for the Japanese, the Germans, or the English. The metaphor was taken to its real-life conclusion.

And like any metaphor made real, the result was a monstrous and fantastic scene. The country was crawling with invisible "spies" and "saboteurs" constantly being caught and exposed. In the street, any passerby could turn out to be a secret enemy. So it goes with any metaphor taken at face value. For instance: "The rain is coming." Let's imagine the rain strolling across bridges, striding through puddles, then starting to run or jump. The result is a kind of live grotesque — not unlike what happened to Lenin's metaphors in the thirties.

But Lenin isn't only guilty of coining phrases like "agents of the bourgeoisie" or "capitalist lackeys," which instantly entered the State's official vocabulary and modus vivendi. He also envisaged the harshest punishments for those who, in departing from the Party line or State policy, appeared *objectively* to be "agents of the bourgeoisie." In 1922, Lenin requested Kursky, people's commissar of justice, "to broaden the application of capital punishment," especially for agitation and propaganda, and "to find a formula which establishes a connection between these acts and the international bourgeoisie" for the criminal code. Note: it is precisely this "connection with the international bourgeoisie" that entitles a person to be shot. And for this, the person doesn't have to have been literally recruited by foreign services; that his statements or writings *objec-*

*tively* help the international bourgeoisie is sufficient. In another letter to Kursky, Lenin found the right formula and proposed it as his personal draft of the corresponding article for the criminal code: "Propaganda or agitation objectively promoting . . . the international bourgeoisie" is punishable by death (or exile abroad).

In the early twenties, expulsion was applied to prominent professors, philosophers, and writers whom, in the face of Europe, it would have been awkward to shoot or imprison for protracted periods.

According to Lenin's formula, "propaganda or agitation objectively promoting . . . the international bourgeoisie" automatically merited the harshest sentences. But with the application of this formula under Stalin, even the mildest criticism of the State and Stalin was regarded as bourgeois agitation and propaganda. And this criticism didn't have to be uttered: the suspicion of an unorthodox thought was enough; a slip of the tongue or a misprint was ample. The widow of the poet Eduard Bagritsky, a man greatly esteemed in the 1930s in the USSR and officially recognized as one of the best revolutionary poets, landed in prison and then in camp after she went to the NKVD (a successor to the Cheka) to petition for her sister's husband, the poet Vladimir Narbut, who had just been arrested and later died in a camp. "Why," she asked the Chekists, "do you just grab everyone indiscriminately?" When they laughed at her she screamed, in a fit of rage: "Nothing gets through to you!" For this exclamation she was arrested on charges of preparing an armed assault on Soviet power. Material evidence of her terrorist intentions was discovered during a search of her apartment: an old saber, given to Bagritsky by a distinguished Red Army commander, hanging on the wall over the ottoman.

Another typical case: A man went to see his friend, an official of some kind, at his office but found that he was out. The official had promised to do something for his friend and then hadn't done it. The friend decided to leave him a note. For lack of anything better to write on, he grabbed a newspaper that was lying on the desk and scrawled: "You scum, you broke your promise!" He didn't notice Stalin's speech right next to his angry, impromptu note. But somebody else did—and called the NKVD. The poor devil was promptly arrested.

The mass arrests in the thirties mainly affected privileged people. Earlier, with collectivization and the dispossession of the kulaks, it was the peasantry that had suffered most. But in principle, anyone could be made to suffer, regardless. One simple old woman dreamed that she gave herself to Kliment Voroshilov, the commissar of defense. The next morning, in the communal kitchen, she told her dream to a neighbor, who quickly denounced her to the NKVD. The old woman was sent to camp for her "crime": "for having unethical dreams about the leaders." There are innumerable stories like this one and countless variations on the theme of "bourgeois agitation."

The repressions in the 1930s were of enormous benefit to their instigator, Stalin.

First, there was the wholesale liquidation of the Party's active ranks, deemed dangerous by Stalin given their connection to revolutionary tradition and to Lenin. Stalin loathed this elite, if only for its popularity at a time when he was still a virtual unknown. It was a bastard's envy of the revolution's legitimate children. Thus it wasn't enough to simply exterminate them, Stalin dragged them through the mud. It became dangerous for any prominent Party member or old revolutionary to keep a journal or to write his memoirs for the desk drawer. If someone found out, he would instantly suspect that the writings contained something that either conflicted or could conflict with Stalin's line. And this suspicion alone could lead to the author's death.

Having eliminated the elite, those who "knew too much," Stalin undertook his second coup, the revision of history to suit his own taste. So that under Lenin the ubiquitous top man turned out to be Stalin, while his rivals — Trotsky, Bukharin, Zinoviev, Kamenev, and others — turned out to be subversives. It was no accident that the height of these repressions coincided with the publication in 1938 of *The History of the Communist Party of the Soviet Union (Bolsheviks), Short Course,* a rewrite of the Soviet past according to Stalin, edited and partly written by him. This manual on the history of the Party and Marxism-Leninism became required reading for any literate Soviet citizen, especially "ideological front" workers. It was the bible of Stalinism.

The spirit of the *Short Course* was emulated in films and historical novels, one of the most famous of which was Aleksei Tolstoy's *Bread* (1937) about the defense of Tsaritsyn (now Volgograd) during the civil war. Grossly distorting and garbling the facts, it depicts Stalin as a great military strategist and leader of the revolution. Tolstoy owed his exceptional rise to this very weak work.

The third boon for Stalin in the wake of the repressions was the replacement of cadres and the emergence of a new type of Party and State leader. The Party underwent a social and psychological sea change. The veterans who had been eliminated were generally replaced by people without a past, by the rank and file from the provinces who hadn't been in the revolution or in the underground and had joined the Party for their careers. These were simple people for the most part, with limited horizons and little education: the basis of what Milovan Djilas calls the "new class." As opposed to the old guard, these people were not burning with revolutionary enthusiasm; they thought and acted unquestioningly, dully doing as they were told to do by the higher-ups. They became the ballast of the Stalin throne.

With their rise, the entire style of life changed. The barely educated but very dutiful functionary was now in charge.

Stalin's fourth triumph was in transforming the country into a servile state, where people were treated like slaves and had a slave's pyschology. Collectivization had enslaved the countryside, depriving huge numbers of people of even the most elementary independence. But the prisons and torture, camps and executions of the 1930s extended this servile system across the board. Stalin forced society to live in a state of terror, a terror that left its permanent mark on every Soviet citizen. Before, the concept of the enemy had had a class connotation. But now the enemy could be any Soviet person, himself unsuspecting and unable to secure any advance guarantee that he wasn't an enemy. According to a then-current anecdote, three men were sitting in a prison cell when one asked another what he was in for. It turned out that the first man was in for criticizing Karl Radek, the distinguished journalist, while the second, arrested later, was in for singing Radek's praises. The third man sat slumped in silence. "What are you in for?" they asked. And he said, "I'm Karl Radek . . ."

This state of terror sometimes turned into mass hysteria or a mass trance, with people searching high and low for spies and saboteurs while any one of them could turn out to be a spy or saboteur tomorrow. Every one of those already in prison knew that he was not a spy, that in his case they had made a mistake, but as for the others who had been arrested, he thought that they were most likely genuine enemies. Olga Berggolts, a known poetess, was arrested at the end of the thirties and then, by some exceptional fluke, fairly quickly released. Many years later she recounted her reactions to prison. This was at the time of the Spanish Civil War, and most Soviets sided, naturally, with the Republicans. When the young Berggolts, a staunch Communist, found herself under arrest, she thought with horror about being locked up with fascist murderers, spies, saboteurs, and all kinds of counterrevolutionaries. For her, this was the worst thing. Shoved into a communal cell, she entered it as if it were a big cave, full of filthy, venomous "vermin" with whom she would now have to share her bread and shelter. She was instantly surrounded by these "vermin," who threw themselves at her as someone fresh from the outside. She recoiled in disgust. But then she heard one of these "enemies of the people" ask: "Tell us, is Madrid still holding?!" The prisoners in this communal cell were all Communists worried about Madrid.

Mass fear caused the wildest and most absurd things to happen. Some of those imprisoned, for example, considered it their moral duty to slander as many of their friends and acquaintances as possible so that they too would be arrested. And they urged other political prisoners to do the same. The theory was that if an awful lot of people were arrested the leadership would understand that it was all a big mistake and would begin reviewing cases.

On the outside, fear bred lies and denunciations. For this summary justice was accompanied by general meetings at all enterprises and institutions where people, collectively or individually, were supposed to stigmatize the "enemies of the people" and welcome their being put to death. People were trained to rejoice in these executions and to greet the death sentence with thunderous applause. And since it's not always pleasant to lie, people persuaded each other and themselves that all this was right and good.

In 1920 Lenin said: "A good Communist is also a good Chekist." With this phrase he obliged Communists to engage in detective work. Stalin went further: on principle, every Soviet citizen should help the Chekists, it was his sacred duty. Thus wives sometimes informed against their husbands and sons against their fathers — not out of meanness but out of the best intentions.

All this, of course, served Stalin's purposes. The result was the ideal selection of people to have power over: people who didn't dare have an opinion of their own, who meekly submitted to any shift in his policy. This is essentially how it was in 1939, when Stalin made his nonaggression pact with Hitler. And today many Stalinists still view fear as a positive and necessary element in Soviet society, as its driving force. Even now that one knows that the existence of these myriad "enemies of the people" was a complete fraud that cost millions of innocent lives. In Russia I argued many times and in vain with a young Stalinist who insisted that Stalin had been right to torture and kill so many people, even if they were proven innocent. The advantage in all this, he contended, was that Stalin instilled a fear in people that kept them right in line with the leadership, which is why, after the bloody purges of the 1930s, we won the war with Germany. Fear forged the moral and political unity of the Soviet people and the Soviet State. As a result, he said, the USSR is the first power in the world today.

This was largely Stalin's logic too: better to let the innocent die than to let a single enemy slip through or dissent take root.

Finally, Stalin's fifth gain from the trials during the thirties was the extraordinary elevation of his own dictatorial persona and the cult around this persona, which reached its apogee precisely during this period: Stalin had razed all the tall trees around him so that he alone remained, towering and infallible.

## STALIN: HERO AND ARTIST OF THE STALIN ERA

In 1934, at the First Congress of Soviet Writers, one Party leader, Emelian Yaroslavsky, declared: "What has our Party given us? It has given us figures of incomparable beauty, of iron will, of fantastic, selfless devotion [I'll omit a string of superlatives — A.S.], the matchless characters of Lenin and Stalin. [Applause] . . . Where, in what work," Yaroslavsky asked reproachfully, "have you shown us Stalin in all his magnitude? [Applause]."

Thus, among all living men — so the theory goes — Stalin is the first positive hero, a notion that in Soviet art focuses on the figure of the leader. The Stalin era can be symbolized by this scene, later recounted by Khrushchev, however apocryphal or not: Stalin strolling with maniacal delight among his own statues.

In principle he could treat this as an onerous but necessary task, displaying his likenesses to the supplicant crowds for their moral and aesthetic edification. But as an intelligent person, he could also be irritated by the fuss over his busts, portraits, and similar effects connected with the cult. Stalin's daughter, Svetlana Alliluyeva, claims that he disliked ovations, that they made him angry. In one famous incident, Stalin turned up at the theater unannounced and proceeded straight to the government box. In a panic, the theater's director suddenly noticed there wasn't a single bust of Stalin in the foyer and only one in the hall. A mad dash during the first act produced a second bust, which was promptly installed in the foyer and adorned with fresh flowers. At intermission Stalin ambled past the apparition and, pointing at it, muttered maliciously: "And when did this get here?"

But it was Stalin who propagated this cult. He thought of himself on a divine scale. Aleksandr Orlov, in *The Secret History of Stalin's Crimes* (1954), writes that when Yenukidze tried to defend Lev Kamenev and Grigory Zinoviev, Stalin said: "Remember, Avel, he who is not with me is against me!" And he had Yenukidze assassinated. As a former seminarian, Stalin could not have failed to know to whom these words belonged — taken from the Gospel according to Matthew.

One may wonder if Stalin genuinely believed his own fantasies about himself as an exceptional being or about the mass repressions and executions. Some hold that Stalin could not have believed in the fairness of these arrests and trials since he had concocted them himself. But others, like Khrushchev, claim that he lived in the fantasy world of his imaginings. Obviously, like any true artist, Stalin both believed and didn't believe his imagination.

During the thirties Stalin distanced himself greatly from even the top bosses of his ruling apparat. Stalin's estrangement elicited if not objections, then secret smiles from the old revolutionaries. To them, putting a Party leader on such a pedestal became neither the leader nor the Party. And Stalin had the wit to realize this.

In *Moscow 1937*, Feuchtwanger describes a conversation he had with Stalin. The episode is entitled "100,000 portraits of the man with the moustache":

> To my remark about the tasteless and extravagant adulation of his person, Stalin shrugged. He excused his peasants and workers, saying they were too busy with other things to cultivate good taste, and joked a bit about the hundreds of thousands of monstrously enlarged portraits of the man with the moustache, portraits that danced before his eyes during the demonstrations. I pointed out that even people who did have taste displayed busts and portraits of him — and what busts and portraits! — in the most inappropriate places, such as the Rembrandt exhibit. Here Stalin turned serious. He suggested that these were people who had been late to acknowledge the regime and so now were trying with redoubled zeal to prove their devotion. He also intimated that this could be the work of saboteurs trying to discredit him. "A bootlicking fool," he snarled, "does more harm than a hundred enemies." Stalin added that he tolerated the fanfare only because he knew what naive joy these festivities afforded their organizers and because he knew they concerned him not personally but as one of many who consider building a socialist economy in the Soviet Union more important than permanent revolution.

Stalin was undoubtedly dissembling. He couldn't cow Feuchtwanger the way he could his own subjects, so he deceived this foreign writer, hoping to please him. And he did please him. Feuchtwanger extolled Stalin in the Western press, especially for his modesty. But of interest here is how Stalin explained the personality cult. The reference to "permanent revolution," whose theorist was Trotsky, wasn't haphazard. In fact, Stalin appropriated this theory, applying it in his own way. Collectivization, the purges of the thirties, and much more besides may be seen as a form of permanent revolution. But Stalin valued the portraits and alleluias as proof of his victory over Trotsky, once his greatest enemy and rival. A victory that was crowned by the executions of the thirties and, soon thereafter, by the assassination of Trotsky. At the same time Stalin, with characteristic finesse, tried to blame his own personality cult on mythical "saboteurs" out to discredit him. In so doing, he untied his hands for future executions, even of those most devoted to him. Finally, Stalin excused this cult as nothing but the naïveté of his workers and peasants. But the secret idea here, it seems to me, is one that Stalin put into practice: the idea that this was the only way one could or should rule this naive people — or any people.

Some historians say that Stalin possessed one uncanny ability. He could read people like no one else, he could see right through them. Hence his knack for picking cadres, destroying the talented or independent ones while retaining the yes-men incapable of competing with him, who feared this more than fire. Aside from being able to parse people, Stalin was adept at playing them off against one another to serve his own purposes. He could, for instance, recruit one opponent, use him to discard a second opponent, then sic a third opponent on the one remaining, and finally shoot the third as the hangman of the other two. Thus in the mid-twenties Stalin toppled Trotsky with the help of Zinoviev and Nikolai Bukharin, who themselves would later pay as fictional members of the Trotsky-Bukharin conspiracy. Stalin's victims were linked one to the next, often having played the role of the executioner before being executed. Iona Yakir's death sentence was signed by Marshal Vasily Blyukher (among others), who himself was later shot. "One of the essential principles of the assassinations under Stalin was the annihilation of one group of Party officials by another, later destroyed by a third group of assassins," writes Varlam Shalamov in "The Resurrection of the Larch."

Not an educated man, Stalin nevertheless read a fair amount. He was a great admirer of Joseph Fouché, the French minister of police in the early 1800s, who survived several regimes and was a master of intrigue; having read Stefan Zweig's book on Fouché, published in Russia in the early thirties, Stalin said delightedly: "Now, there was a man! He outwitted them all, made a fool of everyone."

Stalin was also fascinated by Machiavelli — master of the arts of politics and government — for whom he had enormous respect. Stalin must have particularly valued Machiavelli's scruple-free recommendations on how to take and consolidate power.

Among Russian historical figures, Stalin revered Ivan the Terrible. Aleksei Tolstoy's drama eulogizing Ivan IV earned him a personal phone call from Stalin, who praised the work. But according to the record of this conversation preserved in the archives, Stalin added that the tsar did have one failing: between executions of the boyars, he was tortured by pangs of conscience and repented of his cruelty.

Sadism aside, Stalin also possessed, it seems to me, something of the craziness of the terrible tsar Ivan Vasilyevich. Svetlana Alliluyeva indicates that in 1952 her father "twice asked the Central Committee to retire him. Everyone cried out that that was impossible. . . . Was he expecting anything else from that unanimous chorus?" asks Svetlana in *Only One Year* (1970):

> Did he suspect that someone would agree to replace him? No one would have dared. Not one of them could make up his mind to take Stalin seriously. And besides, did he really want to retire? This recalled the ruses of Ivan the Terrible who, complaining of old age and fatigue, periodically withdrew to a monastery and ordered the boyars to choose a new tsar. On their knees, the boyars would beg him not to abandon them, fearing that anyone they chose would be decapitated on the spot.

Stalin played Ivan the Terrible. The ex-Chekist Orlov, who remained in the West, tells in *The Secret History of Stalin's Crimes* how Stalin once gave himself a special pseudonym to be used by Soviet agents involved in top-secret operations abroad: Ivan Vasilyevich. "A transparent pseudonym," says Orlov. "It was the name of the tsar who was dear to Stalin's heart, Ivan the Terrible."

Unlike Ivan the Terrible, Stalin didn't seem tortured by his sins. But for all his callousness, he was emotionally mercurial and, apart from his theater of men-marionettes, he could play on his own heartstrings. Svetlana recounts:

> I think father saw something of himself in *Boris Godunov,* his favorite opera and one that he repeatedly went to hear in his last years, often sitting alone in his box. Once he took me with him. Boris's monologue and the Innocent's recitative sent shivers up my spine and I was scared to look at my father. . . . Perhaps at that moment he [like Boris — A.S.] had "blood-stained children in his eyes"? Why did he always go to that particular opera?

A talented director, Stalin was also a gifted actor by the accounts of Khrushchev and many other memoirists who describe, for example, Stalin kissing Kirov — whom he had had assassinated — laid out in his coffin. Or Stalin grieving over the body of Georgy Ordzhonikidze, whom he either killed or drove to death. Writes Abdurakhman Avtorkhanov (*Memoirs*): "I was at that meeting, not far from the Mausoleum, on a snowy February day in 1937. I watched Stalin: what profound sorrow, what enormous grief, what fantastic pain, were etched in his face! Yes, Comrade Stalin was a great actor!"

Then again Stalin could charm people with his gentle good manners. He knew how to maintain an impenetrable mask, behind which the unpredictable lurked. . . . With a single, unhurried inflection, he could impart a profound wisdom to the most trivial platitudes. Just as he could use words to disguise the real meanings of his speeches and decisions.

Power fascinated Stalin as, among other things, a game with human lives. Having a profound knowledge of people and holding them in as profound a contempt, Stalin used them like putty in the crafting of his own design, in imposing his own personality and fate on history. In his eyes he was the only actor-director on the stage of all Russia and all the world. In this sense, Stalin was a born artist. Hence this divergence into a cult of his own person, which separates him from Lenin. Hence his capricious despotism. And his concoction of the show trials, choreographed as engrossing thrillers and colorful spectacles. And his impassive public mask — the mask of the wise leader, sure of his rightness and infallibility — concealing the passions that must have seethed within. Stalin could hypnotize a crowd — and liked to do so — with his calm. He was forever toying with his victims, as if power gave him a kind of aesthetic satisfaction.

Stalin liked to lure his victim with displays of affection laced with intimidation, knocking him off balance in a game of cat and mouse. This was how he dealt with the devoted A. V. Kosarev, secretary of the Komsomol's Central Committee, at a Kremlin banquet in 1938. After Molotov toasted all the guests, including Kosarev, each one went up to Stalin to clink glasses. When Kosarev's turn came, Stalin hugged him and kissed him and whispered in his ear: "If you betray me, I'll kill you." Kosarev blanched and returned home very shaken to tell his wife (from whom we know this) what happened. Kosarev, of course, never betrayed Stalin who, a few months later, had him shot.

All this wasn't just a mood or a whim, but a well-thought-out game. Stalin loved to keep a man on tenterhooks, retaining him in a high post while arresting his wife, brother, or son. And before ordering the execution, he might even raise his victim still higher, so as to give him an illusion of security.

One day Stalin asked Otto Kuusinen, a top Party official, why he hadn't petitioned for his son's release. "Obviously," said Kuusinen, "there were serious reasons for his arrest." Stalin smiled — and had the son freed.

As if he needed to test the force and magic of his power. Submissiveness might be rewarded with kindness, but not necessarily: a person could grovel all he wanted and still be trampled. In this game with human lives, the important thing to Stalin was to imbue his power with an impenetrable mystery, a supreme irrationality. Already irrational by nature, Stalin thickened the brew with his own dramatizations and embellishments. This corresponded to his artistic side, to his desire to give his power a mystical quality, and to his secretive inner workings.

Compared to Stalin, Lenin gives the impression of an open man, as open as a dictator can be. Lenin didn't have anything particular to hide in that he spelled out almost everything in his rational constructions and activities. Stalin, on the other hand, had a lot to hide, notably the fact that he placed himself immeasurably higher than the others. He had to conceal his machinations and dark instincts. Consequently, Stalin's name and persona are surrounded by all sorts of stories, some of which agree with the facts, others of which conflict, but never so radically as to seem unbelievable.

This is one reason I've included so many anecdotes about Stalin, both entirely and partially documentary, written and oral. Without them, one is hard pressed to understand the enigma of Stalin. By all rights, these vignettes should all be anthologized in a big book called *Historical Legends and Anecdotes About Comrade Stalin*. Historians of the past, like Suetonius, pieced biographies together largely from anecdotes and entertaining landmarks in the life of one hero or another. And this quasi-folklore serves as a historical source in the study of distant eras. It doesn't so much matter whether it's truth or invention, since conjecture can contain more of reality than the facts. The same can be said of stories about Stalin: one can't vouch for their factual authenticity, but the important thing is that they correspond with the era and with its image of Stalin and his metaphysical personality.

Certain passages in Vasily Grossman's novel *Life and Fate* (1980) revolve around these kinds of anecdotes:[1]

> One evening Stalin appeared in the Metro. Slightly tipsy, he sat down next to a young woman and said:
> "How can I help you?"
> The woman said:
> "I'd very much like to visit the Kremlin."
> Stalin reflected a minute before answering and then said:
> "I might be able to arrange this for you."

Another example:

> They say that Stalin once called the editorial offices of a youth newspaper and the deputy editor answered:
> "Bubekin speaking."
> Stalin said:
> "Who's Bubekin?"
> Bubekin said:
> "You ought to know!" and slammed down the receiver.
> Stalin called back and said:
> "Comrade Bubekin, this is Stalin speaking, please explain to me who you are."
> They say that after this incident Bubekin spent two weeks in the hospital recovering from nervous shock.

---

1. *Translator's note:* Before Grossman's death in 1964, the KGB confiscated all but two of the manuscripts of *Life and Fate*. Of the surviving two, one was kept by Grossman's friend the poet Semyon Lipkin, who sent it to the West. It was first published by Editions l'Age d'Homme (Lausanne) in Russian in 1980. Harper & Row came out with an English-language version in 1986. In 1988, Knizhnaya Palata Publishers (Moscow) produced the first Soviet edition.

From these anecdotes and many others, it is obvious that Stalin loved not only to flaunt his power but to use his position to perform ingenious "tricks," the most benign of which was a game he invented with the little Svetlana, recorded in their correspondence. In *Twenty Letters to a Friend* (1967), Svetlana writes that Stalin would affectionately call her "the proprietress" and reduce himself, the all-powerful proprietor, to the rank of her humble "secretary" or poor "little secretary" along with the other members of the Politburo. Then he would sign his own sonorous name, "Stalin." Stalin liked to jokingly disparage himself to his little girl, as if to show that he was so powerful that his supreme power didn't mean a thing to him.

Stalin was apparently a great humorist as opposed to Lenin, who once confessed sadly to Gorky that he had no sense of humor. Lenin, after all, was a scholar and a rationalist who didn't need humor, whereas Stalin, with his irrational, artistic nature, reveled in his humor — black humor mostly, but humor nevertheless. It was one more tool he used to control people's lives and fates, to bring them good or evil. As if he were above good and evil. Stalin played deliberately on this ambivalence: turning evil into good and good into evil. So that he could be affectionate while showing his claws, threatening to kill; a menacing gesture might just as easily end in a reward. The endless possibilities for substituting evil for good and vice versa were the stuff of Stalin's unfathomable mystery, of his black secret. Ultimately, the best expression of Stalin's black humor was the corpse. Not just any corpse or the corpse of an enemy, but the corpse of a friend who loved Stalin and whom Stalin for some reason didn't trust . . .

Stalin's black humor also came through in politics. As we know, Stalin had Kirov killed and then ascribed his assassination to his ideological adversaries — Trotsky, Zinoviev, Kamenev, and others — thus triggering a succession of show trials. A brilliant move, tactically and politically. But at the same time Stalin turned Kirov, a relatively obscure Party official, into a renowned leader post facto, a great historical figure and his own best friend; their names became linked in people's minds. Stalin even renamed a series of cities in his victim's honor: Kirovsk, Kirovograd, Kirovokan, and so on. And this desire to immortalize Kirov, to put him on the map, wasn't just a function of Stalin's wanting to cover his tracks but above all, in my view, an exercise in black humor. As if Stalin were compensating the dead Kirov by making him a national hero. Possibly this was his way of thanking Kirov for having been murdered.

Stalin loved art — literature, film, theater, music, dance — much more so, surprisingly, than Lenin, who showed little interest. Stalin's artistic tastes amounted to a bizarre blend of crude, barbaric passions and a subtle sense of the creative process. This is natural, since Stalin was a plebian and a despot with unusual artistic tendencies. We find nothing of the kind in the intellectual Lenin, compared to whom Stalin was a savage. But this savage read a lot more fiction than Lenin who, as a rule, stuck to politics and science. Stalin kept a keen eye on Soviet literature which, it's true, paid dearly for this. But this vigilance also attests to Stalin's aesthetic sense, prompted as much by the concerns of a chief censor as by personal convictions about art. The combination produced absurd judgments as well as occasional glimmers of real insight. On the one hand, Gorky's very weak poem "A Young Girl and Death" inspired Stalin to write: "This thing is stronger than Goethe's *Faust*" — a comical assessment, the height of vulgarity and incomprehension. On the other hand, Stalin was able to see in Mayakovsky the best Soviet poet, and not just out of political considerations. Though Viktor Nekrasov's *In the Trenches of Stalingrad* (1946) didn't contain a single eulogy to Stalin, he praised it as the best novel about the war. And among the writers who were ideologically alien to him, Stalin had a weakness for Mikhail Bulgakov, whom he allowed to stay alive. Stalin went to see Bulgakov's *Days of the Turbins* (1926) seventeen times at the Moscow Art Theater, though he banned this play from production anywhere else. He had evidently seen a great writer in Bulgakov, whereas the Soviet literary establishment wanted him liquidated. About Dostoyevsky, Stalin once remarked to his daughter that he was "a great psychologist." "He must have found something in Dostoyevksy," Svetlana surmises, "that concerned him profoundly, but he didn't want to say what exactly" (*Only One Year*).

And yet, Stalin's aesthetic tastes were primitive. For example, he loved the color illustrations in the weekly *Ogonyok,* which he often had framed. This fondness tells us something, as does Stalin's passion for the theater or the movies. He saw his favorite films — like

*The Happy Boys* and *Volga-Volga* — fifty times. However ludicrous, this all points to a penchant for art.

Stalin's psychology, dark, complex, and poetic in its own way despite the grossness and appalling cruelty, is evoked by Fazil Iskander in his novel *Sandro from Chegem* (1979). In one chapter, Stalin is shown in the mid-thirties, in Abkhazia, at a banquet in his honor. A national folk ensemble is singing and dancing, while all the applause is going to him. Stalin raises a glass to the host, his devoted friend Nestor Lakoba, whom he will soon destroy. Then, with morbid inspiration, he listens to the Georgian song "Fly, Black Swallow, Fly," imagining himself as that black swallow while meditating on his fate as the supreme leader who loves no one, who cannot and must not love anyone, since this is his tragic lot. These pages are among the best that uncensored Soviet prose has produced on Stalin, precisely because they convey his irrationality.

## The Mystery and the Magic of Stalin's Power

Though corrupted by power, Stalin understood its nature perfectly and made secrecy its mainspring. Stalin wasn't just a ruthless dictator, he was a kind of hypnotist who managed to convince the people that he was their god by shrouding his cult in the mystery he knew power required. Witness the unpredictability of his decisions (when he had both friends and enemies killed), his black humor, and even his laconic speech. Stalin spoke very slowly between long pauses, creating an illusion of enormous import, no matter how flat the phrase, and superhuman wisdom. Though Stalin didn't say or write anything wise, the sheer inscrutability of his words and acts signified his "wisdom," his ability to see and know all, his divine powers, his omniscience. Stalin's ubiquitous secret police penetrated every pore of Soviet society and, repressive functions aside, added to the aura of supreme mystery around the workings of the omniscient almighty.

In a similar vein, Stalin tried to pass himself off as a leading light in all branches of science. Though not a scholar, he affected a universal erudition. This explains, in particular, his contributions to linguistics, a field which would seem far removed from his own. By setting forth his authoritative views here, Stalin showed everyone that his intellect extended to everything, that nothing escaped

him. Some claimed that Stalin had a photographic memory allowing him to read a thousand pages a day: rather than having to scan
every line, a glance at the page was enough for it to be imprinted in
his memory.

When Stalin died, many people thought that everything had
died, even those who weren't politically attached to the regime or
worshippers of Stalin. It's just that Stalin had become a synonym for
the entire State, for life on earth. "Stalin's name . . . is life!" wrote
the poet Aleksandr Tvardovsky. It's no accident that during the war
soldiers mounted an assault with this one device: "For the Motherland! For Stalin!" Stalin was the Motherland. He was often deferen-
tially referred to as "the Proprietor." Everyone knew that the
Proprietor was Stalin.

Stalin's posthumous "reappearances" were legend. This "mysticism" matters to us here only as an example of the magical power
Stalin possessed in the minds of Soviet people, including those who
didn't love him. Stalin's ghost appeared as a kind of demon. The
noted writer Leonid Leonov recounted this curious incident in a
private conversation. This happened after the Twentieth Party Congress (1956), where Khrushchev had denounced Stalin, and the
latter's name was being crossed out everywhere. Leonov and his
secretary had just spent an evening removing every reference to
Stalin in a book of his due to be reissued. She then left — only to
fall on the stairs and break her arm. In superstitious horror, Leonov
seriously insisted that this was Stalin taking revenge and added that
he too had felt poorly ever since. So Stalin, like an evil spirit, put
hexes on everyone who crossed him.

Of interest to us here is this dark fascination that Stalin exercised
in death as in life, a fascination which is explained by the
profound mystery in which he cloaked his power and his own
person.

Schematically, Stalin's magic has two faces: the light and the
dark. One half of Stalin's personality belongs to the bright light of
day, when the people rejoice, when buildings are built and parades
parade, when the art of Socialist Realism thrives. But the principal
business is done at night: arrests, executions, political intrigues,
and governmental sessions associated with binges of black humor

and sinister buffoonery. This nocturnal style of life corresponds to the mystery with which Stalin invested the very notion of power. Which is why it's so interesting to read about Stalin. The mystery sucks you in, swallows you up. Aleksandr Orlov's book is called *The Secret History of Stalin's Crimes:* this sounds like music or an absorbing novel à la *Mysteries of Paris, The Mysterious Island, Mystery of Two Oceans.* Stalin, you might say, was able to transform the history of Soviet society into the secret history of his own crimes.

Glancing back over the Stalin era, I can't find one artist who would have been worthy of Stalin, who could have matched his formidable irrationality, his "nocturnal" spirit. During Stalin's lifetime, only he himself could have been that artist, since he had eliminated all those who might have rivaled him in art or in life, while leaving most writers to go the radiant road of Socialist Realism, limited to his diurnal aspect. But one mysterious book eluded Stalin and reached us many years later, a lasting monument of and to that unique epoch.

I'm referring to Bulgakov's *The Master and Margarita,* first published in 1966, more than twenty-five years after the author's death, but written when Stalin's irrationality was at its most brutal. Bulgakov's novel is a product of Stalinist "problems," though not confined to them. Woland, or Satan, favorably disposed toward the Master, is to a certain extent Stalin favorably disposed toward Bulgakov: a somber, black, and yet idealized Stalin.

On March 28, 1930, Bulgakov wrote the Soviet government that the critics and censors had so hounded him that he, in his despair, had burned the draft of a novel about the devil (an earlier version of *The Master and Margarita*). Bulgakov asked the government to give him his freedom, to let him emigrate, or to find him some kind of employment. In the same letter, he recommended himself as a writer who preferred "black and mystical colors."

Three weeks later, on April 18, Bulgakov received a call from Stalin: "So, are you really fed up with us?" These words evidently struck Bulgakov, since he reproduced them in *The Master and Margarita,* where Woland, after the grand ball, asks Margarita: "Now then, have we really worn you out?"

Satan's grand ball represents a kind of apotheosis of evil, the quintessence of crime, which reached its maximum concentration in Stalin. The villains of the world have all congregated at Woland's, at Stalin's.

The novel contains numerous other allusions to Stalin, like this toast addressed to Pontius Pilate: "To us, and to you, Caesar, father of the Romans, the most beloved and the best man of all . . . ." But the main thing is not these indirect and direct references to contemporary reality, rather it's the novel's atmosphere, shot through with Stalin's somber currents. It's the mass psychosis that has locked society in a vicious circle of denunciations, where the secret police, the prison, and the interrogations are presented as a sort of theater in imitation of Stalin's own theater of denunciations and repressions.

I would like to try to convey the tragic dimension of *The Master and Margarita* in its correspondence to Soviet history of the period and Bulgakov's own life.

The role of the devil, of the dark genie Woland who, for some mysterious reason tolerates the writer, the Master, is the role that Stalin played in Bulgakov's life. Stalin knew about Bulgakov but, having cornered him, let him be. All things considered, Bulgakov should have been shot, and it's highly possible that, had Stalin suspected the existence of *The Master and Margarita,* Bulgakov would have been killed, the manuscript incinerated, and the ashes scattered to the winds. Instead, other writers were caught and shot, including the most proletarian, the most faithfully devoted to the Party. *The Master and Margarita* depicted the debauchery and bedlam of this literary world that had sicced itself on Bulgakov, publicly branding him the never-shot White Guard, and now suddenly this world was dying a worse death than the White Guard. Bulgakov survived by some obscure irony of fate and, played out, described in his novel his strange friendship with Woland who, having unleashed all this witchcraft, turned out to be far better than those he had put to death. People turned into demons, and the chief demon into a Maecenas. The only ones protected by Woland, master of evil, were the Master and his Margarita (and it's she — Bulgakov's wife — who saved the manuscript of the novel), because he knew who was who. The mysticism of this relationship between the writer and the leader was even reflected in the graphic proximity of their names, where the W in Woland is like an inverted M, emblem of the Master and of Margarita. "He believes in the mutual knowledge / Of these two extreme principles," Pasternak wrote on the similarly mystical theme of the relationship between the Poet and the Leader (specifically, between Pasternak and Stalin).

Yes, Stalin could inspire not only horror and love, but also faith in his magic powers. Among theosophists, persecuted and far from supporting the regime, there was a rumor that Stalin knew something that no one else guessed, that he was the incarnation of the Great Manu of India. Bulgakov's fascination with Woland is more understandable since through him Stalin appears as an astounding conjurer and unique artist in his profession (hence his sympathy, in the novel, for the other professional, the Master, for the writer Bulgakov), all wrapped up in the art of confounding and deceiving people, of creating mirages and hallucinations. In Stalin, the orchestrator of executions and show trials, the perfidious wizard towering over everyone in the eerie solitude of an omniscient, omnipotent evil spirit, Bulgakov must have sensed an artistic streak, which he exaggerated in his dreams about Woland.

Of course, neither Woland nor Bulgakov's novel can be reduced to this Stalinist element, just as the book can't be called an autobiography. But *The Master and Margarita* gives us a better understanding of Soviet history, which at one point became all tangled up in the game of a Magician who, for a protracted period, was able to infuse it with the force and aspect of the fabulous fantastic, of a mad, nightmarish farce. It's no accident that the events in Bulgakov's novel revolve around an insane asylum that ends by enveloping all of Moscow.

Neither of one mind with Bulgakov nor a mystic, Khrushchev nevertheless compared the Stalin era to an insane asylum, where he survived by chance: he drew "a lucky lottery ticket," as he says in *Khrushchev Remembers* (1970), which saved him from winding up an enemy of the people. It was Khrushchev's good luck to have studied at the industry academy with Stalin's wife, to whom he defended Stalin's positions; she, in her naïveté, passed these conversations on to her husband, who never forgot that Khrushchev was his man. Even Stalin, incidentally, once let it slip that "we are living in a crazy time."

In 1937 Trotsky wrote that Stalin's criminal behavior had acquired "truly apocalyptic dimensions"; he called his falsifications "monstrous" and likened them to a "nightmare" or a "delirium." Epithets that well convey the morality of Stalin and his epoch, however weak the link with Marxism. The "mystical writer" Bulgakov managed to discern the reality in a way that no "realist" did. He showed that Soviet history had entered a realm beyond human comprehension, a realm of demonic powers.

Several years ago, *Literaturnaya Gazeta* ran an article by V. Kaverin noting the topicality of *The Master and Margarita* both at the time of its writing and now ("Looking It in the Face," June 18, 1986). Kaverin calls this novel, where the "fantastic marked by a contemporary poignancy" reigns, "fresh air" that has finally blown into Soviet literature: "For years we pretended that literature never departed from the truth. Meanwhile, literature had become purposeful, but hollow." Further on, Kaverin asserts that under Stalin "a certain social atmosphere evolved, the fruits of which we haven't been able to eliminate to this day." The Stalinist spirit lives on . . .

In the secrecy of his rule, Stalin undoubtedly leaned on the old Russian tradition of autocracy, even if his power surpassed that of all the tsars. Interestingly, soon after Lenin's death, Stalin once let the cat out of the bag, declaring that Russia needed a tsar. At a dinner the conversation had turned to the pressing question of how to run the Party without Lenin. Suddenly Stalin said: "Don't forget that we are living in Russia, in the land of the tsars. The Russian people like to see one man alone at the head of the State." No one noticed the remark, nor did it occur to anyone that Stalin had himself in mind for the role of emperor. But this proposal materialized, and on a prodigious scale. If Lenin laid the foundations of one-man rule, Stalin was able to imbue it with a religious, even mystical quality. From Russian traditions, he had gleaned that the tsar must be terrible, even terrifying, while offering the people his smile as the supreme kindness. Stalin's oriental nature may also have influenced his monarchistic style, evoking the ancient despots of the Orient. But at the same time it expressed Stalin's feel for the strictly Russian national character.

In his Russocentrism, Stalin sometimes resorted to prerevolutionary arguments. In 1945, for example, in honor of the victory over Japan, Stalin made the following speech:

"The defeat of the Russian forces in 1904 during the Russo-Japanese War left painful memories in the people's consciousness. It left a black stain on our country. Our people knew that the day would come when Japan would be beaten and the stain liquidated. We, the older generation, waited forty years for this day. And now this day has come."

Surprising rhetoric, given that at the time of the Russo-Japanese War, the unpatriotic Bolsheviks were rooting for Russia's defeat in the belief that this would benefit the revolution. And of course by 1945, everyone had forgotten about the score to be settled with Japan. But not Stalin.

Stalin's monarchism also showed in the revival of prerevolutionary practices. So that, while the word "officer" had long been considered an insult, epaulets, ranks, and titles were reintroduced in the army. If this touched and pleased some older émigrés, it could shock people brought up on Soviet norms and Leninist traditions. This was the logic of the new, Stalinist epoch, with its attempts to restore certain monarchistic forms and customs. Stalin was feathering himself a tsarist nest.

It's funny that Stalin imposed one-man rule everywhere when he alone was ruling the entire country. Even literature had its hierarchy, the pillar of Socialist Realism being Gorky, with Mayakovsky for poetry. The top theater director was Konstantin Stanislavsky. The government had its Jew: Lazar Kaganovich.

But one has to admit that Stalin's personality cult found popular support; it wasn't only imposed by force. The mysticism of his power appealed to people. They were impressed by his grandeur, his inaccessibility, his mystery. This speaks, in my view, not just of the Russian people's attachment to its tsars but also of its affinity for power stamped with the seal of an irrational mystery. One might even suppose that herein lies a sign of the religiousness of the Russian soul, distorted in the deification of Stalin, a tsar invested with quasi-divine powers. This explains how the Russians could prefer a dictator to a parliament. Most reacted with astounding indifference to the dispersal of the Constituent Assembly — their parliament — treated by the Bolsheviks with a contempt that communicated itself to the people. Because parliamentary power utterly lacked the mystery that surrounded the tsar.

Even today, many in Russia still equate Stalin with a time of order that disappeared with him. Because Stalin was all-knowing and all-powerful. I once tried long and hard — and without success — to dissuade a worker who assured me that the simple people lived much better under Stalin, since the bosses feared him, while he periodically — every ten years — had them shot: this was the only way to run the country. According to this logic, the bosses became slack after ten years and had to be eliminated and replaced by new bosses who hadn't had time to let themselves go; thus Stalin was only thinking of the common good in systematically liquidating the ruling cadres, the executions bespoke his kindness to the simple people. And if you point out that simple people were also shot, you're told: "That's how you have to treat us. That's why there was real order under Stalin." Such was the magic of his power.

This power and its magic cost Stalin. He was very alone and trusted no one; hence his gloominess, which then turned into a persecution complex. There was one anecdote that went around while he was still alive in which, by analogy to cognac, he was called "maniac three stars" — an allusion to the three gold stars given to a Hero of the Soviet Union, an award he had bestowed upon himself.

Stalin's suspiciousness was a function of his having killed so many people that it always seemed to him that someone wanted to settle the score; so he had to go on endlessly killing new friends who had become suspect.

His persecution complex was especially aggravated toward the end of his life which, consequently, was not easy. They say that at the dachas where Stalin lived there were generally several bedrooms and he moved from one to the next. Fresh linen was laid out in each room, and Stalin made his own bed. Before going to sleep, he looked under the bed with a special lamp. It seems that he rarely worked at his desk, preferring to move around the room with his chair, dodging would-be snipers. He also seems to have had several doubles. Not to mention the permanent guard and ubiquitous sur-

veillance that shadowed everyone, the government and Politburo
included.

There are those who claim that Stalin was killed. This strikes me
as unlikely. No one in his entourage could have contemplated such
a thing, while all the daredevils who would have been capable had
been destroyed long since.

Retribution caught up with Stalin only after his death, which
elicited unseemly jubilance in many people. Reportedly the first to
rejoice that the tyrant was dead was his most faithful and terrifying
servant, Lavrenty Beria; possibly this was calculated to absolve himself of responsibility for many crimes of power. But there were also
simple people who exulted openly.

"Personality cult" is a rather narrow term and somewhat absurd
insofar as it reduces the content of the Stalin era to Stalin's personal
mistakes and failings. But these so-called mistakes diverted the
entire country and its history from the path prescribed by the
original doctrine. Even so, the concept of a personality cult conveys
an important aspect of Soviet civilization. The word "cult" implies
a religion, religious worship, religious rites. But in this case, it's a
religion without God, who is replaced by the State power and its
flesh-and-blood representative: Stalin. Thus the deification of Stalin
is a manifestation of the Soviet State's ecclesiastical nature. The
State of scholars under Lenin gave way to a Church-State under
Stalin, though the necessary conditions for such a transformation
existed much earlier: the religious worship of an omnipotent power
that enjoys the right to resort to any means of violence, covert or
overt. Marxist ideology itself, as we have seen, has something in
common with religion, only without God, and with communism in
place of the Heavenly Kingdom and historical necessity replacing
divine Providence. And even before Marxism, Russian socialism
possessed its own religious potential.

Stalin's cult evolved naturally from all of this, except that early
socialism deified man in general, whereas Stalin deified himself as
the personification of State power.

And the State turned Church embraced everyone — their soul
and their consciousness. To disavow the Party doctrine was subversive, tantamount to a crime against the State. All this began with

Lenin, who ordered comrades shot for "bourgeois propaganda," but Stalin completed this unification of the country, of social groups and people's own thoughts. Soviet writers bragged, not without reason, about the harmony of the Soviet world: the past was dominated by discord and people lived in enmity; but we are happy because we are living in the century of great unanimity, which will never end, which will gather up all of humanity.

Dostoyevsky claimed that Catholicism had transformed the church into a state, whereas our Orthodoxy, he said, would ideally like the State to transform itself into the church. Dostoyevsky's dream came true, but topsy-turvy; the Godless State transformed itself into a Godless Church with unlimited claims on the human soul. Thus Stalin doesn't just speak, he officiates, and every one of his adversaries, real or imagined, must confess his sins before being shot.

Hence the enormous importance of uniformity. There is one science: Marxism; one eminent Marxist: Stalin; one "creative method" in art and literature: Socialist Realism; one basic history book; and so on. All originality is dangerous and suspect. Conspicuous stylistic deviations are forbidden. The fight against "formalism" is a fight for the Party standard, for a strict, ecclesiastical form in art and literature. This extends to everyday life: beards and long hair on men are seen as a sign of nonconformity; men shouldn't wear narrow pants; women shouldn't wear pants period, or miniskirts . . .

If Lenin required of Marxism a concrete analysis of the historical situation, Stalin wanted exact prescriptions: all speeches had to conform to strict criteria, including set quotes from Lenin and Stalin, and God forbid one should misquote. The form constricts and congeals; here again it resembles the religious devotion to the holy letter. In the 1930s and later they even imprisoned people for misprints in a newspaper or a book, since these were interpreted as hostile attacks. True, there was one benefit: Soviet publications contained precious few misprints. Stalin's lessons stuck in people's minds.

The cult of the leader clearly began with Lenin, who enjoyed unquestioned authority. Curiously, this cult gained a religous dimension when Lenin died and his body was embalmed and placed in a mausoleum — perhaps the most graphic display of the Soviet State's ecclesiastical nature. An especially macabre display, since Lenin in his mausoleum implies the worship of a corpse. Initially, the Soviet State fought Orthodox religion, removing holy relics from the churches, desecrating and destroying them. Then it turned Lenin into an artificial relic. Holy relics assume faith in God, in the immortality of the soul, and in the resurrection of the dead; here, in the absence of genuine faith, they preserve the dust. Krupskaya reportedly objected to the mausoleum, but they ignored her and mummified Lenin for the sake of the State. Their prototype was probably the mummies of the pharaohs. But in ancient Egypt, this rite relied on faith in God and in a kingdom beyond the grave; and the pharaoh, to himself and to the people, was a truly deified monarch, not just the head dictator.

Lenin's mausoleum, in the heart of Red Square — regarded as the symbolic center of the country and the entire world — functions as a kind of cathedral. The successive Leaders file out onto its rostrum to show themselves to the people during parades and demonstrations. It's a cathedral built for a corpse, without faith in God, with faith only in the idea and the legitimacy of one's own cause, faith in one's own deified power.

Many years ago, when I was still a student, I learned that in our country they tortured political prisoners to extract confessions of guilt. I relayed this fact to a friend of mine who was much older and already a Party member. Fortunately, he wasn't an informer. But his utterly sincere response, not prompted by fear, was this: "Don't talk to me about any torture. Even if this is true, I don't want to know about it. Because I want to believe, I have to have faith." At the time, I was taken aback that someone would wittingly, in the name of faith, close his eyes to the reality.

All this speaks of Soviet civilization's religious foundation. Since then, many things have changed in the country and the faith in communism has been badly eroded, though the State continues to maintain its ecclesiastical exterior. The faith is gone but the dead shell remains, strong and solid like a petrified coat of mail, nostalgic for the Stalin era, which precluded change. Because then, order prevailed, and the power was not a soulless mechanism but a mystery.

# 5

# The New Man

THE REVOLUTIONARY FLAG READ: "Everything anew."
But to create the "new man," a single revolutionary leap forward
was not enough. The coup d'état would have to be followed by a
long process of elimination of everything that was old in man and in
humanity. An arduous task given that the "old man," in Marxist
parlance, was the product of centuries of slavery. To recast the old
psychology would require the creation of utterly new conditions of
existence.

On the other hand, the old psychology could and must be
changed with persistent social and moral coercion. Hence the endless lectures to Soviet citizens and to the entire world, hence the
moralistic and didactic posture assumed by the Soviet power as it
instructs, criticizes, exhorts, and preaches. It is a prison cum
school, a school for defective or problem children, where the education goes hand in hand with punishment and incarceration, themselves a method of education.

Soviet civilization in miniature is thus a camp, also known as a
"corrective labor colony." For the camp's aim is not just to hold
criminals behind the barbed wire, but to amend them. This by two
means: labor, in accordance with the famous Marxist thesis that
labor is what made the monkey a man; and moralistic, ideological
pressure exerted on the criminals by the authorities (the "new
men").

This idea of the new man is the cornerstone of Soviet civilization.
The State could not have survived as long as it has without the
support of a man of a new social and psychological type. Without

him, one could not have built socialism. This is the gist of these
lines by Mayakovsky written in 1918:

> *We fired for a day or two*
> *Then we thought:*
> *We'll clean the old man's clock.*
> *That's what!*
> *Reversing one's jacket,*
> *That's not enough, comrades!*
> *Go on, turn yourselves inside out!*

The government had a similar plan. In 1922 Bukharin wrote that
the revolution's principal task was "to alter people's actual psychology." He returned to this subject in 1928 in an article-program
published in *Izvestia:* "In our system of scientific planning, one of
the first priorities is the question of the systematic preparation of
new men, the builders of socialism."

This is the mass production of the new man in the likeness of
Communists, supposed to embody the ideal and the standard. The
original concept included all sorts of wonderful qualities — man in
his plenitude finally revealed thanks to the revolution. The oldest
proletarian poet, F. Shkulev, in a poem pretentiously entitled "I
Am a Communist," wrote in 1919:

> *I love the dawn, the pure air*
> *And the pale blue sky,*
> *The murmur of the silvery brook,*
> *The fields and forests of this land.*
> *I love this longed-for freedom,*
> *The mute quietude,*
> *The howl of the storm,*
> *Good days and bad . . .*
> *I am a Communist, I am a Communist.*
>
> *I sing of labor,*
> *Pure as the sun.*
> *Riches, sloth, I despise.*
> *I am a Communist, I am a Communist!*

But to contemplate nature, to love the pure air and pale blue sky, one needn't be a Communist. The definition of the real Communist (or new man) is far more contained and precise, citing but a few, if highly developed virtues peculiar to the new psychology.

First, there is a boundless devotion to the supreme goal, the building of an ideal society on earth. In other words, a fanatical faith in the idea of communism.

Second is the ability to shift resolutely from words to deeds. The new man, forever remaking the world in an image closer to his ideal, is not a dreamer but a doer.

And third, the new man has the habit of representing the masses or the class, which effects its own ideal through him. The new man is in no sense solitary; even if circumstances should compel him to act alone, he still senses the unseen collective behind him. This collective is called the "Party," the "class," or even "the entire Soviet people," and ideally consists of new men. In short, the new man toils not for himself but for the great common cause, his one interest in life.

The most egregious sin, from the perspective of the new man, is egoism or individualism, the desire to live for oneself as opposed to the common good. And since this is the case with most people, the new man must transform human nature itself and eradicate the "original sin" of individual egoism, personified by the "bourgeois." The bourgeois lives unabashedly for himself at others' expense, at the proletariat's expense, capitalist property being the proof.

The bourgeois, however, is not only a social category but a universal psychological phenomenon, an intrinsic part of human nature. This explains why, even after the eradication of the bourgeoisie, "bourgeois vestiges" remain in people's consciousness: individualism, laziness, depravity, freedom, un-Communist ideas or views. Though various, these vestiges all derive from the same bourgeois interest in personal profit, in oneself and in the individual generally as soon as he diverges in any way from the common cause. Hence the necessity of stifling all personal aspects in others and in oneself. Hence the new man's distrust, even hatred, for the mere idea of a personality, the still-to-be-slaughtered bourgeois, as it were, lurking in every one of us.

The new man prides himself on not having anything of his own, on not distinguishing between the individual and the social. What's mine is ours, what's ours is mine. And the new man gives freely of his time. As Mayakovsky put it:

> *We load our wood*
> *Into our carriages, on our rails . . .*
> *The work is hard, backbreaking*
> *And we do it for free.*

Lenin attached great significance to *subbotniki* — voluntary working Saturdays. He saw them as "communism in action," in that people worked disinterestedly, of their own free will. It's only later that *subbotniki* became compulsory. Originally invented by the Communists for Communists and all comers, they were intended to cultivate that new type of man for whom the personal and the common were so much of a piece that he was ready to work for free, in the name of the idea itself of building communism.

This new breed of man did exist in fact, his most outstanding feature being the heroism without which the new man would have been inconceivable. For this heroism united the three cardinal virtues: a fanatical faith in the supreme goal; the ability to translate that faith into action; and a desire to strive not for one's own glory but for the general good. Ideally, these heroic feats should not have afforded the new man any personal success or profit and even should have remained anonymous. In *Chapaev*, Furmanov notes that in some units during the civil war, soldiers and commanders refused decorations on the grounds that either everyone should be decorated or no one. This idealism certainly did not benefit the power itself, since these decorations were also part of the educational effort to produce a new breed of men. Decorations were soon institutionalized, and Soviet people are still proud to receive them. But this initial refusal suggests how strong the sense of equality was at the beginning of the revolution. The new man — or whoever thought of himself as that — did not want to stand out in any way from the masses; he labored not for himself but for the common cause, in the name of the supreme goal: communism.

These verses by Nikolai Tikhonov convey the image of the new man:

*Life taught me with rifle and oar,*
*Lashed with wild winds against*
*My back like knotted cords,*
*Life made me calm and capable,*
*Simple — like nails of iron.*

For the noted Soviet literary critic Aleksandr Voronsky, these lines attested to the birth of a new man, unknown in old Russia: "In slack, flabby, Oblomovian old Russia, a new breed of men has appeared — simple and tough as nails" (1923).

This cult of the heroic is generally endemic to Soviet civilization, where the people are the "heroic Soviet people" who don't so much work as engage in "heroic labor." Every stage of Soviet history has its heroes, models for the edification of the masses: the test pilot Chkalov; the polar explorers led by Papanin, who spent an entire winter on a block of ice; the cosmonaut Gagarin; and so on.

Not surprisingly, Soviet literature abounds in educational novels depicting the transformation of an old man, or just an ordinary one, into a new man. Gorky's novel *Mother* (1906) was unanimously declared a Socialist Realist archetype. It's also the ideal educational novel: an old, ignorant, illiterate, downtrodden woman gradually turns into an ardent, conscious revolutionary, a fighter for the working-class cause.

But it was Nikolai Ostrovsky's *How the Steel Was Tempered* that proved to be the best real-life primer for successive generations of young Soviets. This novel was particularly popular for being autobiographical: the hero was a perfectly real person with a heroic past and present. Even the novel's writing had been a heroic feat: the author, previously unknown, was gravely ill, confined to his bed and blind. This, in effect, was his last service to the fight for communism, his last debt to society.

Some thirty years later, Aleksandr Solzhenitsyn, in his story "Incident at Kochetovka Station" (1963), seemed to respond to Ostrovsky and the notion of the new man. The title suggests the polemic:[1] Ostrovsky's hero, Pavel Korchagin, embarks on his heroic life at a little station called Shepetovka. At Solzhenitsyn's similar-sounding Kochetovka, the young Lieutenant Zotov is assistant stationmaster. The action takes place in late 1941, when Soviet forces had beat a panicky retreat. Troop trains are passing through the station, bound for and returning from the front; Zotov has his hands full. Also passing through are soldiers who have escaped from the German encirclement. One of them, Tveretinov, an actor turned volunteer who fell behind his unit, has no documents (he destroyed them all during the encirclement). He asks to board a train going to Moscow. Zotov's heart goes out to this intellectual, he talks with him and wants dearly to help. Then suddenly, an absurd suspicion tells him that Tveretinov is actually a German agent in disguise. And he arrests him: "What are you doing! What are you doing!" Tveretinov's voice rings out like a tolling bell. "Don't you see that what you're doing is irreparable!!" In the end, Tveretinov disappears into the depths of the NKVD and Zotov can never forget him. But Zotov — this is Solzhenitsyn's principal achievement — is not cruel. It's just that he was molded by the society and Soviet novels. As a boy he dreamed of going to Spain to fight; all his life he has ached exclusively for the common cause. Now his dream is to die at the front: "Zotov had no desire to stay in one piece now that the war had begun. His little life meant only what he could give to the Revolution." In essence, Zotov is a version of the new man: an idealist and a romantic, with a kind, gentle nature besides. And here this great idealist, whose dream it is to die, sends another man to his death for no reason. He does this based on his own notions, also romantic, of vigilance.

## MORALS OF THE NEW MAN

The new man manufactured by the Soviet system of education is nowhere near as wonderful as he seems in the poems and novels

---

1. *Translator's note:* Kochetovka is the name of an actual station where the incident in fact took place in 1941; all other place names in the story are real. When the liberal *Novy Mir* published the story in 1963, "Kochetovka" was changed to "Krechetovka" to avoid any association with the literary journal's conservative rival *Oktyabr,* then edited by Vsevolod Kochetov. In 1978, when the YMCA Press (Vermont–Paris) published Solzhenitsyn's collected works, "Kochetovka" was reinstated.

hymning the heroism of the revolution and the civil war. His inferiority is most evident in the moral sphere. Especially since the idea and even the term "new man" are not original with the revolution but with religion. Christianity proposes to the believer that he expunge the "ancient man" from himself, in other words, that he cleanse himself of his sins and become, with God's help, a new man. But those who follow this path never call themselves new men; they consider themselves sinners and ascribe everything good and holy that they do to God, whose will is done through them.

The new men created by the revolution also show religious qualities: fanatical faith in communism, the idea of sacrifice, rejection of personal profit, and renunciation of self. But here a strange shift occurs in the moral sense. Morality is not rescinded, but it is reduced to a secondary role, subordinated to the interests of class and to those of the common cause. A new concept takes hold, that of "Communist morals."

Lenin, speaking in 1920 to young Communists about their future, declared: "Our morality is entirely subordinate to the interests of the class struggle of the proletariat. . . . We say that morality is that which serves the destruction of the old exploiter society and the unification of all workers around the proletariat, which is creating the new society of Communists. . . . We do not believe in an eternal morality."

From this fundamental declaration, it naturally follows that a person is permitted everything, that anything is moral if it serves the interests of the working class and the good of the cause. It is moral to murder, to steal, to lie . . . just so long as one doesn't do this for oneself. Lenin, for example, in "Communism's Childhood Disease ('Leftism')" taught Western Communists how to infiltrate trade unions: one must, "if need be, resort to any subterfuge, ruse, or illegal means, dissemble and conceal the truth."

It's strange after all this to hear Lenin on his deathbed saying that Stalin had "no common honesty, no simple human honesty" (Trotsky, *Portraits*). That's some admission!

The psychology of the Communist bears comparison to that of the terrorist Socialist Revolutionary who, despite the blood on his hands, was faithful to the revolutionary ethical norms drawn up by the nineteenth-century Populists.

In 1912, a curious novel appeared by Viktor Ropshin — *That Which Wasn't*, about terror and the psychology of the terrorist Socialist Revolutionary, and based on personal experience. Ropshin was the pen name of the famous revolutionary Boris Savinkov. Ropshin-Savinkov's hero asks himself the following: How can one reconcile murder and other sins necessary to the revolution with notions of morality? Because the revolutionary who has no moral sense is just a common murderer.

> When I joined the Party, I thought I had it all figured out. . . . Almost everyone thinks that. Violence? In the name of the people, even violence is permitted. Lies? In the name of the revolution, lies are permitted. Fraud? In the name of the Party, fraud is permitted. Now I see it's not that simple. . . . Can the end justify all means? Can everything really be permitted?

No. In the opinion of the author and the hero of this narrative, there is no end, no matter how lofty, that justifies all means. Be it the interests of the people, the Party, or the revolution, these cannot legitimize murder and violence:

> Yes, you have to lie, cheat, kill, but you don't have to say that this is permitted, justified, that this is fine. You don't have to think that by lying you are sacrificing yourself, that by killing you are saving your soul. No, you have to have the courage to say: this is evil, cruel, terrible, but it is unavoidable . . . yes, unavoidable. . . . Terror is not only sacrifice, but also lies, blood, and shame.

In short, the old-style Russian revolutionary thought that bloodshed was a necessary but extreme measure, a sin (in the old, Christian sense). He did not preach terror, did not turn it into indiscriminate killing; he maintained a moral face. Such a concept is utterly alien and incomprehensible to new men of the Communist type.

But let's return to Savinkov's hero. The consciousness of the terrible moral sin on his soul does not keep him from doing his "work," as he refers to terror: He could not abandon it, his "work," not because it would have been unworthy to desert the battlefield, not because his comrades were dying, not because he had "fallen in love" with terror. He couldn't abandon it because he thought that only death crowns the bloodstained cause, because he was awaiting his own death as reward and deliverance.

To put it another way, the old-style revolutionary counterbalanced his sin with his death. The new-style revolutionary also stands ready to sacrifice, but this is neither connected with the notion of sin, nor intended to serve as atonement. Because both the sin and one's sacrifice are justified in advance, the only difference being what the Party and the revolution command: to kill or to die. Before his execution, Savinkov's hero arrives at a morally more refined understanding of sin. He realizes that even "death is not an atonement, that even one's own blood cannot justify murder, that . . . one must not look for justifications, since woe be to the one who killed. . . . And he also saw — and this was the most precious to him — that to kill is harder than to die, and he understood with joy that death was longed for and not frightening."

Another idea that occurs to him is of interest to us from a historical standpoint. His "work" puts him in contact with yard-keepers and draymen whose total lack of morality astounds him, and he thinks: "Here we are struggling, giving our lives . . . And here they . . . will defeat us in the end. . . . Defeat us with their superb stupidity, their full bellies, their silly smugness, their pleated boots and their rigid assurance."

In the end, this is indeed what happened. The draymen defeated the revolutionary intellectuals. The Leninist Bolsheviks are hardly draymen, but they already have that rigid assurance about themselves and the absolute legitimacy of their cause. Unlike Savinkov's hero, they are not torn between morality and the sin of violence. Which is partly why, incidentally, the none-too-numerous Bolsheviks could outweigh the Socialist Revolutionaries, who were supported after the revolution by most of the peasantry. The Socialist Revolutionaries would be destroyed as enemies of the revolution, and Savinkov senses this. His hero is rebuffed by a firm opponent: "You know, your point of view is bad. Yes, bad. It's the point of view of the ones who are being beaten, of the romantics, I'd say."

This is true, even if some of the Bolsheviks could also be romantics. Only not moral romantics like the old revolutionaries who, for all their terrorism, held the old-fashioned (and in this sense romantic) view that to kill was not good: they did not consider that the end justified all means. Lenin did. One reason he won.

Socialist Revolutionary leader Viktor Chernov discussed Ropshin-Savinkov's novel in the journal *Zavety*. His article, entitled "Ethics and Politics," posed the same question as the novel: How can moral norms be reconciled with the acts of a revolutionary obliged to flout these norms as soon as he enters the fray? The revolutionary cannot possess, says Chernov, the moral maximalism of a Lev Tolstoy, with his theory of nonresistance to evil (or, we may add, the religious maximalism that makes murder impossible). He must preserve the ethical minimum, since it confines the violence and guarantees that the real revolutionary will not turn into a murderer or despot.

Chernov tries to establish this moral minimum, this inviolable code of ethics, which the Bolsheviks would later violate: "Revolutionary despotism is on the same level as counterrevolutionary despotism. Revolutionary ethics rejects the instinct for revenge both of those who oppress the people and of those fighting for their liberation. It repudiates the persecution of ideas, be they retrograde or progressive."

Lenin called this kind of reasoning rotten bourgeois liberalism, more dangerous than the fiercest enemy. This was logical: to win, one had to reject universal ethics, to give moral norms a Party and class character.

Not that the new man was immoral. In some ways he was morally superior to ordinary people: he lived not for himself but for the general good, for all people or, more accurately, for "his own." But his morality was warped by the conviction that to murder his enemy was not evil but good, and that evil, on the contrary, was in mercy or compassion for his enemy.

In 1918 the very mediocre and now forgotten proletarian poet Vasily Knyazev produced his "Red Gospel," a versified code of Communist morals called on to replace the Christian Gospel and reprinted several times that year. Knyazev, calling himself a Second Christ, stated fundamental laws of ethics. Yet he did not seek his own aggrandizement as the newfound Messiah. He spoke in the name of the victorious revolution:

*People, heed the words of the prophet:*
*Get out of treachery's way!*
*In battle, nothing is more fatal*
*Than the vice of mercy!*

Later, in the thirties, Gorky's famous formula — "If the enemy won't give in, we'll destroy him" — was taken up in the Soviet press and judicial practice alike. But Gorky's slogan, at least, was pure form. Knyazev's appeal, on the other hand, is absolutely precise and terrifying: kill even those who ask for mercy. Finish off the wounded with your bayonets, shoot any prisoners:

*Take no prisoners —*
*A bullet in the head will do*
*For restorers of the throne!*

Or:

*Blessed is he who knows no mercy*
*In the fight against his enemy!*

This was the essence of communism's moral code: mercy equals treason. Or as Lenin wrote: "Sentimentality is no less a crime than speculation in time of war."

These "Red Commandments" sparked the moral indignation of the Russian intelligentsia and its best representative, Vladimir Korolenko. Faithful to the Populist revolutionary tradition, veteran of tsarist prisons and exile, Korolenko defended all the aggrieved regardless of their political ties. Out of ethical considerations, this intellectual, this righteous man, rose up against the October Revolution and against the new Communist morality. Given Korolenko's enormous authority, not only as a great writer but also as the conscience of the Russian intelligentsia, the Soviet power could not allow itself to destroy him. Instead, Anatoly Lunacharsky, the government's most liberal and cultivated member, began debating with Korolenko in an exchange of letters which, of course, led nowhere but did lay out the positions: Korolenko's universal morality versus Lunacharsky's Communist one. Without ethics, Korolenko argued, there can be no revolution.

When Korolenko died in 1921, Lunacharsky wrote a eulogy,

entitled "A Righteous Man," which reopened the debate as to whether one could spill blood endlessly and how this squared with morality: "Righteous men are appalled by the blood on our hands. Righteous men are in despair over our cruelty. . . . The righteous man will never understand that love 'demands expiatory victims,' that it is not only a question of self-sacrifice (this he understands), but also of the sacrifice of others."

If a bit grandiloquent, Lunacharsky makes it clear that the revolution's right, its moral philosophy, is unlimited violence. Another of his remarks sheds important light on Communist morality and the psychology of the new man: "Righteousness and the most unsullied appearance undoubtedly include something that is deeply unacceptable for revolutionary epochs."

I don't know if Lunacharsky suspected what he was saying here: that the new man should be stained with blood, the blood of others, as the supreme symbol of his righteousness. This reduces the moral code of the righteous revolutionary to that of an executioner and an informer. And the sad thing is not that countless executioners and informers appeared from who knows where, the antithesis of the new man with his heroism and ascetic renunciation of self. The sad thing is that this new man, in order to be new, turned executioner and informer. Bloodstained hands were no longer the exception but the rule — a historical, even psychological necessity.

## THE EXECUTIONER AS MORAL MODEL

The new ethics found their real ideal — or moral model — in the person of Feliks Dzerzhinsky, president of the Cheka. The Chekists' job was to fight the internal counterrevolution. In other words, they did the dirtiest, vilest work involving surveillance, searches, confiscation, arrests, interrogations, executions, the organization of networks of spies and informers, of prisons and camps. The Cheka was the dictatorship's most frightening instrument, sowing terror throughout Russia. But Dzerzhinsky, the new government's premier executioner, fairly shone in all his blood-red, merciless glory. In the system of new ethical values, this chief hangman and jailer became the preeminent moral model. This may seem like a perversion, a sort of pathology of the new society. But if one considers communism's moral code and the psychology of the new man, there's nothing pathological or unnatural about it. For the supreme morality consists in giving oneself entirely to the service of the idea and of society, overstepping all conceivable bounds of personal and universal morality in the name of duty. Thus Dzerzhinsky, in assuming the function of first executioner, became a holy martyr, the incarnation of virtue. His bloody role, far from diminishing his prestige, only increased it.

The revolutionary — according to Russian tradition — is someone who has known tsarist prisons and torture. He is the revolution's noble man. He has achieved this perfection through his experience and hates nothing more than torture and prisons, against which he lives and fights. Now he is faced with a new feat: that of becoming the actual hangman and jailer. This was — it seemed then — a painful necessity of the moment, the vital one. Everyone killed, but the chief murderer, manager of the prisons and the torture, had to be a man with a crystal-clear soul. In staining it with blood, he became in the eyes of his worshippers a truly great martyr who had sacrificed himself on the altar of revolutionary cosmogony, for the creation of a new world and a new man.

Hence the surprising similarity between Dzerzhinsky and Christ: both gave themselves to redeem man's sins. Except that Christ redeemed man's sins with his death and resurrection, whereas the new saint, Dzerzhinsky, takes sins upon himself — mass murder and torture — which he commits in the name of the creation of a Heavenly Kingdom on earth. So that in Soviet iconography the Crucified Lord is replaced by a Holy Executioner.

Dzerzhinsky's life and psychology prepared him for this role as the revolution's moral model. As far as one can objectively judge this enigmatic man, he had many merits. Not a cruel person, he had a good and noble heart; his temperament classed him as a religious type. Of Polish origin, he was a fervent Catholic until the age of sixteen, and even planned to be a priest or monk. Once his older brother Cazimir, who was not a believer, asked him how he imagined God. "God is in my heart!" the young Dzerzhinsky said. "Yes, in my heart! And if I were ever to come to the conclusion like you that there is no God, I would shoot myself. I couldn't live without God."

Some people claimed that as president of the Cheka, Dzerzhinsky remained a Catholic in his soul, secretly praying to the Holy Virgin Mary between tortures and late-night interrogations. This is probably legend, but it matches, as sometimes happens, a certain psychological reality: Dzerzhinsky had in effect transferred his youthful religiousness to the revolution, had transferred his ardent faith in God to communism.

He also loved nature, flowers. He had a poetic temperament. And . . . he adored children. In a letter to his sister in 1902, when he was twenty-five and already a confirmed Social Democrat, Dzerzhinsky wrote: "I don't know why it is that I love children more than anyone else . . . I could never love a woman as much as I love them, and I don't think I could love my own children more than other people's . . . Very often it seems to me that even a mother cannot love them as passionately as I do."

This seems incredible: someone who loves children more than anything else and more than anyone else, even a mother, becomes an executioner. But revolutionary ethics are based on such reversals. The purest and most loving person should be the first to kill. He sees this as his sacrifice for children. And children are our future, communism. Dzerzhinsky's love for children was lifelong. The executions did not keep him from setting up orphanages and colonies for homeless children. After the civil war, aside from his work as chief Chekist — as people's commissar of internal affairs — he also occupied important economic posts. But according to his wife, his dream — dashed by an early death — was to one day trade in all his police and economic posts and become people's commissar of education, devoted solely to children and the youth. Isn't that a wonderful prospect — in the spirit of communist morality — the chief executioner converted into chief educator?! Into creator of the new man.

Dzerzhinsky possessed one more quality that equipped him to be the revolution's moral yardstick: exceptional energy and lifelong devotion to the struggle. He spent the two decades that preceded the revolution working underground between periodic arrests and escapes. His time in exile and prison — often in solitary confinement or at hard labor — totaled eleven years. And if he loved children most of all, the thing he hated most of all was prison. He was able to study the prisons better than many Bolsheviks and knew them from the inside. The revolutionary struggle for him was primarily the destruction of prison, in the literal sense as well as in the larger, social sense.

Out of hatred for prison, Dzerzhinsky became the first jailer after the revolution and the founder of a prison system of a kind that history, most likely, had never known. This was not a betrayal of his ideal — the ideal of freedom — but a concrete struggle for that ideal. As head of the Cheka, he wore the halo of a prison martyr and the reputation of a righteous man. You could never suspect this man of sadism, or of self-interest, or even of a special predilection for prison and police work. He did bloody work not out of love for the art but out of hard political necessity, this being the mission entrusted to him by the Party. And he showed no mercy, only fantastic energy and will. Dzerzhinsky is still glorified as the "knight of the revolution," a fitting image, since it assumes an ardent faith, a purity and nobility of soul, combined with an iron strength and will to act. Even outwardly, Dzerzhinsky had something of the knight ascetic: a pointed beard, gaunt face, and fine features. He preferred the austere life of a soldier-monk. Dzerzhinsky's deputy, Yakov Peters, once described his office in Lubyanka, the heart of the Cheka:

> It is in this building, in the plainest, smallest room . . . that Comrade Dzerzhinsky lived during the first years of the revolution. In this room he worked, slept, received guests. A simple desk, an old screen hiding a narrow iron bed: such was the setting of Comrade Dzerzhinsky's personal life. He never went home to his family except on holidays. He worked round the clock, often conducting the interrogations himself. Wrung out with exhaustion, wearing high hunting boots and an old, threadbare tunic, he took his meals at the same table as all the other Chekists.

An ascetic environment — whether genuine or for show — was generally typical of the first revolutionaries. It was meant to point up the fact that the person who had given himself to the revolutionary cause possessed nothing or almost nothing of his own. In 1918 Dzerzhinsky, already president of the Cheka, wrote his wife that his entire life had taken place "in the heat of battle. The life of the soldier who knows no rest because he must save the burning house. No time to think of one's own or of oneself. Work and the hellish fight. But in this fight, my heart has remained alive, the same as it was before. All my time is just one, endless struggle to remain at my station until the end."

Dzerzhinsky did remain at his station until the end, working until the last minute. He died suddenly and relatively young, in 1926 at the age of forty-eight, of a heart attack. His comrades attached symbolic importance to his death, saying that his whole life had been a revolutionary flame, that he burned himself out, having given his heart to the revolution.

During his lifetime, Dzerzhinsky commanded enormous authority within the Party. He was virtually the only one who had some influence over Lenin. His professional abilities aside, Dzerzhinsky obviously appealed to Lenin for the fact that he put the Leninist theory of violence into pervasive, unflinching practice, at the same time combining this cold-blooded cruelty with an unimpeachable morality. Thus was born in the history of Soviet society the cult of the holy executioner Dzerzhinsky. A very important cult for the government in general and for the development of the Cheka's punitive apparatus in particular, but also from the moral and educational standpoint, since Dzerzhinsky became the example of the new man worthy of all emulation. This was impossible to do with Lenin, too great and too unique in the system of Communist values; not everyone can be such a genius, a leader and politician of that caliber. But there can and must be many "knights of the revolution"; so Dzerzhinsky is to be emulated. In his poem "Fine!" (1927) Mayakovsky raises Dzerzhinsky's ghost or phantom, which one night on Red Square crosses his path

> *in a crumpled trenchcoat,*
>> *with a pointed beard,*
> *another man,*
>> *steely*
>>> *and sinewy.*[2]

2. Translation by Dorian Rottenberg in *Mayakovsky,* vol. 2 (Moscow: Raduga Publishers, 1986), p. 269.

This is the "Feliks of Steel" whose image should serve Soviet youth henceforth as moral ideal and guide.

> *To a young lad*
> > *plunged*
> > > *into meditation,*
> *after whom*
> > *to model his life,*
> > > *just commencing,*
> *I would say,*
> > *without hesitation:*
> *model it*
> > *on Comrade Dzerzhinsky.*[3]

An unsettling recommendation, if one thinks about it, that one should emulate an executioner, of all people. That Soviet youth should sacrifice their pure souls to become, if need be, a Chekist, an informer, a spy, an executioner. This transgression of oneself, of one's own conscience, is an act of the highest revolutionary morality. Mayakovsky was a deeply moral person, with a pure and tender soul, but as a real revolutionary, he understood that the road to a radiant future was paved with blood and filth. That to rid the world of violence forever, one must commit the supreme violence — against oneself and against others. That to demolish prisons everywhere, one must first build a new and vast prison in which to amend humanity. And for all of this, one needed many Dzerzhinskys . . .

Mayakovsky was not alone in this notion of ethics. In 1929, Eduard Bagritsky devoted a poem to Dzerzhinsky: "TVS." It tells of a tubercular poet (Bagritsky himself suffered from bad asthma) who is so exhausted that the entire world disgusts him; he must work but hasn't the strength. He is feverish, delirious. Then Dzerzhinsky's ghost appears at his bedside:

> *Triangular face,*
> *Triangular beard . . .*

---

3. Translation by Rottenberg in *op. cit.*, pp. 269–270.

Sitting down beside the sick man, he begins to teach him: one must overcome all personal afflictions and rise to the demands of the century. This reference — to the voice of the century — is characteristic. The new men were compelled to educate themselves and the masses not by subjective impulses but by the laws of history. It is not we who are cruel; it is the century, the times, and the revolution that demand cruelty, hard as this may be. Dzerzhinsky speaks to Bagritsky in the voice of the century:

> *The century lies in wait by the roadway,*
> *Staring fixedly like a sentinel.*
> *Don't be afraid, go stand beside him.*
> *Your solitude is no different.*
> *You look around: enemies lurk;*
> *You reach out: no friends come;*
> *But if he says: "Lie," you will lie,*
> *But if he says: "Kill," you will kill.*

Soviet literature of the twenties and thirties reveals an odd and unusual friendship between writers and Chekists. Mayakovsky, Bagritsky, Svetlov, Lugovskoi, Babel, and Gorky all associated with Chekists as friends and as connoisseurs of literature. Many writers depicted the Chekist as a new breed. As if they were drawn to this type of person, to this profession, invested with supreme and mysterious powers. As if they felt a certain spiritual affinity for this kindred member of the Soviet elite. The trusted writer and the responsible Chekist: both work with human material, with the complexities of psychology. Both must have subtlety and insight, an ability to read into hearts. Both must reform humanity: one with words, the other with deeds. If writers are the engineers of the human soul, Chekists are the surgeons of the human soul. And there is nothing morally reprehensible to a Soviet writer, or any other citizen, about befriending a Chekist. For he is the most moral of us all, beyond reproach, a fearless knight standing guard over the conquests of the revolution. As Dzerzhinsky taught his collaborators, a Chekist must possess three things: an ardent heart (or a faith making one ready for anything), a cool head (exactitude), and clean hands (no interest in personal gain). That these clean hands were stained with blood didn't trouble anyone, since a Chekist never broke the moral commandments except in the interests of the common cause, and this elevated him morally in the eyes of society since his mission was the hardest. Condemning people to die and executing them isn't pleasant, after all; it demands enormous will, self-possession, and violence to oneself. As Bagritsky says of Dzerzhinsky:

> *O Mother revolution! How bitter*
> *The nakedness of the three-edged blade . . .*

In 1927, Mikhail Svetlov wrote one of his best poems, "The Carouse," about the romantic supper of an elite coterie of Red Army commanders and Chekists. The poet looks on as they drink to 1917, to the civil war, to the battles and crusades to come. They are relaxed and luxuriating in the animated heart-to-hearts that typify this sort of male reunion. But surprisingly, this affectionate enthusiasm is mainly reserved for the cruelty and violence wrought by these Red commanders, if mixed with a mournful note: it is a sad historical necessity to have to kill and to torture. The poet addresses one of the revelers:

> *Tell me, please,*
> *My dear,*
> *My shy friend,*
> *Tell me about*
> *How Poltava blazed,*
> *How Dzhankoy shook,*
> *How Saratov crossed itself*
> *With the sign*
> *Of the last cross . . .*

This shy comrade was evidently the undoing of a number of Russian cities. Then Svetlov asks another drinking companion to recount

> *How we eked along without bread,*
> *How we suffered without water,*
> *Without arms,*
> *A regiment of cadets.*

But the poet's first and most rhapsodical toast goes to the president of the Cheka:

> *Drink, Comrade Orlov,*
> *President of the Cheka!*
> *The skies may glower,*
> *Stifling their alarm,*
> *Stars smashed to bits*
> *By the blow of a bayonet!*
> *This night as merciless*
> *As your signature.*
> *Drink, Comrade Orlov,*
> *Drink to the new crusade!*
> *Leap ahead, the horses*
> *Of despairing days!*
> > *The sentence is set,*
> > *The mandolin sings,*
> > *And the trumpet-executioner,*
> > *Is hunching over her . . .*

The fraternization of poets with executioners, the rhyming of their toil, the cult of violence, the negation of moral precepts in the name of a greater, Communist morality: all of this ended badly for the poets, for the people, and for many of the executioners too. Under history's pen, the new man acquired a bestial image, largely the result of bolshevism's rejection of ethics.

In 1936, not long before his tragic end as a victim of the purges, Bukharin was in Paris and admitted privately to the gravest doubts about the road taken by Soviet history and the Party. Sensing his imminent death, Bukharin now felt a kind of nostalgia for the forgotten, universal morality. This was the man who, a decade earlier, had called for the remaking of people's psychology in the Communist mold, who had cited the "systematic preparation of new men" as the main task before Soviet society. By the mid-thirties this was a fait accompli and then, suddenly, Bukharin remembered about morality. His interlocutor in Paris, Boris Nikolaevsky, was very surprised: "Nikolai Ivanovich, it seems you have come to believe in the Ten Commandments?" Bukharin replied: "They're not that bad, the Ten Commandments." An avowal, in essence, of the fallibility of the entire system of Soviet education, of the entire moral code of communism. But by then it was late to be remembering the biblical commandments: the only ones who did were the ones faced with death. Meanwhile, the new man was in place. And he was parroting another commandment:

> *But if he says: "Lie," you will lie,*
> *But if he says: "Kill," you will kill.*

With time, this significant "he" telling one to lie and to kill became much more simplified. It was no longer the twentieth century, the epoch, or historical necessity that was giving the orders: it was Comrade Stalin himself. Simpler still: "he" was the top boss who knew better than anyone what, at a given moment, was required of the Soviet man. Consequently, the moral imperative of the revolution, the bargain with one's conscience, became business as usual. And the new man became a pedestrian servant, an obsequious slave, a mechanical executor.

## THE ROLE AND PLACE OF THE INTELLIGENTSIA

If one looks closely at the actual processes involved in forming the new man, then it becomes apparent that the intelligentsia was consistently presented as one of the most serious opponents, if not the most dangerous, morally and psychologically. This may seem strange since the intelligentsia had no material clout. Deprived of the right to vote and freedom of speech, it was going through its own internal crisis, being divided as to which way to go. Yet it was perceived as the principal opponent of the "victorious class" and the new man; this was like some original sin. Numerous Soviet novels of the twenties and early thirties allude to this theme of "the intelligentsia and the revolution": Konstantin Fedin's *Cities and Years,* Yury Olesha's *Envy,* Maksim Gorky's *The Life of Klim Samgin,* and so on. Their authors are themselves mostly intellectuals. But intellectuals who have moved over to the camp of the victorious class, from where they criticize and denounce the intelligentsia. One gets the impression that now it is the number-one enemy, and not the bourgeoisie, swept away, liquidated by the revolution. That it suffers from an inferiority complex that demands to be overcome. A huge complex: individualism, humanism, flabbiness, spinelessness, a tendency to compromise, halfheartedness, no Party spirit, introspection, freedom of thought, skepticism, and so forth. And all these sins add up to one thing: treason. But this charge doesn't apply to some reactionary or conservative segments of the intelligentsia, attached to the old system or to the White movement. This applies to the liberal, even prorevolutionary intelligentsia. The new man dealt his heaviest blow there on the theory that the intellectual was an opportunist and more dangerous than any outright enemy since, with his halfheartedness and other defects, he had betrayed the working-class cause. The intellectual hero of Fedin's *Cities and Years* (1924) sympathizes with the revolution, but because of his spinelessness and personal egoism he takes pity on an enemy and helps him to escape, thus earning himself a death sentence for treason. This was a typical scenario for early Soviet literature, which made short work of the intellectual by contrasting him to the staunch proletarian, the revolutionary Leninist, the Bolshevik, the Chekist, or even to the plain muzhik, who may have been crude, ignorant, and given to anarchist pranks, drunkenness, and debauchery, but was a faithful soldier of the revolution and therefore purer and more upright than the intellectual slush.

It's not difficult to guess that all this reviling of the intelligentsia concealed an educational and even self-educational task. The new man must free himself from universal morality (referred to contemptuously as "abstract humanism"), from doubts about the legitimacy of the Party line, from efforts to think, to reason, to criticize, to defend his individual freedom and independence. For the new society, the threat lay in the intellectual, moral, and spiritual needs that exist in every human soul. These were the basis for the image of the unstable intellectual who became the pariah of Soviet literature. In fact, literature was attacking man in general and itself in particular, or the intellectual remains of its own creativity. If the moral model became Dzerzhinsky, then reluctance to follow his example became a betrayal of the interests of the revolution; and literature frightened not only readers but itself with this bugaboo. If you show pity, you are a traitor. If you stand apart from the class struggle, you are a traitor. If you defend not belonging to the Party or personal independence, you are a traitor.

But before the new society, the Russian intelligentsia felt itself guilty of inconsistency. Until the revolution, the intelligentsia had been highly democratic in the main, prorevolutionary, pitying and loving the people, believing in a beautiful if somewhat misty socialism, dreaming of the advent of a new man — from who knew where — who would purify all of society. But when this man arrived and started shooting, the intelligentsia recoiled in horror, as if he were Frankenstein's monster. And the new society reproached the intelligentsia for this inconsistency, which it interpreted as treason.

When a collection of articles entitled *Landmarks* appeared in 1909, Lenin denounced it as an "encyclopedia of liberal apostasy." This "apostasy" was the work of a small, moderate group of intellectuals who, after the bloody horrors of 1905–1907, decided to revise their traditions and tried to define a third route, between the extremes of the tsarist reaction and those of the revolution. The authors of this modest and unique collection were appealing to the intelligentsia to do calm, creative work; to reject revolutionary obsession and despotism; to search for more positive, constructive solutions than nihilistic denial or conservative safeguarding of the past. At the same time, they recalled the eternal values of religion, of morality, and of the individual. This was enough for Lenin to accuse them of treason: as if the entire liberal intelligentsia should follow blindly behind him to what would become his dictatorship. But such was the logic of bolshevism.

All this repeated itself on an infinitely grander scale in 1917. The Bolsheviks not only betrayed freedom and democracy, prohibited an independent press, and wrought mass terror, they also demanded that the intelligentsia rejoice in all this. The intelligentsia, with its liberal and humanistic nature, could not rejoice, but trembled with fear, silently indignant, laughing, mourning its ideals, and, yes, showing its inconsistency and instability by vacillating between the Reds and the Whites. If this was proof of the intelligentsia's softness, weakness, and indecision, it also reflected profound morality and spiritual firmness. One example is the stance of the poet Maksimilian Voloshin. He lived in the Crimea which, during the civil war, was constantly changing hands. First the Reds, then the Whites would win, and on the heels of every victory came a bloody reprisal. Neither Red nor White himself, Voloshin saw this inter-

necine war as a tragedy of history. Yet another. But his position of
the wise man "above partisan concerns" did not prevent him from
sympathizing or helping, as much as he was able, anyone who was
in danger. Risking his own neck, Voloshin saved Reds from Whites
and Whites from Reds, trying to protect the individual. The
breadth of Voloshin's historical views and his tolerance allowed him
to understand that in this terrible war both the Reds and the
Whites were, each in their own way, both right and wrong. That
most horrible of all was the implacable enmity in both camps
toward anyone who thought differently:

> *Both here and there between the rows*
> *The same voice sounds:*
> *"He who is not with us, is against us!*
> *No one is indifferent! The truth is with us!"*
> > *But I stand alone between them,*
> > *In the roaring flames and smoke,*
> > *And with all my heart*
> > *I pray for one and all.*

But in the new conditions of the victorious revolution, to pray for
one and all was considered hypocrisy and a crime, because this
minimized the social contradictions and wrested from the revolution its main weapon, the thesis about the class struggle. In this
sense, the White officer who shot at Reds was, from the latter's
point of view, preferable to that lousy intellectual conciliator who
wouldn't shoot at anyone, out of his so-called humanism: the White
who fired confirmed the theory of Marxism-Leninism and justified
the violence, while the waffling intellectual threw everything into a
cocked hat and showed the greatest contempt for the proletarian
religion.

It is striking how Russian history repeats itself with this problem
of the intelligentsia in the revolution. Forty years after Voloshin's
poem, Pasternak's *Doctor Zhivago* was published around the world,
revealing him to be the spiritual father and forerunner of the "dissidents." And once again, Pasternak and other intellectuals were
cursed from Soviet rostrums and accused of treason. Pasternak's
"treason" consisted in the fact that his hero had been loathe to shoot
at Whites or Reds during the civil war and, horrified by the cruelty

of both camps, had prayed "for one and all." As if to refute Soviet
literature, which for so long had so doggedly denigrated the intelligentsia, Pasternak depicted the purest intellectual, his sad fate in
the new society, and his feat: the feat of not killing, of refusing on
moral grounds to obey the laws of the class struggle, where people
annihilate each other for ideological or political reasons and require
that everyone do the same. The Soviet press was especially indignant over the famous episode in which the hero, forcibly recruited as
a doctor for the partisans, is obliged to take part in the battle. Not
wanting to kill anyone, this intellectual purposely fires wide of the
mark. I still remember the livid rage of the Soviet writer-officer
Konstantin Simonov: better that Zhivago-Pasternak had been with
the Whites and shooting at Reds than that uncertainty — loyalty to
neither camp — that traitorous uncertainty. That's the sad thing:
for the Soviet government and society, the enemy became the very
fact of being humane, of not participating in the fight.

This "class" approach aside, men of the new breed felt an acute
psychological revulsion for the intelligentsia with its complex, am-
bivalent, and contradictory nature, characteristics that generally
corresponded to its situation as the former occupier of the vast
mental terrain between the simple people and the tsarist bureaucracy, between East and West, between Russia and Europe. The
intellectual admitted the multiplicity of truths, subjected everything — himself included — to doubt and analysis, and merited his
reputation as the "critical spirit." This psychological type was out
of place in the world of socialism, built on unambiguous, black-
and-white foundations. What complexity could there be if there
was only one truth, objective and absolute in its scientific infallibility?

Intellectual narrowness and linearity guaranteed the victory of
bolshevism. Not surprisingly, the new literary dynasty of Socialist
Realism was partly founded by Gorky who, at the beginning of the
century, had launched a new type of hero, the proletarian revolutionary, glowingly described in his 1901 play *The Petits Bourgeois*:
"Only these men, straight and hard as swords, will succeed." From
this time on, Gorky chastised the intelligentsia for being too self-
involved, confused, and incomprehensible.

True, later, during the revolution and the civil war, during the terror and famine, Gorky thought better of his criticisms and defended the intelligentsia which, in his horrified state, he declared to be the best thing about Russia. But this was only a temporary relapse, or "mistake," as Soviet critics still say, and Gorky soon made amends. In the mid-twenties, having embraced the revolution and socialism in Russia, he rejoined and even led the smear campaign against the intelligentsia. His opus, *The Life of Klim Samgin* (1927–1936), is a collective portrait of the prerevolutionary intellectual who is so caught up in the swirl of competing political and ideological currents that he turns into a gray, faceless blur. This is the personification of the footloose intelligentsia, deceiving itself and others as it careens between liberal and reactionary views. Klim Samgin counts as a potential traitor and main enemy of the revolution, even if he does nothing, even if he does not fight, only philosophizes and argues every point. This, precisely, is the essence of his treason.

The novel was never finished. When Gorky died in 1936, the power let it be known that he had been killed by enemies of the people: a routine provocation, more grist for the trials of 1937 and 1938. But Gorky was involuntarily involved in this provocation, having spent the last decade indicting intellectuals on charges of treason and sabotage. It was as if these enemies, these Klim Samgins, had finally taken their revenge. Konstantin Simonov responded to Gorky's death and also to the trials with these verses written in the spirit of the times:

> *And with a ruthless death sentence*
> *We finished writing the saga of Klim Samgin.*

This also finished the saga of the intelligentsia.

The Soviet power, especially at the outset, had not been able to manage without the old intelligentsia, notably in the domain of exact sciences and technology, so necessary to an industrialized nation. But in enlisting intellectuals to do useful work, the State did everything to limit their line of inquiry, forcing them to stick to their specialty and swallow Marxism-Leninism as a world outlook. In short, the State wanted to recast the intellectual in the mold of the new man. Bukharin spoke very frankly about this in 1925 at a debate in Moscow devoted to the fate of the Russian intelligentsia. The eminent philologist P. Sakulin took the liberty of saying that the new power "had infringed on the freedom of scientific investigation" and that this could harm the development of Russian science. Bukharin, himself the most intellectual leader, countered: "When people advocate creative freedom, we cannot but ask ourselves about the freedom to promote monarchism [in 1925, the scientific intelligentsia was not promoting monarchism, this was just a standard demagogic procedure, which Stalin would later use on Bukharin — A.S.] or vitalism in biology, or giving Kantian idealists free rein with their substance in philosophy. Given this kind of freedom, our universities would produce cultural workers who could do just as well in Prague as in Moscow. But we want workers who do well only in Moscow. . . . It is vital that our intellectual cadres be ideologically trained in a specific way. Yes, we will stamp our intellectuals, we will manufacture them just like in a factory."

Under this regime, the intellectual was no longer an intellectual, but a mechanical Soviet yes-man hooked up to some narrow specialty or other. The narrower, the better. The simpler, the better. Bukharin wasn't bothered by the prospect of Russian science lagging behind the world level. The stamp was the important thing.

And intellectuals, for the most part, succumbed to this stamp in fairly short order, since all the interesting and useful work, all the access to science, the arts, the press, and education was in the hands of the State. One had no choice but to pose as a new, stamped man. Though playing this part wasn't easy. First one had to renounce one's self, one's past, one's milieu, one's intellectuality. This was the beginning of the intellectuals' pilgrimage and repentence before the victorious class. This was (and remains) the essence of the reeducation, or elimination of the "ancient person" in oneself for the sake of a new career. This process cuts through all of Soviet history, from October to the present.

This said, it would be a mistake to think that the reeducation was a total sham, tolerated only under duress. Many intellectuals were sincerely drawn to the revolution and strove willingly, even gladly, to conform. Communism's high ideals aside, the intellectuals were also motivated by their perennial guilt over the fact that the people had labored, living in poverty and ignorance, while they philosophized, reveling in the blessings of enlightenment and civilization. They felt they owed a debt to the people for the sin of their own social and cultural superiority. The popular nineteenth-century term "repentant noblemen" — which conveyed this psychology — referred to the better part of cultivated Russian society.

The result was various tendencies: "going to the people," revolutionary radicalism, a Tolstoyan "return to the simple life," the intelligentsia's compassion for the "poor folk." But even so, many "repentant noblemen," not finding suitable employ, consumed themselves with remorse and agonizing self-analysis. Thus was born the "superfluous man," central to so many Russian novels.

For some intellectuals of this "superfluous" type, the revolution was an answer to their prayers: together with socialism, it seduced them with the idea of doing something useful.

One highly interesting document on this score is by Marietta Shaginyan, decadent poetess turned prominent Soviet writer, having reforged herself in accordance with Party prescriptions. Written in 1922, it has a strange title: *How I Was a Weaving Instructor (A True Story)*. During the revolution, Shaginyan found herself an unexpected occupation that filled her with joy. Joy that she — an intellectual and a bourgeois poetess — had finally found real work. She didn't care that it wasn't her expertise, she saw it as a service to the people:

> The October absolutism was for us . . . the only really real thing on earth, the first and the last, perhaps, which made life worth living. That which the best people had thought endlessly about, dreamed about, prayed for — expiation, the hour of sacrifice, the hour of our redemption before life's martyrs — was finally upon us. One had to understand this precisely as an expiation, and convert everything that followed into the joy of a duty fulfilled.

Shaginyan's revamped psychology, her moral transformation, suggests three causes:

First, Shaginyan longed, like the "superfluous man," to be useful and, like the intellectual, was extremely surprised when she turned out to be capable of doing something real.

Second, not just the work itself, but the sense of connection with the greater, historic cause of the revolution gave Shaginyan joy. A joy that she experienced as one of self-sacrifice, since she, a poet, had abandoned her own work for something unknown but replete with a greater significance.

Third, her interlude as a weaving instructor was brief. Had she been left at this work for the rest of her days, I suspect her romantic enthusiasm would have flagged: millions work for the common cause without experiencing the least bit of joy. The fact that Shaginyan missed writing and went back to it allowed her to romanticize this odd chapter in her life.

In the conditions of the new society, many people found themselves work. And if the intelligentsia virtually disappeared, it was not as a scientific class but as the gamut of thinking people in Russia. Accorded the joy of doing, people were deprived of the right — indispensable to the intellectual — to think and speak freely.

## THE MAN OF THE MASSES

However bitter the battle with the intelligentsia in the twenties, it was not the heart of the question about the new man, which was primarily a social debate. A debate as to whether the new system would be able to manufacture a new psychology; the fate of the State and world history depended on the answer. The intellectual was not the point here, or even the Communist, who was already set as the ideal model of the new breed. But Communists were a minority and needed reinforcements, bases, support systems . . . among the masses. Thus, all the attention, education, and energy, as well as hopes and dreams, were invested in the man of the masses.

Soviet, socialist society arose and conquered as the materialization of the Marxist teaching about classes and the class struggle. The new man was perceived as the living manifestation of the proletariat's and to some extent the peasantry's special class nature. It was from this social base that he was supposed to emerge, not just here and there, but in huge numbers, en masse.

Consequently, social origin became the critical factor in determining people's lives and fates. A proletarian was by definition a good person, worthy of trust and attention. At the beginning of the revolution, proletarian origins could save a criminal from prison or even death.

This is somewhat reminiscent of the feudal-aristocratic approach wherein pure blood or noble origins guaranteed a privileged place in society. After the revolution, this role of the elite went to the working class and the poor peasantry. The only difference being that whereas the nobility had been a tiny minority, this new elite was the majority of the population. The State obviously did not have the means to provide this majority with real privileges, and more often than not the worker remained a worker; but he could always, like the nobleman flaunting his title, point to his proletarian affiliation.

The idea of the proletariat's "class purity" also echoed Rousseau's notion of the "natural man," innocent by nature, perverted by civilization. After the revolution, that "natural man" became the proletariat, whose class nature was innocent and whose failings were the fault of the bourgeoisie. Therefore, to create the new man, one could and must start with the proletarian psychology; it was the tabula rasa, a beautiful innocence of soul on which the new calligraphy of communism, answering the proletarian nature, could be effortlessly inscribed.

At the beginning of the revolution, some proletarian ideologists jealously guarded their class primacy; certain poets and writers continued to work at factory jobs though they could easily have earned a living from their writing and though this situation hurt their professionalism. They needed to be on the assembly line in order to feel, socially and morally, like the real proletarians of whom would be born a pure, unalloyed culture.

This idea of a new culture born of the machine tool or the wooden plow was soon exploded, since these poets who showed such prodigious "proletarian enthusiasm" remained literarily as ignorant as they were before. Nevertheless, worker and peasant origins are still prized in Soviet society. Many leaders made a point of advertising their working-class genealogy, guarantee of their ideological and political purity, of their devotion to the cause.

This not only had an abstract meaning but also assumed concrete forms of a highly rigid and restrictive nature. Take that specifically Soviet phenomenon the questionnaire, one or many of which must be filled out every time one applies for a job, enters an institute, goes abroad, and so on.

Originally, the questionnaire was intended to cull people according to class, the crucial question being the one about social origin. For most of those with bad origins (noblemen, former bureaucrats, merchants, clerics), the doors to the new society slammed automatically shut. They could not find jobs or enter universities; they were deprived of ration cards and of the right to vote. During the twenties and thirties they were called *lishentsy* (deprivees). Sometimes, social origin alone was enough to invite a person's arrest or death.

The questionnaire sifted people, dividing them into categories depending on their past affiliation to one class or another. The questionnaire decided whom to discard or destroy, whom to allow to linger on, whom to invite to join in the life of the new society, whom to promote in his work or studies.

Representatives of the toiling masses, people with working-class origins, were a kind of "pure race" in which the State placed all its hopes. As the State's support system, this category enjoyed the greatest opportunities as well as the benevolent attentions of the Party in its efforts to fashion the new man. That man must be — initially — socially pure, of impeccable origins. Later he must be educated in the Communist spirit and given some training. Thus, State-sponsored instruction for the masses mushroomed after the revolution, with three principal aims in mind: first, to teach workers to read and write, to eradicate illiteracy nationwide; second, to inculcate Marxism-Leninism in the masses as the only correct theory, as a guide for action; third, to promote the applied sciences and technology, to turn workers and peasants into mechanics and engineers, into the new cadres needed to replace the old scientific intelligentsia.

The masses responded gratefully to this sudden access to knowledge: they all started studying. The philosopher and historian Georgy Fedotov described this period in the twenties this way: "A hunger for knowledge has gripped the masses, especially the younger generations." But, he adds bitterly:

Russia is teeming with half-baked intellectuals and semi-learned types, but one rarely meets a "cultivated" person in the old sense of the word. The new school doesn't produce them. . . . What is typical of the revolution is this extension of culture to include the masses "fresh from the machine tool and the wooden plow." This rash democratization conceals a danger: an abrupt drop in the level, causing the spiritual waters to run shallow. . . . The old cadres are thinning out and being replaced by a new type: practical-minded barbarian specialists, suspicious of the great cultural riches.

This dual process meant, on the one hand, an extraordinary extension of culture or, rather, education to the broad masses of illiterate and semiliterate Russians; and on the other hand, a substantial drop in the cultural level. The dissemination of knowledge gained in breadth but lost in depth. Both this gain and this loss suited the State. And also the masses, all those who for the first time had access to some kind of culture.

An interesting detail: in the first Soviet schools for children or adults, one of the first lessons written on the slate was "We are not slaves. The slaves are not us."

As if by spelling out these phrases, one could break the slaves of slavery. These grammar lessons coincided with the Soviet power's first steps. Initially it seemed that with the help of rudimentary knowledge applied to a pure class consciousness, the new man would finally be born. And he was born. But this was not a free man, this was what I would call a self-satisfied slave. His self-satisfaction derived from two sources: from his social position and consciousness first, and from his superficial learning second. His origins, his belonging to the victorious class, seemed to open all the doors. Seemed only, since this was largely an illusion. In reality, this man remained a slave of the State and of the society, but he did not realize this because the oppression and exploitation had been impersonalized. Before the revolution, when he worked in a factory, he worked for the bourgeois, for an actual person. Now the bourgeois was gone and the factory belonged to the impersonal State, running everything in the name of the people, of the working class. Meanwhile, the worker was told: "You are working for yourself, you are the master. And not only of this factory, but of the entire country." In fact, he was master of nothing, not even of his own fate. But nominally he was considered the master. And they encouraged his sense of class superiority vis-à-vis people of bourgeois origins, the intelligentsia, and the rest of the world beyond the bounds of the Soviet Union. He was constantly having it drummed into him: "You are the best, you are the first, you are in the avant-garde." Not because of his personal qualities or merits, but because of his social class. When this high opinion of himself had sunk in fully, he became a self-satisfied slave. In the famous Soviet song written by Lebedev-Kumach in the thirties, he boasts:

*There's no other land the whole world over*
*Where man walks the earth so proud and free.*

This slave not only does not feel his slavery, but sees himself as the freest man there is, and dreams of converting the workers of the world, suffering in capitalist chains, to the same state.

Now let's imagine that this slave goes to a vocational school, or a technical college, or even an institute. This is not particularly difficult: in the Soviet Union, candidates of worker or peasant origins and those directly from production have generally enjoyed a huge advantage in entering institutions of higher learning. This is done so that society's uppermost layers will be composed not of intellectuals but of "our own people," kindred spirits socially and psychologically of the top Party echelons. This education — whether primary, secondary, or university-level — renders the self-satisfied slave even more self-satisfied. On top of his class superiority, he now has the complacency of the semieducated man. Not because instruction in the Soviet Union is poor, but because even at the higher levels it is often exceedingly specialized. A graduate of a technical institute may have a perfect grasp of how machine tools are put together and yet remain, culturally and intellectually, the same simple worker he was before taking courses.

Moreover, any discipline in the humanities is steeped in Marxism-Leninism, the only philosophical doctrine studied in the USSR. Highly unsophisticated and also incredibly self-satisfied, it is received as the only truth by the self-satisfied slave, whom it both elevates and teaches not to think. He spouts Marxist clichés and entertains no doubts. He can study long and hard and yet think very little. Because to think is to search, to doubt, to ask questions. But if the world is easily and simply explained, why think?

This standardized man — the man of the masses — is undoubtedly the most frightening thing that Soviet civilization has produced. And continues to produce. He is the backbone of this civilization. He represents this new breed, mass-minted by the

Soviet State and society. His spiritual, moral, and even intellectual profile places him immeasurably lower than the most unenlightened muzhik. In exchange for the good qualities found in simple people, he has acquired impudence, familiarity, and arrogance, as well as a habit of judging and explaining everything in the most primitive terms. This is a savage who thinks that he knows it all, that he is the pearl of creation.

To make this man did not require much time or effort. For every one of us is inhabited by an egoistical "I," engendering envy, malice, pride, and other vices. In normal people this egoistical "I" is somehow tempered and contained by a moral sense or education. But let's imagine that they gave this personal egoism a class form ("You are the leading class! You are the great victorious people!") and carte blanche. Imagine that they cultivated this egoism which, equipped with nothing but the barest bit of schooling, grew by leaps and bounds. Here you have the new man.

To present this type in his pure state, I will cite Mikhail Bulgakov's *Heart of a Dog* (1925), a brilliant satire on the new man, his literary portrait.

In the novel, Professor Preobrazhensky, eminent scholar, surgeon, and biologist, performs a fantastic operation. Hence his name ("Preobrazhensky" evokes the Transfiguration): he transforms nature. This typical representative of the old Russian intelligentsia is tolerated by the Soviet power only because of his world renown and splendid operations, but he himself finds the Soviet power hard to bear. Not because he is a reactionary who favors capitalism, but because the revolution has turned everything upside down — both daily life and people's brains. At lunch one day the professor — Philip Philippovich — is talking with his friend and associate Doctor Bormenthal when what sounds like choral singing wafts down from somewhere above: the tenants are holding another general meeting under the direction of the *domkom,* or house committee.

Hearing the ritual choral response, Philip Philippovich exclaims mournfully:

> "Why is it that the electricity which, if my memory serves me, had gone out twice in twenty years now regularly goes out once a month? . . ."

"It's the general rack and ruin, Philip Philippovich. Economic collapse."

"No," Philip Philippovich argued with utmost assurance. "No. . . . What is this general ruin of yours? An old crone with a crutch? A witch who has knocked out all the windows and extinguished all the lights? Why, there's no such thing! . . . It's this: if I begin to sing in chorus in my apartment every evening instead of operating, it will lead to ruin. If, coming into the bathroom, I will — forgive the expression — begin to urinate past the toilet bowl, and if Zina and Darya Petrovna do the same, I'll have ruin in my bathroom. Hence, the rack and ruin are not in the bathrooms, but in the heads. . . . It is impossible to serve two gods! It is impossible at one and the same time to sweep the streetcar tracks and settle the fate of Spanish beggars! No one can succeed in this, Doctor, and least of all people who, being generally behind Europeans by some two hundred years, still aren't too sure of how to button their own pants!"[4]

So the revolution and its aftermath, Soviet civilization, have turned the whole system on its ear. The same thing happens when the unsuspecting Professor Preobrazhensky performs his astonishing experiment on a dog. He finds a lone, hungry mongrel on the street, takes him home, and replaces his pituitary gland with that of a man just killed in a brawl. After the operation, the dog, Sharik, gradually turns into a person — endowed with all the traits he had as a dog and those of the proletarian drunk and thief whose pituitary he has inherited. The nature of this new creature is a class nature, but very inflated by the vivisection (the revolution). In his diary, Bormenthal notes:

"The creature took his first walk around the apartment. He laughed in the hallway, looking at the electric light. Then, accompanied by Philip Philippovich and myself, he proceeded to the office. He stands firmly on his hind (*last word crossed out*) . . . feet and looks like a short and poorly built man.

"He laughed in the office. His smile is unpleasant and seems

4. Translation of this and subsequent excerpts by Mirra Ginsburg in *Heart of a Dog* by Mikhail Bulgakov (New York: Grove Press, 1968), pp. 36–37, 60, 67–68, 69–70, 88–89.

artificial. Then he scratched his head, looked around, and I wrote down another clearly enunciated word, 'bourgeois.' Swore. His swearing is methodical, continuous, and apparently entirely senseless."

This is how the class nature manifests itself. It's no accident that one of the first words this "new man" learns is "bourgeois" (addressed to the master of the house and his whole professorial setup). And when, at mealtime, the professor tells him to "stop throwing food on the floor," the "new man" answers unexpectedly: "Leave me alone, louse." But here is his new appearance:

Near the hanging, a short man of unpleasant appearance stood leaning against the door-jamb, one leg crossed over the other. . . . His forehead was strikingly low. The thick brush of hair began almost directly over the black tufts of his shaggy eyebrows.

Bits of straw clung to his jacket, ripped open under the left arm; the tight striped trousers were torn on the right knee and spotted with lilac paint on the left. Around his neck, the man wore a poisonously blue tie with a fake ruby pin.

The professor starts correcting him:

"Remove that rag from your neck. You . . . Sha . . . just take a look at yourself in the mirror, see what you look like. A clown. Stop throwing butts on the floor — I ask you for the hundredth time. And no more swearing in the apartment! No spitting! Here is a spittoon. Take care when you use the toilet. Stop all conversation with Zina. She complains that you lie in wait for her in the dark. Look out! Who said to a patient, 'The son of a bitch knows!'? What is this, do you think you are in a saloon?"

Then the creature demands identity papers so that he can be registered in the apartment. He chooses himself a refined name and patronymic — Polygraph Polygraphovich — to be appended to his hereditary last name, Sharikov. Sharik had been a very good dog, but then he was replaced by an awful subperson, Sharikov. A conversation over lunch:

"Well, and what shall we do this evening?" he [Bormenthal — A.S.] asked Sharikov.

The latter blinked and said:

"The circus, I think, best of all."

"Every day the circus," Philip Philippovich remarked benignly. "It's pretty boring, to my mind. In your place, I would go to the theater for once."

"I won't go to the theater," Sharikov said peevishly and made a sign of the cross over his mouth.

"Hiccupping at the table spoils other people's appetite," Bormenthal commented mechanically. "If you excuse me . . . Why don't you like the theater?"

Sharikov looked through the empty glass as through binoculars, pondered awhile, and thrust out his lips.

"Nothing but fooling around . . . Talk, talk . . . Counterrevolution, that's what it is."

Philip Philoppovich threw himself against the gothic back of the chair and roared with laughter, so that his teeth glittered like a golden picket fence. Bormenthal only shook his head.

"Why don't you read something," he suggested. "Otherwise, you know . . ."

"Eh, I read and read . . ." answered Sharikov and with a quick, greedy movement poured himself half a glass of vodka.

"Zina," Philip Philippovich cried anxiously. "Take away the vodka, dear. We don't need it anymore. And what do you read?" . . .

"Oh, that . . . What d'you call it . . . the correspondence of Engels with that . . . what the devil's his name — Kautsky" . . .

Philip Philippovich put his elbows on the table, peered closely at Sharikov, and asked:

"And what is your opinion of it, if I may ask?"

Sharikov shrugged.

"I don't agree."

"With whom? With Engels, or with Kautsky?"

"With neither," answered Sharikov.

"That's marvelous, I swear. Everyone who says the other . . . And what would you propose yourself?"

"What's there to propose? . . . They write and write . . . congress, Germans . . . who knows them . . . Makes your head spin. Just take everything and divide it up. . . ."

So Sharikov's main idea is social equality: to divide everything equally. But what especially strikes the professor is the exceeding peremptoriness and self-confidence of his judgments.

The story ends well: unable to bear Sharikov's onslaughts, the professor gives him back his pituitary gland in a second operation, and the creature returns to his peaceful canine state, becomes his old dog self.

What to conclude from this very funny and very sad story? That one cannot change human nature in such a radical, revolutionary way and do so with impunity. The changes that occur are, alas, often for the worse.

Let's now look at one more aspect of the Soviet man tied to his class nature: his simplicity. This man is so simple that at times it is difficult for us to understand him. His simplicity has its advantages and disadvantages. On the one hand, it causes him to reject various social conventions as hypocritical, affected, and dishonest. For to be honest means to be simple, in other words, not to wag, not to dissemble, to say what one truly thinks, and so on. On the other hand, this man's simplicity can degenerate, à la Sharikov, into an extremely primitive mentality, into crudeness, vulgarity, boorishness, and familiarity.

Fedotov writes that Russia, after the revolution, was astonishingly renewed in a social and psychological sense. Notably because of the simplicity that bubbled to the surface, moving into the foreground in everyday life as well as in the psychology and relations betweeen people. "In Russia the traditions have been uprooted more radically, perhaps, than by any other revolution ever. Nineteen seventeen has revealed that mentality which is defined by 'simplicity' as the supreme criterion of value."

Taking Fedotov's thought a step further, one might say that this happened primarily because the common people were catapulted to the rank of a social elite. Simplicity generally characterizes the worker and the peasant, but after the revolution, this ingredient became much more concentrated, more potent. Simplicity became an index of real human worth.

On the eve of the revolution, Lenin made this famous remark about the future Communist society: "Any lady cook should be able to run the State." This phrase was repeated many times with slight variations: "We'll even teach (show) the lady cook how to run the State." A sacramental epithet, it signified the new society and the new man. Coming from Lenin, it evoked (as it does today) the highest form of democracy. With two qualifications: First, it assumed that the lady cook should know how to govern, that she should study and thus transform herself into a new-style intellectual capable of fielding complex political questions. Second, Lenin, still thinking in utopian terms, assumed that the new society would be founded exclusively on principles of self-government, that there would not be any special State machinery, and that everyone, lady cooks included, would take turns at the helm of the State without receiving any privileges for this social service. On coming to power, Lenin himself was forced to abandon this democratic idea.

Nevertheless, this wishful Leninist catchphrase took on enormous significance in the new society. And it did come true, but inside out. The cook began to run the State, but without having acquired any knowledge for the purpose, and without having displayed any ability or talent. Culturally and psychologically still a cook, she simply installed herself on the throne. Sharikov won. But I repeat: neither the dog Sharik nor the cook is an inherently vile creature. They only exhibit lowness when they are in a position to command. One sees this in many post-Stalinist Soviet leaders: in their faces, manners, speeches, and styles of governing. Neither miscreants nor monsters, they are just plain cooks. And not even to blame, necessarily, for where they ended up. Any more than Sharik was to blame for ending up a person. The blame is incumbent on the sociohistorical destinies and mechanisms that produced this vivisection. Any Soviet leader, in his rightful place, would undoubtedly make an excellent stableboy, shepherd, drayman, or even engineer. A kind and wonderful cook, at last.

The great Leninist catchphrase, when it came true, turned into a farce, comic and horrible at the same time. And this became the incarnation of the dream about the new man, the cornerstone of Soviet civilization.

# 6

# The Soviet Way of Life

FROM THE METAPHYSICS of the new world, let's turn to its physics: from the heights of ideology and lofty generalizations, let's come down to earth and investigate the molecular makeup of this system, this organism.

What is the Soviet way of life? The term assumes the lowest, simplest, most mundane level of social existence, and characterizes the ordinary life of the average man, of a certain stratum or an entire people. On the other hand, the "way of life" is something enduring and stable, tied to habits, to traditions, to basic forms of existence — the need to eat, to work, to have a roof over one's head and clothes on one's back, to amuse oneself, to reproduce, to bury one's own. But as a phenomenon of Soviet civilization and history, this way of life is transformed and possesses a quality all its own.

It is defined, in effect, by two antithetical tendencies: destruction and creation. Or negation and conservation. In the new society, everything ascribed to the "old way of life" is subject to destruction and negation in the name of the new "Soviet way of life." These negative and destructive tendencies are so substantial and so entrenched in the life of society that the term "Soviet way of life" or "new way of life" sounds like so much nonsense or like an oxymoron, the marriage of mutually exclusive concepts. Indeed, any "new way of life" might as well be called the "new old stuff" insofar as "way of life" always includes something old, something enduring.

Taking this word game a step further, the Soviet way of life may be described as "permanent uncertainty" because the permanent and the uncertain here are closely linked, creating a kind of precarious balance.

A simple illustration from everyday life would be that perfectly standard and abiding Soviet phenomenon: lines. Lines for bread, for meat, for potatoes, for stockings, for cars, for refrigerators. Lines in the baths and lines in the cafeteria. Lines in which people stand for hours on end, or from morning till night and from night till morning. Lines stretching on for blocks and lines stretching on for years. What do these lines represent? Man's abiding need for his daily bread versus the absence or, rather, shortage of that bread. Stability founded on uncertainty, on instability. The new anchored to the old. So that the endless line has become the living image of the Soviet way of life.

Like anything else, Soviet life has of course changed over the space of seventy years. Precipitous drops in the standard of living have been followed by periods of relative improvement, and vice versa. But almost invariably Soviet life exhibits this uniquely consistent instability, the basis of the contradiction between old and new or the interaction between destructive and creative forces. The Soviet power does not specially organize or create these lines. They are a spontaneous phenomenon, constructive and creative, born of socialist insufficiency, of hunger and misery or, more broadly, of destruction.

What is more, the conditions of life dominate the consciousness and existence of Soviet citizens precisely because a normal or civilized way of life is either nonexistent or has been reduced to a bare minimum, itself often hardly accessible. This is another mystery of Soviet history: the conditions of life become a value. They are played up, highlighted, and extolled because they have been destroyed or are deficient. It is no accident that in conversation, on the street or at home, among friends or strangers, one constantly hears the question "Where did you find that?" Not where did you buy that hat, but where did you find it? Where did you find that meat? Even, where did you find that toilet paper? Basic necessities become an achievement, a value for which one must struggle. In other words, daily life moves into the foreground once conditions make it a struggle. However primitive and paltry, it takes on bloated, hyperbolic features since a person's very existence depends on it.

## CONDITIONS OF LIFE AT THE TIME OF THE REVOLUTION

The destructive tendencies aimed at the old way of life and at the way of life in general were acutely felt as early as the first years of the revolution. The country was reduced to rags. The war and its disastrous aftermath — hunger, devastation, epidemics, gangsterism — were, of course, to blame. But at the same time, the revolution had upset the entire system of daily and economic life, thus aggravating the disasters, and left the harsh imprint of a strictly Soviet way of life on people's existence. Too numerous to list here, the changes included endless requisitions, evictions and "consolidations" (when strangers were forcibly moved into one's apartment), the destruction of private property, the decimation of entire estates and classes, and the ensuing chaos. As a result, certain people won: those who had been nothing became all, at least nominally.

This process entailed astronomical costs and losses. An objective eyewitness, Vladimir Korolenko, wrote in his journal in 1919:

> "My home is my castle," say the English. But for the Russian now, especially if he is a "bourgeois," there is no sanctity of hearth and home. Nothing is more hideous than this orgy of requisitions. Like everything else here, it knows no bounds. "Institutions" requisition the apartments. They proffer one and seize another. The "consolidation" is also dubious: they often evict entire families to make room for a much smaller family of Soviet employees.

These upheavals were especially painful to individuals and groups ripped out of their accustomed milieu and thrown into the most excruciating circumstances. Not just the old rich or the aristocrats suffered, but any person ill equipped to cope with the daily, hourly struggle for existence. Even given a few privileges because of their work or their rank as a scholar or writer, they still found themselves in untenable, unthinkable situations, the ones that give us an idea of the Soviet way of life then.

It is a way of life turned inside out, but a way of life nevertheless. Marina Tsvetayeva recalls (*My Jobs,* 1918–1919) how, working in an office, she and her colleagues organized an expedition to the country, customary at the time, to search for food. The trip took two months and turned up nothing but half-frozen potatoes.

One hundred pounds per person. First thought: how to get them back. Second thought: how to eat them. One hundred rotten pounds. The potatoes are in a cellar, in a deep, dark crypt. The potatoes died and were buried and now we, the jackals, are going to dig them up and eat them. They say the potatoes were good on arrival, but then someone "banned" them, and by the time the ban was lifted the potatoes had frozen, then thawed and rotted. . . . The potatoes are on the floor: they take up three corridors. At the end, it's more protected, the potatoes are less rotten. But the only way to them is over them. So over them we go: in our bare feet or in boots. Like walking over a mound of jellyfish. We have to pick them out with our hands: one hundred pounds. The thawed potatoes are stuck together in monstrous gluey clusters. I have no knife. So, in despair (I can't feel my hands anymore), I take whatever comes: squashed, frozen, thawed. My sack is already full. My hands, completely numb, cannot tie the knot. Taking advantage of the darkness, I start to cry. . . . I hoist my sack, I drag it. Swearing, kicking. Those behind are pushing. I am blocking the passage. . . . My sack, loosely tied, spills. Gurgling. Sobbing. Squelching. Patiently and not hurrying, I gather them up.

They return home with the potatoes piled on a child's broken sled, dragged across Moscow. Face smeared with tears, later with potatoes. "I'm no better than my sack. The potatoes and I are now one."

This scene points up aspects inherent in the conditions of Soviet life: not just the hunger, but the appalling negligence that is a cause of the hunger. The potatoes are first left to rot, then distributed. One must trample them with one's boots to fill a sack. All this because relations between buyer and seller have been severed. There is no personal initiative, it is forbidden, and officials don't give a damn about anything. Decrees, bans, mandates, permits, and special supplies have supplanted the natural exchange. And Marina Tsvetayeva, Russia's great poetess, says with bitter irony: "The potatoes and I are now one." This is not simply poetic license and not simply irony, but an allusion to the conditions of life that beat a person down, dominating his consciousness and existence like the huge gelatinous mound of congealed, gluey potatoes that Tsvetayeva depicts with such revulsion.

People adjusted variously to these privations and vicissitudes. For Mayakovsky, the asceticism of the revolution contained the supreme meaning of Soviet history; this need forged a genuine unity among men, a moral and spiritual unity that he called the "socialist Motherland." He mentions this in his poem "Fine!" where he paints a fairly grim picture of life in Moscow during the civil war. One detail, for example: it is winter, the heating has broken, the pipes have frozen. Mayakovsky's response rings crude and direct:

> *I pull out a sleigh.*
>      *"Gotta run."*
> *And pick up a cap,*
>      *an ancient one.*
> *"Where to?"*
>     *"The john,*
> *at Yaroslavsky Station."*[1]

To go to the toilet, one must go a long way, as far as Yaroslavsky Station. And one takes a sleigh along to ferry home planks from a tumbledown fence on the way. But this also shows a caring for one's own, for the family nest. Suddenly this picture is lit up with happiness, that of being alive in this age when new human emotions are emerging from the depths of this miserable existence:

> *A land*
>   *where the air's*
>      *sweet and heavy,*
> *a fruit juice,*
>    *you leave,*
>      *for new places panting,*
> *but a land*
>    *you froze with*
>      *will stay forever*
> *deep in your heart*
>     *implanted.*[2]

1. Translation by Dorian Rottenberg in *Mayakovsky*, vol. 2 (Moscow: Raduga Publishers, 1986), p. 248.
2. Translation by Rottenberg in *op. cit.*, p. 250.

And certain things in this wretched existence become—for Ma-yakovsky — symbols of love:

> *I'm holding*
>> *two carrots*
>>> *crunchy.*
>
> *They're not*
>> *for my stew:*
> *I'm taking them to*
> *my sweetheart,*
>> *for her*
>>> *to munch.*
>
> *Boxes of sweets*
>> *and flowers*
>>> *freely*
>
> *I handed out,*
>> *but*
>>> *I recall*
> *that those carrots*
>> *plus firewood*
>>> *(half a billet)*
> *were*
>> *the most precious*
>>> *gift*
>>>> *of all.*[3]

This is life at the time of the revolution, frozen, fixed on the threshold of its annihilation and that of human life in general. Thus these pitiful tokens are prized — not only materially, but spiritu-ally, morally — as expressions of kindness, love, and solidarity. For Mayakovsky, they are illuminated by the humanistic ideals of the revolution, created for the sake of the universal, socialist good. For him, this isn't merely a way of life, but the birth of a new society. Hence the tragic, heroic, and patriotic note in his evocation of hunger, cold, and ruin.

The most extreme poverty, beyond the suffering it brings — or, rather, thanks to this suffering — can elicit the most positive

---

3. Translation by Rottenberg in *op. cit.,* pp. 251–252.

emotions, the most profound spiritual response. During the Second World War, Olga Berggolts wrote about the terrible seige of Leningrad:

> *In those days, daily life*
> *Disappeared, reappeared.*
> *And bravely, being*
> *Came back into its own.*

Here, "daily life" and "being" are opposites, like little and big, trivial and sublime. Of course, "daily life" did not disappear entirely but, reduced to a minimum, it inspired a desire to live for the sake of "being," for the sake of something grand and universal, as opposed to all that is personal, petty, banal. In this situation, a person can experience great joy, an extraordinary inner release, and spiritual uplift. As Berggolts wrote in 1942:

> *In the mud, darkness, hunger, and sorrow,*
> *With death's shadow dogging our heels,*
> *We were so happy,*
> *So wild with freedom,*
> *That our grandchildren would surely envy us.*

Man occasionally finds supreme freedom, enlightenment, inspiration, or closeness to God in moments of extreme duress. The material lack unlocks an embarrassment of ideas. Poverty and hunger are spiritualized, idealized, and men, through the sufferings of war and revolution, purify and strengthen themselves.

But the masses responded to all these horrors in quite another way and snatched greedily at the last scraps of food and warmth. The torment they endured did not elicit anything noble in them, in their minds or souls. They simply died or learned endurance, patience, resourcefulness, how to get and keep a piece for themselves.

While Mayakovsky exulted in "the warmth of loves, of friendships, and of families," other, opposite processes had been set in motion. The hunger and cold bred enmity, mutual suspicion, fear, and alienation. Man became hardened, dulled, brutalized.

Yevgeny Zamyatin's 1922 story "The Cave" stands in stark contrast to Mayakovsky's vision of revolutionary life in "Fine!" It's the same life, but the camera has lighted on different aspects. Zamyatin shows us a wintry, icebound city, the old Petersburg set against what seems to be some prehistoric period, the Stone Age: "Glaciers, mammoths, deserts. Pitch-black crags that look a bit like houses; caves in the crags." The caves are apartments and rooms, the last habitation where men can take refuge from the cold and each other. At the center of the universe, at the center of the cave, stands "a short-legged god with rust-red hair, a greedy cave god: a cast-iron stove. . . . People . . . reached toward it reverently, silently, gratefully. For one hour spring filled the cave; for one hour, the animal skins, claws, and fangs were tossed aside and new, green idea-shoots poked through the crust of the brain's ice-covered cortex."

At the center of the story are Martin Martinovich (Mart) and his infirm wife, Masha. They are intellectuals: noble and refined, incapable of adapting to the new, primitive conditions. Masha remembers that tomorrow is her name day and asks that the stove be lit first thing in the morning. She doesn't realize the wood has run out. So Martin steals wood from a neighbor. The stove is lit, and Masha happily recalls her youth and their love while Martin nods docilely. But the firewood has already been missed, and he must return the logs that are now ashes. Late in the evening, Martin Martinovich reaches for the only things he has left: a packet of letters from Masha and a dark blue vial of poison. He relights the fire for the last time with the letters and is about to consume the poison when Masha notices the vial:

"Mart, if you still love me . . . Please, Mart, please remember! Mart, darling, give me that!"

Martin Martinovich slowly got up from his knees. Slowly . . . took the dark blue vial and handed it to Masha.

She threw back the blanket, sat down on the bed — flushed, rushing, immortal like the water then at sunset — snatched the vial and burst out laughing.

"Light the lamp, there, on the table. Good. Now put something else in the stove. I want the fire to be . . ."

Martin Martinovich, without looking, raked some papers off the table and threw them into the stove.

"Now . . . You go out for a walk. . . . Don't forget to take the key, if you slam the door you'll have no way to get back in . . ."

This scene in Zamyatin suggests a parallel with the moment in "Fine!" when Mayakovsky gives his beloved the best and last that he has: two carrots and a birch log. In Zamyatin, the most precious gift is poison. But as in Mayakovsky, this is an expression of love, the last warmth, the last humanity. Except that in Mayakovsky it's life that triumphs in love, whereas in Zamyatin it's death. Both are right, since Soviet life was then tottering between life and death. First one would triumph, then the other.

One may object that these were extraordinary times: the revolution, the war. That one can't judge ordinary life on the basis of such exceptions. Yes, of course, these were exceptions to the general rules. But exceptions can reflect the rules, albeit in exaggerated ways. Through them one can form some idea of the norm, of ordinary Soviet life in peacetime. War and revolution aside, catastrophes are periodic: collectivization which, in the late 1920s and early 1930s, wreaked as much havoc as the revolution; or mass arrests; or flights to the moon or an arms race that meant restricting the people to semistarvation rations; or the chronic problems in agriculture today. Soviet life at any point is, more or less, the picture of poverty.

## EXAGGERATED SIMPLICITY

In an early story by Mikhail Zoshchenko, someone says: "Ah, my dear sirs and good comrades! Isn't it astounding how life is changing and how much simpler it's all becoming." It is a fact that after the victory of Soviet power man became simpler, as did social relations and everyday life. This simplicity manifested itself in various ways but is best depicted by Zoshchenko, the sad philosopher, reflecting on the Soviet condition:

"No one ever knew the catastrophe that hit. Or if, indeed, it had been a catastrophe. Most likely it was not a catastrophe, but life, simple and ordinary, where two people in a thousand manage to stand up; the others simply exist."

The "catastrophe" here, in the broad sense, is the revolution, which apparently has not affected the masses: life goes on as it always has. The "two people in a thousand" who stand up are heroes, men of ideas. But the others? The others, says Zoshchenko, "exist." Such is the formula for ordinary, everyday Soviet life. All men live to live, but in the Soviet world, one lives to survive.

"Life in the city had changed," Zoshchenko says, "but in general people lived as they had before. If anything, they fought even harder for their right to exist: they swindled, stole, cheated."

If life had both changed and remained the same in that the fight for survival was even fiercer, this meant that the revolution, in the higher sense, had failed. Having changed everything and made everyone equal, the socialist revolution, compared with the capitalist world, had only escalated the daily struggle to survive, to possess some minimal piece of the pie.

Zoshchenko is an especially pertinent observer of the Soviet condition because he is drawn not only to general ideas, but to specific individuals. Not to the outstanding hero and not to the intellectual, but to the representative of the masses, the simple little man with his pedestrian existence.

There were no more rich people in the old sense of the word. But in the context of general misery, the most insignificant and even worthless possession became the greatest luxury. The nanny goat, for instance, in Zoshchenko's 1923 story by the same name, in which the hero, the petty official Zabezhkin, notices an advertisement posted on the street:

"Room to rent for single man."

. . . In his excitement, Zabezhkin turned back up the street and peeked over the gate, then walked away.

"A nanny goat!" said Zabezhkin. "My word, a nanny goat. . . . Pray God, she belongs to the proprietress. . . . With a hint like that, one could even marry. And I will. My word, I will. Let's say that if there's a nanny goat, I will marry. Basta. Ten years I've waited and here . . . Fate . . . Ah, what a pretty affair! A small property. A cow, perhaps, or a milch goat. Better a goat — they eat less."

Zabezhkin opened the gate.

"A nanny goat!" he gasped. "There's a nanny goat by the fence.

With a nanny goat, it wouldn't be hard to live. With a nanny goat, it would be silly even to . . ."

For our hero, the entire world is reduced to this nanny goat, his vision of the good and peaceful life, of material prosperity. And he goes to incredible lengths, gives himself entirely to this task, to this idée fixe: to get into the proprietress's good graces and gain access to her goat.

In "The Nanny Goat," Zoshchenko tells us that despite the socialist revolution, nothing has changed essentially for the little man. And on top of everything, the general misery has turned this pitiful nanny goat into a treasure, an unattainable ideal. Proprietary instincts and desires, far from having disappeared, are thriving in the most unexpected, often monstrous ways.

Poverty and the difficulties of existence are not the sole causes. The Soviet power also changed people's psychology. Certain vices have been exacerbated. One is struck by the outrageous small-mindedness of everyday Soviet life. The sphere of great endeavors and great passions has been reduced to almost nothing, placed out of legal reach, prohibited. Thus passions are seething at the lowest level, at the level of day-to-day existence. One should add that the little people were often oblivious of the social oppression. The masses — particularly in the twenties and thirties — considered that they were on top of the situation, masters of life, always right, and thus unashamed of their base instincts. Hence the distorted, hyperbolic features of what we call everyday Soviet life.

Zoshchenko shows us how a trifle can become fuel for a conflict out of all proportion. In his 1927 story "The Guests," the hostess suddenly turns pale as death and says:

"Well this is an outrage! Someone has just unscrewed the twenty-five-watt electric light bulb in the toilet. Then guests can no longer be allowed into the toilet."

In the end it turns out that her husband had pocketed the light bulb — so the guests wouldn't filch it — only to smash it when he fell asleep on the window seat.

These incidents, with which Soviet life abounds, are not strictly the result of poverty. But people who have known poverty can, even in normal or comfortable conditions, act like penny-pinchers. Not that they are naturally stingy, but it is habit with them to pick at trifles and to suspect one another even when these trifles are no longer a problem.

## THE NEW WAY OF LIFE

In the twenties and early thirties, attempts were made to create a new way of life based on the ideas of socialism. Particularly the planning and building of apartment blocs and mass housing designed for a collective way of life. According to socialist ideologies, one should live and be educated collectively. Living the old way was harmful, they claimed, because people lived isolated, in families or alone, in separate houses or apartments. This fostered disunity, individualism, and proprietary habits. Therefore this way of life had to be destroyed and replaced by one based on the principles of collectivism. Collective labor and collective ownership, cornerstones of the new society, demanded a new way of life: collective recreation, collective child-rearing, collective meals — at the factory as well as at home.

In the 1920s, then People's Commissar of Education Lunacharsky phrased it this way: "The revolution's goal is to make men brothers. . . . The revolution wants to build big houses where the kitchen, dining room, laundry, nursery, and club would be built according to the latest scientific methods and would serve all residents of the house-commune, who would live in comfortable, clean rooms with running water and electricity."

These projects had various names: House-commune, Housecomplex, NLH (New Life House), Proletarian housing. The big dining rooms were called "factory-kitchens" and meals there were meant to replace family meals.

A single person or couple was to be allotted the minimal amount of space, just enough to sleep in and change clothes. Life apart would be restricted in the name of life in the collective. Children were to be raised away from their parents, in their own collectives, guaranteeing them a purer socialist conscience. These projects also earmarked a lot of space for group activities: reading rooms, sports rooms, reception rooms, and so on.

The new way of life had other objectives as well, some of which initially seemed extremely appealing: for instance, to free women from the stove, the laundry, and daily housework, since they should work like men, and study and live collectively. But the key was that the individual and the family would now come second, behind the common cause and the idea of proletarian equality and brotherhood.

These plans never materialized. Some house-anthills were built, but they did not fulfill their function and so were rejected. The new way of life did not take hold for various reasons. The State, for one, was unable to provide for these gigantic projects and unable to supply such daily services as collective meals and laundries. Besides, the Soviet government had never regarded the people's material welfare as more than a distant priority compared with heavy industry and the military.

The utopian character of these projects, the fact that they were contrary to human nature, was one more strike against the new way of life. Even a person raised in the spirit of collectivism wants a corner of his own, his own saucepan, lunch at home with his family and, finally, his solitude. It is impossible, as we know, to live without society, but to be always surrounded by others is a heavy burden.

Ultimately, there was no new way of life. Just as there was no "new man" in the strict sense. Still, Soviet life possesses a number of distinctive aspects, including the fact that the Soviet man is obliged to lead a more collective life than he would like. The communal apartment, for example: this phenomenon is so characteristic that in the Soviet mind the expression "Soviet way of life" first conjures up visions of a communal apartment.

Communal apartments have remained a part of Soviet life like some inadvertent parody of the house-communes of the ideologues' dreams. In a communal apartment, every family lives unto itself and as best it can. But this sort of living arrangement is the result of a chronic housing shortage and an exponential increase in the urban population thanks to the growth of industry and the ruin of the countryside. Thus an apartment originally intended for a single family becomes home for half a dozen or more families, depending on the number of rooms, the largest of which may be subdivided. In the big cities, the so-called sanitary norm stipulates that an individual may not occupy more than nine square meters of living space, plus an additional four square meters per family. It is in these forcibly close quarters that communal living was finally established, with its own laws and coloration.

This way of life, aside from being incredibly cramped, involves constant contact with total strangers. Each family, regardless of size, is confined as a rule to one room. People marry, have children, and continue to live in this one room with parents, brothers, sisters, and grandparents.

A friend of mine — from a fairly well off family of intellectuals — lived in the same small room with his parents and grandmother until he was middle-aged, sleeping on a folding bed that was stowed away during the day and set out each night, part of it tucked under the table. So that my friend slept half under the table.

In a communal apartment, the corridor, the kitchen, and the toilet are "for general use." If there is a bath, it is also shared. As is the telephone, if there is one. These places for general use are the communal apartment's nerve center: small spaces where strangers are thrown together, forced to exchange words and insults in the eternal battle for some fraction of the common space. This accounts for its unusual, if not exotic look. In the corridor, you may see a trunk or a coatrack, or a bicycle hanging on the wall: all can be sources of endless drama and conflict. Someone says he tripped over the trunk in the dark and demands that it be removed; someone else wants to put his own trunk in its place. The kitchen is stuffed with odd-size tables — one managing to take up more space than another — and cupboards, as many as there are families. The gas stove is communal, but there aren't enough burners for everyone at once. Before there was gas, every table had its own portable oil stove, filling the kitchen with soot and smoke. The kitchen is also the place where the laundry is washed and hung up to dry on clothes-lines running back and forth overhead. One line per person. But there is only one faucet for everyone — to take a sponge bath or wash the dishes, to fill the teakettle or a laundry tub. Lots of people and only one faucet . . .

The word "neighbors" has a sinister connotation in the context of the communal apartment. Good relations are rare. More often one's neighbors are hostile, dangerous, alien, in one's way. Any molehill becomes a mountain, any trifle a catastrophe. The suspicion and hatred breed gossip, slander, scandals, fights, and denunciations.

The Communist brotherhood is transformed into the most terrible civil strife. The crowding and the territorial wars aggravate the differences between people — not only materially, but socially and intellectually, in age and even taste. Someone likes to bathe at night, but someone else wants to rinse a child's diapers. One person gets up early and turns on the radio as loud as it will go, another person is always having guests over late at night. And yet another person spends too long in the john. The list of mutual grievances goes on and on. As one might suspect, intellectuals usually fare worst of all in these communal cesspools: they are both a minority and unlike the others by virtue of their education and habits.

Zoshchenko's "Summer Respite" (1929) centers around a prosaic communal dispute over who owes what on the electric bill: there's only one meter for the whole apartment, and everyone uses different amounts. Zoshchenko is mocking those ideologues who claimed that communal apartments would foster friendship and solidarity and thus become the cells of socialist society:

> Of course, to occupy one's own, separate apartment is philistinism. One must live all together, as one big family, and not lock oneself away in one's castle home.
>
> One must live in a communal apartment. In the open. Where there's always someone to talk to. Someone to go to for advice. Someone to pick a fight with.
>
> Of course, there are drawbacks.
>
> The electricity, for example, creates a problem.
>
> You don't know how to divide up the bill. How much to take from whom.
>
> Of course, later on, when our industry has turned the corner and America is at our beck and call, every tenant in every corner can have two meters or more if he likes . . . And then, of course, life in our apartments will shine like the sun.
>
> But for now, indeed, we have nothing but problems.
>
> For example, we have nine families and only one wire, only one meter. At the end of the month, one has to calculate the consumption. Which, of course, leads to serious misunderstandings, if not to blows.
>
> So fine, you say: go by the light bulbs.

So fine, we'll go by the light bulbs. But one conscientious tenant turns on his light for five minutes, the time it takes to undress or to kill a flea. And another tenant chews and chews on something till midnight with the light on. Refuses to turn it off. . . .

There was one tenant, a loader, who literally went off his head because of this. He stopped sleeping and spent all his time ascertaining who was reading algebra at night and who was fixing himself something hot to eat. . . . He was an excellent controller. As I say, he literally did not sleep nights and ran inspections every minute. Ducking in here, ducking in there. Threatening to hack you up with an axe if he discovered any excesses.

Then the orgy begins: every tenant, suspecting the others of excess, tries to personally use up as much of the general electricity as he can. The bill goes up and up. "In a word, when the meter jumped to thirty-eight rubles, the electricity had to be turned off. No one would pay. A lone intellectual pleaded and clutched at the wire, but they ignored him. The electricity was cut."

This incident is neither invention nor hyperbole. I lived in a communal apartment for forty years and can confirm that the light bulb or the garbage pail or where to put the kettle on the stove made for real problems. To Zoshchenko's story, I can add this documentary vignette. We were, my family and I, the only intellectuals in our apartment. In the evenings I would read or write by the desk lamp, sometimes late into the night. The neighbors, naturally, noticed this and suggested I stop reading, turn out the light, and go to sleep earlier. So I began to pay double for my desk lamp. This didn't help. So I installed a separate electricity meter for my room. But then it was pointed out that at night I sometimes went into the corridor or into the kitchen or out-of-doors to walk the dog — at the expense of the communal electricity. So I installed my own hall light and connected it to a switch in my room so that it would register on my own electricity meter. At which point I thought the problem had finally been solved. But then it became a question of my dog. True, he never barked, never ran out of our room, and always sat quietly so not to provoke the neighbors' censure. Still, when I took him outside — twice a day — he did use the communal corridor, and his feet brought in more dirt than those of other tenants, meaning that we should wash the hall floor more often than they. I agreed. But then I was told that my dog, with his four feet as opposed to the usual tenant's two, tracked twice as much dirt inside, making it necessary to wash the floor twice as often. So I began carrying the dog — luckily a small one — through the corridor. In short, it was an unwinnable war. The more money and energy I invested in appeasing my neighbors, the more they hated me. Look at the barin: he installed his own electricity meter, he has a dog, and whereas we wash the hall floor with our own hands, he hires a cleaning woman. Where did he get the money? And why does he stay up so late with the light on? I had a comfortable salary and a few Soviet privileges as a scholar and member of the Writers Union, but nothing would calm them. My way of life differed from theirs, arousing envy and suspicion: What was I really studying? Was I an American spy burning the midnight oil?

This is just one detail to do with the electricity. Others were worse. In the kitchen, every pot on the stove was under lock and key. To stir the soup or to taste it, one had to unlock the pot and then relock it, for fear a neighbor might filch a piece of meat — less from hunger than from spite — or slip something into it: extra salt, dirt from the floor, or just some spit . . .

This gives one a sense of the tension of life in a communal apartment. Socialism's ideologues and organizers hadn't anticipated that human nature could be so unbending or that cohabitation could breed such enmity. For years they blamed the scenes on the accursed capitalist past, on bourgeois vestiges which, they said, would disappear with time. But they did not disappear, they assumed these new forms that make Soviet life what it is.

## THE FIGHT AGAINST THE PETITE BOURGEOISIE

The eradication of bourgeois vestiges in people's life and consciousness was pursued throughout the 1920s and into the 1930s. This coincided with the State policy aimed at liquidating the remains of private property in the country and in the city, at liquidating the petite bourgeoisie: private entrepreneurs, traders, artisans, cottage industries, and prosperous peasants (or, as they were officially known, kulaks). This was not only a political, social, and economic revolution, but also a fight for a new way of life and a new psychol-

ogy of the man in socialist society. The source of all evil, of all vices
— in the way of life and in human consciousness — was "property,"
which caused man to live for himself, not for all, and nurtured his
egotistical nature. Hence the fight against the privately owned
house, against man's small, private world. The conventional revolutionary wisdom held that everything would be fine once there were
no owners and no property. Many works of Soviet literature show
that even the expression "way of life" (or "old way of life") was
linked to the notion of private property. Especially the kind providing a modicum of income and independence. This, ostensibly, concealed the greatest danger of all.

Apropos here is Eduard Bagritsky's poem "Suburban Man."
Written in 1932, at the end of collectivization and the dekulakization of the countryside, it responds to those events. The contemptuously designated "suburban man" is not a kulak or a peasant, but
someone who hasn't yet been touched. He has a little house of his
own outside the city — part of which Bagritsky was then renting —
a small garden, and some livestock. Though he has acquired all this
by dint of his own labor, Bagritsky feels compelled to treat this
owner with great hostility and to portray him in the spirit of the
first capitalist hoarders.

> Not in vain they taught us:
> Hoist it over your shoulder,
> Clutch it to your chest and lug it back,
> To the sheep's cot,
> To man's home,
> To the cabbage-blessed borscht.
> Look at the world
> From inside the granary doors,
> Deep inside where it reeks of rats,
> Don't give anything away:
> Not the leavings or the steam,
> Not a stone or a twig — nothing!

Bagritsky does not and cannot find serious fault with this "suburban man," whose only sin is in owning a house and tending to it.
But this makes him the enemy: the embodiment of the old, self-
centered way of life that now must be destroyed. Bagritsky dreams

of the day, soon to come, when the new age and its men will storm this house:

> *Done battling through forests and rivers,*
> *Faces turned up into the driving rain,*
> *Chekists, mechanics, fish-breeders,*
> *Now step up onto the new-planed porch.*
> *The time has come and we're together again!*
> *Again the horizon in battle smoke!*
> *Look over here, suburban man:*
> *"We've arrived! We're feasting in your house!"*

The tone is overblown. But if one thinks about what is actually happening and about what Bagritsky is anticipating with such enthusiasm, it becomes sinister. The suburban man is being hounded and persecuted by the State. The little, ordinary, simple man. The man for whom the revolution was made. Now this revolution, in its new phase, is chasing him out of house and home, destroying his way of life. Because he is the "petty proprietor" from whom all evil springs.

But as we know, the fall of the petty proprietors and the funneling of people into communal apartments did not rid the new society of the microbe of egoism and self-interest. Before, the petty proprietor grabbed what he could and lugged it home. Now, though already a Soviet man, he is battling his neighbors for his time in the kitchen or the toilet.

The old way of life is always poking through the new. Which only makes it more horrible. All the brutal measures adopted by the Soviet power to restrict the Soviet man do not protect him from his petty egoism; they only aggravate it and transform it into a boundless, petty hatred for his fellow Soviet man.

Aside from the petty proprietor, another reputed source of all evil then was the "petit bourgeois," closely linked to the way of life and sometimes confused with it. The petit bourgeois resembles the petty proprietor in that he too lives for himself and his own well-being: his apartment, his things, his little family pleasures. But the definition of the petit bourgeois is more elusive in the social sense than that of the petty proprietor. The petit bourgeois can be anyone: a small tradesman, a proletarian, a Party official, a onetime hero of the revolution. It's enough to enjoy some level of material prosperity, to have lost one's aspirations and one's ideal, for one to be in danger of becoming petit bourgeois. The words also contain an aesthetic nuance, connoting a certain bad taste. This petit bourgeois taste may be a relic from the past — or something new, acquired under the Soviet regime and a relative material improvement. It is this aspect that interests us: the petit bourgeois as a product of the new society. He adds one more element to the Soviet mix of old and new. In "Rot" (1921), Mayakovsky turns the first postrevolutionary, post–civil war page of Soviet history and is horrified to see the swarms of petits bourgeois crawling out from all the cracks:

> Revolutionary tempests grow quiet, seem far.
> With duckweed the Soviet mishmash gets coated.
> And now
> from the back of the RSFSR
> the philistine's visage
> pokes out, bloated.[4]

This isn't just the old petit bourgeois who sat out the war somewhere and is now emerging into the light; this is also the new, socialist-style petit bourgeois who, thoroughly versed in Soviet ways, feels himself master of the situation. His wife, whom he calls "Comrade Nadya!" in the new Party style, is getting ready for the ball at the Revolutionary War Council — her idea of high society. Her ball gown must be adorned with the Soviet State emblem, the hammer and sickle, while our man means to wear his riding breeches, as wide as the Pacific Ocean, in the military style of the day. These are members not of the old petite bourgeoisie but of the Party's new, bureaucratic elite. And the entire picture of their happiness is built on this blasphemous hotchpotch — in Mayakovsky's eyes — of archaic, petit bourgeois symbols and new, strictly Soviet ones, so that the portrait of Karl Marx is next to the canary trilling in its cage:

4. Translation by Rottenberg in *Mayakovsky*, vol. 1 (Moscow: Raduga Publishers, 1985), p. 82.

*"The revolution's tangled in philistine webs.*
*Worse than Wrangel[5] are philistine habits," he hollered.*
*"Quicker,*
*wring those canaries' necks,*
*don't let canaries beat Communism hollow!"[6]*

The canary is the symbol of the petit bourgeois idyll, of petit bourgeois taste. And in his hatred for the petite bourgeoisie, Mayakovsky fires a cannon at these canaries. Why? Could communism really be beaten by canaries? Yes, says Mayakovsky, since the canary is a sign of bourgeois stability and routine, which are overrunning the revolution and its high ideals. This isn't simply a question of "vestiges of the past" bizarrely juxtaposed with the new, Soviet way of life. In reality, the danger that Mayakovsky fears and is fighting with all his might is that of a petit bourgeois degeneration on the part of the revolution itself. This is not the restoration of the old values, but an ossification, a fossilization of the revolutionary energy and will, stymied by a new triviality and inertia. This explains Mayakovsky's anxiety before canaries, official inkstands, bureaucratic briefcases, and other symbols of the new stability. They heralded the end of the revolution. And the poet's rage was that much greater for the enemy's being so elusive. Neither social stratum nor class, the enemy was everywhere: the microbe of vulgarity and self-interest, that of the petit bourgeois, bureaucratic forces. How could one fight something that was the product of one's own victorious Soviet system?

One must note, however, that behind this routine, retrograde, petit bourgeois way of life, there was a human truth. People cannot burn with revolutionary fervor forever in the name of bright ideals. Their life depends on the present, not some radiant future; they must live in their own house, not on a universal scale. In Mayakovsky's comedy *The Bedbug* (1928), a worker starts showing petit bourgeois symptoms. Amid the endless discussions about universal happiness and the need to remain faithful to the revolutionary ideal,

5. *Translator's note:* Pyotr Nikolayevich Wrangel (1878–1928) was a Russian general who fought against the Bolsheviks during the civil war.
6. Translation by Rottenberg in *op. cit.*, vol. 1, p. 83.

he suddenly objects: "This is not 1919. People want to live for themselves."

This fatal desire to live for oneself (the most ordinary human egoism) became the ballast in the building of the new society. On the everyday level, it seemed to have become ossified, covered with petit bourgeois mold. Even the leaders wanted to live for themselves, and in the 1930s the pejorative term "petit bourgeois," so popular with the Soviet press, was phased out; this mentality had obviously triumphed and did not want to create unnecessary problems for itself. It had triumphed in the ubiquitous person of normal, socialized Soviet citizens living at all levels of the hierarchical pyramid.

Of course, the Soviet State has never given a citizen the total possibility of living for himself; it demands that he live for it, for the State. But having paid the necessary tribute, this man is determined, quietly or not so quietly, to live for himself, putting down roots in the hard Soviet soil.

## THE GREAT OPERATOR

The ways of living for oneself in the Soviet Union are few but various and even surprising. Human nature gets the upper hand and finds the most ingenious ways to sidestep the obstacles and even triumph, at least for a time. Which brings us to another Soviet feature, a specific sociopsychological type whom I will call, for simplicity's sake, the "old fox," a conventional designation embracing so many different aspects of Soviet life that one can fairly say that every Soviet man is, in some sense, an old fox. The one who joined the Party and made himself a profitable career without having the moral right or the ability? An old fox. The one who wangled an apartment ahead of the other fools on the waiting list? An old fox. The one who nipped into the store just as some rare item — sausage or a sheepskin coat — was being put out? An old fox. As a rule, just to live one has to be an old fox.

Any society has its old foxes, with their secret access to power or prosperity. In old Russia, a merchant's proverb said: "Deceive not, sell not." Yet the Soviet way of life is in a class by itself when it comes to the great resourcefulness with which it stamps a person's psyche. One anecdote, which if anything flatters Soviet people, may illustrate the point.

A young American millionaire had given up trying to find a girl with good character to marry: every one had some drawback. For instance, one young English lady he was courting burst into tears the day she lost a diamond necklace. And he thought: If she cries over so little, what will she do when something truly awful happens? No, I won't marry her. At this point the millionaire went to Moscow, where food was being rationed. Walking along the street, he saw a girl laughing. Asked why, the girl said: "Oh, if you only knew. The most wonderful thing just happened! In the store they gave me my macaroni but forgot to detach the coupon from my card!" The millionaire thought: If such a little thing makes her happy, she must have excellent character! And he married the Soviet girl.

This anecdote suggests two things. First, Soviet people aren't as dejected as it might seem. The lives of those who contrive to find something "for themselves" can even be fairly happy and interesting. Second, the Soviet girl is an old fox in that she keeps both the macaroni and her coupon. She skips over the State barrier. And laughs . . .

But the inherently Soviet old fox is not always so innocent. Therefore it is preferable to study this sociopsychological type in his most vivid expression, that of "professional" old fox. For this purpose, I have selected Ostap Bender, the famous hero of Ilya Ilf and Yevgeny Petrov's *Twelve Chairs* and *The Golden Calf,* essentially a single novel written in the late twenties and early thirties. Curiously, this work is hugely popular in the Soviet Union among the broadest audience. To the point that certain scenes and expressions have become part of the Soviet idiom and everyday life. The book is very engaging and very funny, but the pièce de résistance is Ostap Bender himself, whom the authors had the wit to pluck right out of the Soviet air and make the comic center of their adventure.

*Twelve Chairs* and *The Golden Calf* belong to the picaresque genre that flourished in Spain, France, and England in the sixteenth and seventeeth centuries — and turned out to be a perfect fit for Soviet Russia in the twentieth. Ilf and Petrov mined this vein of gold in creating Ostap Bender, whose name and image became household words, so attuned was he to the atmosphere and attitudes of Soviet life.

This is an image of the ideal old fox as almost a positive hero, though the authors were careful not to glorify the mercenary scheming behind his every move. Ilf and Petrov were loyal Soviet writers. They even attempted to condemn Ostap in revealing the vanity of his adventurous pretensions in the world of victorious socialism. But the logic and force of their character is such, the reality of Soviet life is such, that the swindler Ostap Bender comes off as the brightest, bravest, most interesting, and most magnanimous man of all. He is luminous against the dreary background, the inertia of the Soviet routine which, for all its heroic slogans and aspirations, is devoid of life, devoid of chance, since here the individual finds himself subjugated to the State.

Ostap Bender is the Great Operator, a designation that recalls that there were great tsars, great generals, great writers; that there was a Grand Inquisitor; that great feats have been and are being performed under the guidance of great ideas and great leaders, that the great constructions of socialism, as they said then, are under way around the country. But the Great Operator eclipses them all. He's the operator because he's always fiddling with new ideas. "I live on my ideas," he explains. "I'm not a robber, neither a thief, nor a bandit, I'm an ideological fighter." But of a special sort: "I'm an ideological fighter for cash." In other words, a speculator, a swindler driven by the idea not just of riches, but of devising roundabout ways and maneuvers, brilliant machinations to cheat the society in which he is obliged to live. He is a genius of ingenuity operating at the lowest level, that of everyday life, the one place where there's still elbowroom for inventors like him. Big business is off limits, likewise the political struggle. So all this energy, all this talent, all this huffing and puffing, are thrown into the only thing left: the way of life. "On the chest of the Great Operator was a dark blue powder tattoo, a picture of Napoleon in his tricorn holding a tankard of beer in his small hand."

This is the symbol of the new epoch. Napoleon united with a tankard of beer signifies a new stage of human history, that of Soviet history reduced to the level of everyday life. Ostap Bender certainly conducts himself like a Napoleon. But his grandiose ideas and his brilliant abilities are relegated to places where everything is as petty, absurd, and squalid as in a communal apartment.

Ostap Bender is in no way an enemy of the Soviet power. It's just that, as he says, "I'm bored by building socialism." And indeed, independent of the authors' will, we see that building socialism, if perhaps a great thing, is also a very boring one in that it deprives people of all initiative and individualism. In the middle of this boredom, Ostap Bender alone shows initiative and finds rich food in socialism itself for his inventive thoughts.

Thus, though bored by building socialism, Ostap Bender is a product of the socialist, Soviet system. A child of the new society. A modern young man who's in his element in this world. Hence his eminence as an Operator vis-à-vis the other thieves, swindlers, pillagers, moneygrubbers. They all pale beside Ostap Bender for the simple reason that he is a Soviet man, wise to all the ways of — and ways out of — the new system. His philosophy is as simple as it is profound. Appearing before an imaginary court — and, by extension, before all humanity — he says:

"Life, gentlemen of the jury, is a complicated thing, but, gentlemen of the jury, this complicated thing opens very simply, like a box. One need only know how. As for the man who cannot open it, he is lost."

Ostap Bender knows perfectly well how to open this complicated box, Soviet society, because he was raised in the system and knows it like the back of his hand. One of its mainsprings is Soviet demagoguery, which he has mastered to perfection. Which is why he always finds the necessary ideas for his scams. Such as the slogan "Let's Combat Bad Roads with Formula 1"; or the organization of a new industry under the sign "Horn and Hoof"; or the revolutionary origins he accords himself: "Son of Lieutenant Schmidt, hero of the revolution of 1905." His bag contains what any combination traveling musician and conjurer, Soviet rogue and sharper, might need:

Bender squatted over his small suitcase, like a traveling Chinese conjurer over his magic bag, and began pulling out one thing after another. First came a red armband with the word "Bouncer" embroidered in gold. Then came a militiaman's peaked cap bearing the

Kiev city emblem, which he laid on the grass next to four packs of cards . . . and a packet of documents with round lilac seals.

The Soviet signs of power, the signs of a privileged and trusted position in the new society, go hand in hand with the sharper's deck of cards. Everything is forged. But the Soviet forgeries do the trick best of all: everyone bows before a piece of paper stamped with the State seal and before the red armband belonging to the Bouncer.

Let's see how Ostap Bender comports himself as the fictional son of Lieutenant Schmidt. Russia has known many such imposters — from the false Dmitry to Gogol's Khlestakov. Now the imaginary heroes of the revolution and their imaginary sons are following suit. But Ostap Bender does more than just pose, he goes to the City Executive Committee, an official institution, and pulls political strings with the president:

> "Of course, I could go to a private individual. Anyone would oblige me. But, you understand, that would be a bit awkward from the political point of view: the son of a revolutionary turning to a trader or a NEPman for money . . ."
>
> "Indeed, you were absolutely right not to go to a trader," said . . . the president.

The rogue Bender gets his money. His formula "from the political point of view" opens the box every time. So as not to lose his "political vigilance," the executive committee president, representing the State, takes the speculator's bait.

Yet Ostap Bender never commits an out-and-out crime. "I revere the Criminal Code," he says. "None of my four hundred honest ways of appropriating other people's money qualifies as robbery; it just doesn't fit."

Why does Bender shun robbery? Undoubtedly because, as a Soviet citizen who has imbibed this system body and soul, he knows which buttons to press to get rich without special effort or risk. *Twelve Chairs* opens with Ostap Bender in a provincial town without a kopeck. He thinks:

> Tomorrow I could go to the City Commission and suggest that they undertake the exhibition of an as yet unpainted but brilliantly conceived painting: *Bolsheviks Writing a Letter to Chamberlain*, in the

style of the popular painting by Repin, *Zaporozhye Cossacks Writing a Mocking Letter to the Turkish Sultan.* If successful, this operation could net me four hundred rubles.

Bender came up with this idea while . . . strolling through an exhibition at the Association of Artists of Revolutionary Russia. . . . But with the painting . . . it wouldn't necessarily be smooth sailing: one could run into purely technical problems. Would it be proper to paint Comrade Kalinin in a Caucasian fur cap and white felt cloak [Mikhail Kalinin was then head of state — A.S.], and Comrade Chicherin naked from the waist up [Georgy Chicherin was people's commissar of foreign affairs — A.S.]? If need be, one could of course dress them all the usual way, but that wouldn't be the same thing. The effect would be ruined!

Bender's plan is a parody of official Soviet painting: mixing a revolutionary theme with nineteenth-century Peredvizhnik-style realism. Such was the taste of the times: to unite Repin's cossacks with the leaders of the Soviet Union. It's no accident that the idea dawned on Bender at the AARR, the conservative wing of Soviet painting, which triumphed definitively in the 1930s under the sign of Socialist Realism. Ostap Bender was perspicacious enough to guess the direction of Soviet art.

An amusing historical detail that Ilf and Petrov could not have known: Stalin, according to his daughter Svetlana, adored Ilya Repin's *Cossacks* and was fond of reciting the obscene text of the famous letter that the Zaporozhye cossacks did in fact write, while roaring with laughter, to the Turkish Sultan. He had a framed reproduction of this painting, under glass, next to the portrait of Lenin at his dacha.

All in all, Ostap Bender is the picture of the Soviet old fox, able to turn a profit even in these straitened circumstances. Thus he easily blackmails a clandestine Korean millionaire — for a million rubles — by threatening to have him arrested and shot by the GPU. It's only thanks to the protection of the Soviet State and the Soviet way of life that such operators could thrive. Ostap Bender is their composite image, but ennobled by the humor with which he treats this society and himself. He laughs at the fact that only an old fox can win, that not to perish, one has to be an old fox.

To the official literary critic, Ostap Bender is an alien element in Soviet society, a negative character to be rooted out. But this judgment does not correspond to the plot of the novel, to its influence, or to readers' perceptions. One true episode connected with Ostap Bender's posthumous fate may illustrate.

In the 1950s, during the relatively liberal period after Stalin's death, law students at Moscow University organized an evening's entertainment around a comic show trial of Ostap Bender, who was, after all, a criminal. One should also note that this practice of public trials was in keeping with the spirit of the times. Many of the big court cases were accompanied by meetings, at factories and the Academy of Sciences alike, intended to demonstrate the Soviet people's unanimous support for the sentence. A sort of musical accompaniment to the State Tribunal.

Thus these student lawyers, with their moot court, were acting within the norms. But as specialists, they incorporated their own knowledge of the subject. One played the prosecutor, another the judge, a third the lawyer, and a fourth the accused. The whole thing ended in a terrible scandal because this court acquitted Ostap Bender — or gave him too light a sentence. One student was expelled from the Komsomol, another from the university. But the one who suffered most was the lawyer who, carried away in an impassioned defense, made the mistake of saying: "Ostap Bender is the favorite hero of Soviet youth!" True enough. Not that the youth actually admired or imitated him, but he inspired sympathy. The sly old fox was more fun and more popular, brighter and warmer, than the heroes of official virtue. Ilf and Petrov were not wrong in choosing Ostap Bender as Soviet reality's leading representative.

## THE CRIMINAL WORLD AND THE RULING CLASS

In real life, of course, nothing is as romantic as in the novel. The Great Operator is apparent not in certain people but in certain tendencies that permeate Soviet society from top to bottom. Tendencies that assume countless different forms. All sorts of operations are conducted "on the left" — beyond the State's control, for personal gain: corruption, speculation, connections, underground industries, and the black market. Theft at the place of production has become a way of life for the factory worker and collective farmer alike. The State inevitably fights this, taking the severest measures. At one time a pilfered spool of thread could earn a person ten years in prison, the verdict having been determined by the usual demagogic means: the spool of thread was unwound, measured, and duly registered as a "theft of 50 (or 100 or 300) meters of sewing material." The man who pocketed the single spool might just as well have stolen several hundred rolls of linen or silk.

The Soviet Union remains the only state among civilized European nations where the death penalty is consistently enforced for major misappropriations. And the principal offenders are not burglars or bank robbers but those who have managed illegally to organize their own private business, say a sideline produced at a factory and sold "on the left," benefiting not the State but those who worked overtime to manufacture the goods, as well as the factory director who, alongside the official, socialist production, carved out his own little corner of capitalism.

Very often these operations do the State no harm. They afford excess profits, obtained in a roundabout way, that of personal initiative. But the State has always been jealous of private means of enrichment that elude it. And therefore these Great Operators find their heads on the block when they fail to bribe the bosses in time, when they fail to draw the State into the business.

In a normal society, with a normal organization of labor and production, these operators, these Ostap Benders, could enrich themselves and the State. But the paradox of the Soviet economy and system is that the State has till now invariably put prestige before profit. Such are the metaphysics of the Soviet power, built on the opposition of the State and the individual and, consequently, on the suppression of the individual by the State.[7]

But human nature prevails; the spirit of the Great Operator does not die. Soviet life abounds in intrigues worthy of detective novels. Take the workers in the tram depot who, at their own risk and peril, revived an old tram, already consigned to the scrap heap, and put it back on track as their own private enterprise. Outwardly, it

7. Recent events seem to indicate a shift in the blind opposition to the entrepreneurial spirit, but whether it is merely tactical, based on dire economic necessities, or a profound shift, remains to be seen.

looked like any other State tram; but inside, the driver and conductor were not working for the State, and the passengers' kopecks were not going to the public treasury. This was a private enterprise inside socialist city transport. Long after the crime was uncovered and the criminals imprisoned, people were still gleefully recalling the story of Moscow's private tram.

Another ingenious example of private enterprise: At a Moscow market, there was an invalid who sold trinkets. He also had a sideline; for a sum, he could get any person into any university or institute. No mean feat in Moscow, where the competition is extraordinarily stiff and some can resort to special connections, patronage, or a bribe. Naturally, loving parents came running to the miracle-working invalid who, being very honest, warned that there were no guarantees and promised to refund the money if he failed, a promise he kept. But his many successes made for a vast and generous clientele. How did he do it? Very simple. He didn't! He didn't go anywhere, didn't do anything, and generally had no connections whatsoever. But he reasoned that those truly determined parents who were paying him were probably paying everyone else they could think of as well. And any one of those bribes might do the trick, but they would never know which one. Finally, there was always the chance that the actual applicant might be diligent and succeed on his or her own merits.

This scheme is particularly interesting for its being concocted out of nothing except shrewdness and an uncanny sense of the Soviet system, with all its gears and levers. The invalid made money out of thin air, literally out of Soviet air, without expending an ounce of energy or doing anyone any harm. Undoubtedly a Great Operator.

In the USSR, the incidence of what is officially known as "misappropriation of socialist property" has risen sharply. Theft of socialist property is severely punished, much more severely than that of private property. The State protects itself better than it protects its citizens. Under Stalin, crimes connected with State property were often treated as political (meaning the most serious) offenses. One peasant, guilty of having felled a tree in a forest, was charged not with stealing but with so-called sabotage, making him a political enemy.

Millions of people misappropriate "socialist property." I'm referring here to systematic petty theft, if not always perceived as such by the offenders. For instance, going into the woods and filling a sack with grass for one's cow is officially considered theft. The grass is State grass, even if the State doesn't use it. This sort of petty larceny may accompany a person from childhood to the grave, a lifetime habit.

At the same time there are sections of the socialist economy where theft is so rampant as to seem a requirement of the profession. This applies to the entire trade and distribution network. The arrest of a store director for embezzlement, of the man behind the counter or the bookkeeper, of a restaurant manager or a supplier, is a routine occurrence that surprises no one. Sometimes a person in this sort of position has to steal, even if he wants to remain honest: he has to pay tribute to his boss, who then pays his own boss, and so on, so that virtually everyone in the establishment is involved in the ring, and not individuals but whole collectives go off to prison.

All this is accompanied by massive corruption, which encompasses the militia, the courts, the organs of control, and the Party leadership. Many goods and services cannot be obtained except by greasing the palm of the person distributing them; this is done for a train ticket, for a piece of good meat. Bribes, I've been told, were even accepted at the Presidium of the USSR Supreme Soviet when Kalinin was president. People came from all over the country to see Kalinin — to make a request or a complaint — often waiting a month or a month and a half for a few minutes' conversation with him. Kalinin received them all very warmly, paying no attention to the time. His secretary did this for him, striding in with an abrupt "Your time is up." The length of one's time, however, depended on the size of one's bribe. The secretary could be persuaded to stretch the five-minute limit to seven or even ten minutes, given proper compensation. And if the president's own secretary was selling minutes, one can imagine the extent of the corruption in the Soviet Union.

In the broadest sense, then, I would say that every Soviet citizen is, by definition and necessity, a criminal. For the simple reason that survival in socialist society is somehow always a matter of breaking the law. Unless, of course, one wants to become the last of the scoundrels and pursue a Party career up the ranks of the socialist elite, for whom no law is written.

This is why there are so many inmates in the Soviet Union. Everyone is guilty of something and waiting to be caught. But next to this mundane phenomenon, there is also organized crime: professional thieves, robbers, and bandits.

Every country has its criminal world, its mafias. My aim is not to describe it as it exists in the USSR but to isolate its strictly Soviet features. Its origins reach back to the distant past, while more recently this world has fed off new sources such as the revolution, the war, the famine, and destruction. But there are other factors too, the first being, in my opinion, the "criminalization" of Soviet society as a result of the destratification of the people and the individual. Russia had been strictly divided into estates: nobility, merchants, clergy, peasantry, petite bourgeoisie, workers. These relatively self-contained groups had their own status and traditions. Suddenly these partitions came crashing down, throwing everything into confusion. The huge peasant masses, who composed the majority of the Russian population, were uprooted and scattered to the winds, or artificially tied to their place of work and birth as slaves of the State. This confiscation of the land from the peasants — who for centuries had lived for that land, who to a degree had supported the revolution and the Soviet power for the sake of the land they promised — told fatally on the people's sociopsychological makeup. The people were no longer people but masses, human dust. This dust naturally churned up criminals: people who had lost their social niche, their place in the sun, their land. Socialism brought about society's desocialization. Man, deprived of his roots and his ties, deprived of what gave his life meaning, found himself naked; he became a rogue and a marauder whose only friends belonged to the same underworld based on an upside down morality, based on the "thief's law."

According to this "law," the only real man is a thief. In fact, here the word "thief" signifies "man." An example from Stalin's time: A convoy of several thousand prisoners had arrived at a camp and was waiting at the gates, under guard, to be admitted to the zone.

Someone from inside cried out: "How many men?" And someone in the crowd called back: "Five!" Out of the entire convoy, there were only five thieves, only five real men who denied Soviet laws and human laws in favor of their own thief's law.

The second aspect of Soviet society's criminalization is, I would say, purely psychological and linked to poverty and shortages. The logic is simple: If everyone steals, why shouldn't I? But if everyone steals a little while pretending to be honest, I will be a true thief, an honest thief. And morally I will be superior to the restaurant manager, the store director, the Party leader, who all steal while pretending to "build socialism." Hence the cynicism, hidden or outright, that permeates Soviet society. Stealing becomes an act of valor. What keeps a person from stealing is not shame or conscience but fear of punishment. If a man conquers his fear, if he is a real man, he must be a thief.

A third aspect is the odd nature of property, which belongs to everyone and to no one. If it belongs to everyone, then it belongs to me. So why don't they give it to me? And if it belongs to no one, why do certain groups and categories use it as if it were their own?

This raises another problem of Soviet life, that of privileges and restrictions. Formally, everyone in socialist society is equal, everyone is a toiler — or should be. Any property affording the smallest income independent of the State is suspect and must be liquidated. At the same time, the numerous members of a vast ruling class enjoy the better things in life though they work less than anyone else. Society is thus divided into two classes: rich and poor, a distinction that is most acutely felt on the day-to-day level. Yet this is socialism, not capitalism, which makes this class division seem doubly absurd. During collectivization, the peasant who owned two cows was sent to Siberia as a "kulak" while the district committee president next door, with access to much more than the value of two cows, prospered. But it was the peasant who was considered a bourgeois, not the president. Better yet: the president "liquidated" the peasant as a bourgeois.

This perennial paradox is not so paradoxical. The peasant, with his two cows, tried to live on his own initiative, his own labor, his own interest in life. Whereas the district president seems to live for the State and so receives legal recompense: an entire district plus all the cows and all the peasants. He lives like a king. But he possesses nothing of his own, only the power and wealth conferred on him by the State whose interests he protects. So the new division into poor and rich is not the result of free capitalist competition but of intervention by the State, which accords privileges to its servants and imposes restrictions on its slaves. There is no bourgeoisie in the strict sense, but there is a striking contrast between the life of the upper classes and that of the lower classes, between the masters and the slaves. And this contrast between opulence and misery is even more awful under socialism than it is under capitalism. Because socialism does not cease proclaiming the classless society. It hypocritically conceals its own structure. And since this is difficult to conceal, it puts fences around the houses of the rich to keep the poor from seeing how they live. It erects walls, not only social but material, in the form of special stores, exclusive dachas, and envelopes containing fat bonuses for top officials. A closed society emerges, divorced not only from the outside world but from itself, thanks to all sorts of impermeable internal partitions.

The division of society into leaders and subordinates began early on, during the first years of Soviet power. Property was divided despite the fact that most Communists had been against this before seizing power. But now it turned out that the Communist leaders were an elite deserving better treatment from the State than simple proletarians. This instantaneous degeneration was described by Vladislav Khodasevich in *The White Corridor* (1937), a reminiscence. The time is late 1918–early 1919; the place is the Kremlin. Playing at patron of the arts, Olga Kameneva, the wife of Lev Kamenev (then one of the revolution's first leaders, shot in 1937) and the sister of Trotsky, has invited Khodasevich to her apartment in the Kremlin, off the White Corridor.

At that time, the White Corridor was occupied by dignitaries. The Kamenevs, Lunacharsky, and Demyan Bedny lived there. Every apartment had three or four rooms. One's existence was rather secluded, lacking neither in comfort nor originality. Since the simple people were not admitted to these precincts, one didn't have to pretend. . . . The ladies, ignorant until then of everything but *The*

*Erfurt Program,*[8] were anxious to gain some polish. They bought their clothes at Lamanova's, patronized the arts, fought over the automobiles and organized "salons." They dutifully patronized the proletarian writers, but preferred to receive the "bourgeois" writers "at home," on an equal footing.

Khodasevich, as a "bourgeois writer," is admitted to one of these new salons:

> The table in the dining room wasn't simply "set," it was disguised. Set with dainty bell-shaped faience cups which, as everyone knows, were not meant for tea, but for chocolate. Possibly when the spoils were divided, this was all the Kamenevs could get hold of: cups from the imperial service rimmed with gold and decorated with the black double-headed eagle. On small matching plates, there were hunks of barely buttered black bread, and in the sugar bowl, gray cubes of "played" sugar bought from Red Army soldiers who had won them at cards. This was the disguise: the meagerness of the refreshment was intended to show us that in the Kremlin they ate the same things we did.

Of course, one isn't obliged to believe Khodasevich who, in observing these nouveaux riches, fixes maliciously on every faux pas. One cannot take literally, for instance, his remark about the Kamenevs' acquisition of the imperial chocolate cups. Still, Khodasevich has caught the style of the new, socialist elite: the tsar's cups and modesty, hypocrisy meant to disguise the line between those at the top and those on the bottom.

The Kamenevs' little boy, Lyutik, the apple of his mother's eye, creates an especially painful impression: "It sickened me, terrified me, just to listen to her. Not so long ago another little boy — about the same age as their son and wearing the same little sailor's costume — had been racing around this room: the heir to the throne whom the Bolsheviks murdered, whose blood was on these happy parents' hands."

Ten years later this plundered prosperity would adorn the "golden childhood" of Stalin's daughter, Svetlana. In *Twenty Letters*

---

8. *Translator's note: The Erfurt Program* refers to a Marxist program adopted by Germany's Social Democratic party in 1891 in Erfurt.

*to a Friend* she writes rhapsodically about this period at the end of the twenties, when her mother was still alive and before her father had sequestered himself — like a wolf at bay — in his new houses and dachas surrounded by guards.

> We also had another house. Yes, sweet friend, imagine that in the old days we had another house entirely: cheerful, sunny, filled with children's voices, with warm, merry people, filled with life. My mother was the mistress of that house. She created that house and imbued it with her spirit. My father was not a god there, not a "cult," just an ordinary paterfamilias. This house was called "Zubalovo," after its old, prerevolutionary proprietor."

A picture of bliss, but the last sentence gives one pause . . . Evidently the house had not belonged to Stalin but was requisitioned from an old owner at the time of the revolution. Svetlana seems oblivious of this, however, cooing about how wonderful the old house was in her mother's time, when everything was the old way: the furniture, the maids, and the governesses.

> Mikoyan's dacha had been kept exactly as its previous owners had left it before emigrating. On the veranda, a marble dog, the master's favorite; in the house, marble statues brought from Italy; old French tapestries on the walls; stained glass in the downstairs windows. The park, the garden, the tennis court, the greenhouse, the hotbeds, the stable, everything remained as it was. I always felt such pleasure entering that dear house filled with old friends, entering the dining room with its same carved sideboard, its same old-fashioned chandelier, its same clock on the mantelpiece. Now Anastas Ivanovich's ten grandchildren run around on the same lawns beside the house, have lunch at the same table under the trees where his five sons grew up, where Mama used to come.

This is all very touching, and a little sinister. Because the house is someone else's. A stolen house. Anastas Mikoyan — a Central Committee member in the 1920s — didn't bring those statues from Italy or all those tapestries . . .

But Svetlana is jubilant: "We children," she writes, referring to the progeny of the Party leadership, "grew up, in effect, in a little country seat with its country ways."

When one reads this, one can't help asking various rhetorical questions. For instance, was it worth it to replace the lords of old with others, only cruder and of proletarian origin? What sort of a golden childhood can this have been, built on the blood and the property of others, perceived not as stolen happiness but as one's own, ancestral home? Yet in Svetlana's view, this still had nothing to do with greed, covetousness, or a craving for luxury. Stalin, she says, dressed very simply: "In summer, he wore a semimilitary costume. . . . He wore the same coat for fifteen years, and as for the bizarre, too-short deerskin coat lined with squirrel which he must have had made just after the revolution, he wore it with his fur hat every winter till the end of his life."

This detail indicates that the old Bolsheviks to whom Stalin belonged maintained their revolutionary habits and traditions. They didn't try to become bourgeois: that would have been a travesty. But little by little, everything changed, and a taste for luxury and comfort (in their Soviet interpretation) took over. The shame of being rich was replaced by cynicism: professing the socialist faith, they lived or aspired to live the bourgeois life. But they were obliged to conceal this from their people. And sometimes from themselves.

All these difficulties and contradictions of Soviet life, in the metaphysical sense, may derive from the fact that this life has been upset to the point where one can hardly call it a life. On the bottom, chaos and penury reign. At the top, everything has been stolen from others. Which makes for a strange result: man continues to fight for his happiness, and even more zealously than he might do so ordinarily. He cheats, steals, subdivides socialism into all sorts of internal compartments, in his desire to create something lasting. All in vain. There is no life in any real sense. The way of life seems cursed for its having been built on a wasteland where there is neither individual nor society, only the State.

# 7

# The Soviet Language

THE SOVIET LANGUAGE is not utterly new or distinct from the language of prerevolutionary Russia. But the fissures and shifts that occurred in it were so significant and so radical that some scholars and poets have called it a linguistic revolution comparable to the one that took place at the beginning of the eighteenth century under Peter the Great.

Here I will cite one paper presented in 1921 by the then noted literary critic A. Gornfeld. This erudite liberal, who had sympathized with the revolution, strove to produce a sober, unbiased analysis of the Russian language in the first three or four years after the revolution. In so doing, Gornfeld thought he could avoid the extremes of modernism and conservatism.

> A breakthrough has occurred right before our eyes, one might say, on the language front. Language, an organic creation, vast and all-encompassing, usually enjoys a sedate and placid existence. It evolves slowly, methodically, its movements as imperceptible, at any given moment, as those of the hands of a clock. But here as everywhere, there are jolts and abrupt transitions. . . . And new words, new turns of phrase, and new expressions come rushing into the language in an irrepressible torrent.

### THE RENAMED WORLD

Thus, with the revolution the language is roiled and its lexicon revamped. Even Gornfeld, in his reserved, academic manner, uses some of the new idioms, unthinkable in the past. If he can talk about a "breakthrough" on the "language front," this is because at this point in history everything has become a "front." After that of the civil war, others emerged: the bread front, the labor front, the education front, the ideology front, the literature front, the left front of art, and so on.

Which language did the new government inculcate? It aimed primarily to change the official and administrative language connected with the concept of "the State," to replace the old juridico-State terminology. To discard, for instance, the concepts of autocracy and empire in favor of those of "dictatorship of the proletariat," "Soviet power," and "soviet of worker and peasant deputies." Ministers could no longer be ministers, since the word was associated with the tsar or the Provisional Government, with bourgeois notions of an old-style republic. The appelation "minister" was, if anything, insulting; now anyone who fulfilled this function would be known as a "people's commissar" (or *narkom* in the abridged form).

Military ranks and posts also changed nominally: generals, admirals, officers, and even soldiers were unacceptable. Soldiers thus became "combatants" or "Red-Armyists." Officers were "commanders." "Kombrigs" (brigade commanders), "komdivs" (division commanders), and "komandarms" (army commanders) replaced the colonels and generals.

Everything old had to disappear: even the language of the new world must be entirely new. In these new names one detects two somewhat contradictory tendencies. First, the language — the expression of the idea, the ideology — races ahead of life; it must express something new, something which, however, does not yet exist in reality. Therefore, the language tries to rename everything using labels that indicate only a potential meaning, an ideal that may never materialize. Take that most influential of all revolutionary slogans, which has preserved its magical significance right up to the present day: "All Power to the Soviets!" This formula was pure incantation; the soviets have never exercised real power. They are a fiction that nevertheless entered the life and the language, and even became the name of the State: "Power of the Soviets," "Land of the Soviets," "the Soviet Union." In other words, the word supplanted the reality.

But here the second tendency appears: the practical impossibility of creating a new, ideal language. Hence the attempts to invent a

half-synthetic, half-natural language. To replace certain key words
with neologisms, or to tack new epithets onto old words. Though
few, these epithets have insinuated themselves everywhere in the
language and left a distinct mark. For instance, it's not "State
power" but "Soviet State power"; not "republic" but "Soviet republic"; not "people" but "Soviet people"; not "man" but "Soviet
man." This epithet is like a label affixed to the language indicating
that all concepts now have a new semantic and lexical emphasis.
Thus, if there are certain things that "man" can do, these things are
forbidden to "Soviet man."

Other epithets had this same supplementary or corrective function: "worker" or "worker-peasant," "revolutionary," "socialist,"
"Communist," "State," and so on. In the Soviet Union everything
belongs to the State, all institutions and enterprises are "State."
Unnecessary as it might seem to mention this every time, this is the
prefix for all sorts of new contracted compound words: *gosunivermag*
(State department store), *gosplan* (State plan), *goskontrol* (State control); every university is designated as "State," though no private
universities exist. Even the circus is "State." An incident from
1923: A famous conjurer was traveling around Russia as an independent artist (this was still possible then). On the posters, he
billed himself as a priest and a magician, but in performance, he
claimed to be sponsored by the State, by an institution he called
*Gosfortuna* (State Fortune). This is symbolic. The ancient word "fortune" changed into *Gosfortuna:* this is the Soviet language that
intrudes everywhere in an effort to inject everything with a new
officialness. This language is politicized: the State wants to impart
not only new meaning to its words, but also an overt political cast.

The new names of State institutions were generally long, complicated, and harnessed to stock political epithets such as "people's," "socialist," "Soviet," and "State." To pronounce them
properly was an arduous necessity that led to the invention of myriad abbreviations and acronyms.

In the twentieth century, abbreviations have proliferated around
the world in response to the accelerated pace of life, to develop-
ments in technology and a more schematic, even mathematical
language. The look and sound of many of these words remind one of
an algebraic formula.

But in this respect too, the Soviet language has its own coloration. In order to name itself, the new State introduced a new and complex terminology, which for simplicity's sake had to be contracted: "Russia" became the Russian Soviet Federated Socialist Republic, Union of Soviet Socialist Republics, or the RSFSR, USSR. Though these abbreviations were modified through the years, every new modification implanted itself in the life, the language, and people's consciousness. The political police, first known as the Cheka (short for *Cherezvychainaya Komissia,* or Extraordinary Commission), was later called the GPU (State Political Directorate), then the NKVD, the MGB, and finally the KGB. The Soviet man keeps all these letters in his head, without always knowing what they stand for. Over the years, the ruling Party has been called the RSDRP (b), the RKP (b), the VKP (b) — the "(b)" stands for Bolshevik — and now the KPSS. Simultaneously, a veritable abracadabra has emerged: *RKKA, Rabkrin, Tseka, Glavbumsbyt, Sovnarkhoz, Ossoaviakhim, Gum, Tsum, Torgsin,* and many more.

To the ordinary Russian, this all sounded originally like a nonsensical language, devoid of meaning yet portending something mysterious and sinister, since certain letters threatened life while others constituted its foundation, like some magic formula for reality.

In one of Yevgeny Zamyatin's stories, dating from the first years of the revolution, there is an intellectual whose invariable word of greeting and farewell — *"Chik"* — scares people half to death since death is exactly what it means to them. To them, the word has a sinister sound. Someone has his throat slit: *"Chik."* Someone else is liquidated with a bullet in the back of the head: *"Chik." "Chik"* is associated with the Cheka and Chekists, whose principal activity it is. But Zamyatin's character, pronouncing this word with an ominous smile, goes on to explain that it stands for an old, courtly expression meaning "It is my honor to greet you." Zamyatin surely did not invent this but took it from the real life and language of the revolutionary epoch.

The renamed reality seemed unsteady and unreliable, especially in matters of geography. The names of cities and streets changed. The new names multiplied, invading every corner of the country. St. Petersburg became Leningrad, and Tsaritsyn became Stalingrad, but this was not enough; many cities were given variations of the same name and so were easily confused: Stalingrad, Stalinabad, Stalinogorsk, Stalino; Voroshilovgrad, Voroshilovsk; Kirov, Kirovsk, Kirovograd, Kirovokan; and on and on. The Soviet power's insistence on renaming everything smacks of something irrational. As if the State were in a hurry to substitute names for the reality. Samara became Kuibyshev, Nizhny Novgorod became Gorky, Perm became Molotov, Yekaterinburg became Sverdlovsk, Pishpek became Frunze, and so on, ad infinitum. Not that these new names invariably stuck: Molotov became Perm again, Stalingrad is now Volgograd, and who knows which city will be called what tomorrow.

In all cities, even the smallest ones, many streets were renamed in accordance with the new Soviet nomenclature. As a rule, a provincial town's main street is Soviet Street or Leninsky Avenue. The main square is Freedom Square or Lenin Square, especially given a statue to the man. Earlier, it might have been Stalin Square, with a statue to Stalin. The lateral streets, too, even the saddest and dirtiest, have heroic names: Red Army Street, Marx-and-Engels Street, Cosmonauts Street, Socialist Street . . . The effect can be comical: little dead-end alleys once called Cow's Cul-de-sac or Goat's Cul-de-sac renamed Communist Cul-de-sac or Marxism-Leninism Cul-de-sac, turning this sonorous title into a parody.

Numerous institutions were now named after someone: a factory named after Lenin; a fine arts museum named after Pushkin, even if Pushkin had nothing to do with it; a theater named after Gorky; a ballet named after Kirov. Hence the witticism about the statue of Pushkin named after Gorky.

This new solemn style, however foreign to the Russian ear, had a definite influence on the language and society. The most popular first names in Russia — Ivan and Nikolai — fell into disgrace and disuse in the 1920s. Why? The name Ivan was too traditional, too common, and the people, newly empowered and emboldened, shunned it in favor of grander-sounding names borrowed from the former aristocracy: Anatoly, Viktor, Aleksandr. Valery came into fashion in the 1930s (after the famous pilot Valery Chkalov). If the Nikolais — the name of the last Russian tsar — were now few and far between, the Vladimirs — in honor of Lenin — were legion.

The rare Russian name Feliks was revived, after Feliks Dzerzhinsky. And when Stalin named his daughter Svetlana, he was not alone.

Many other names after the revolution were made up: antitraditional concoctions to the glory of the new society such as Lenina for a girl or Vladilena (a contraction of Vladimir Lenin), Stalina or Stalnira, Marksina or Engelsina. At the end of the thirties, I even knew of a little girl named Elektrifikatsia, which seemed almost as sublime as the Electra of ancient Greece. Boys were perhaps even more affected as the objects of their parents' greatest hopes. There were Zhores (after the French socialist Jean Jaurès), Revolt, Mir (Peace), Marlen (Marx-Lenin), and even a Traktor.

In the twentieth century, all languages have incorporated scientific and technical terminology. The Soviet language is no exception but for the fact that it often transforms these terms into political symbols. The words, aside from designating new objects introduced into use and production, attest to the fact that the society and the individual have entered the stage of socialism. Thus the name Traktor doesn't just refer to the farming vehicle but is also a symbol of collectivization, of man's inclusion in a grand design. It is pronounced with exultation and panache, waved about like a banner, a medal, an emblem of triumph. Everyday speech is full of these "beautiful" words, such as mechanization, industrialization, electrification, melioration, chemicalization, aviation, radio, antenna, accumulator, commutator, automat, cadres, et cetera. These terms are punctuated with exclamation marks implying some greater meaning. Behind the word "cadres," one hears Stalin's famous dictum "The cadres decide everything"; and behind the word "electrification," the Leninist formula "Socialism equals Soviet power plus the electrification of the entire country."

As a result, people endeavor — appropriately or not — to use these "exalted" words, which they may not even understand or know how to pronounce properly. But this is the sacred language of the Soviet State, handed down from above — through the press and the leaders' speeches — and toward which the masses are, or in principle should be, striving. Words replace knowledge: it's enough to know a specific set of words to feel on top of the situation.

Here we encounter another tendency in the Soviet language: the

desire to express oneself "scientifically." Or, in fact, pseudoscientifi-
cally, with a profusion of specific political, economic, or technical
terms.

All this is undoubtedly tied to the scientific utopia at the base
of Soviet civilization. Hence the endless isms, such as socialism, capitalism, imperialism, Trotskyism, revisionism, idealism,
materialism, and so on. Modeled on these abstractions, new pseudoscientific terms are created from ordinary and even vulgar words.
Thus the expression "I don't give a damn" produced the "I-don't-
give-a-damnism" — the indifference toward the State's ideals,
words, and deeds — against which everyone was supposed to fight.
Socialism has battled constantly against this "I-don't-give-a-
damnism," against the natural reaction on the part of a man who
doesn't give a damn about these constructions or this language.

Thus there exists at the core of the Soviet language a specific
jargon that the leaders use among themselves and with the people.
They speak not in words but in what I would call word-signals, the
implied significance of which no one, not even they, can explain.

One finds oneself faced with an institutionalized morass of abstract words that mean nothing but are nevertheless pronounced
with aplomb. This is the top, elite floor of the Soviet language and,
at the same time, its metaphysical foundation.

## The Spontaneous Element of Speech

The other, opposite aspect of the contemporary language is the
living, popular idiom, or spontaneous element. It too underwent
substantial changes with the revolution. The language of the people, having finally acquired its full rights of citizenship, engulfed
the literary language, consumed it. The street invaded the language. Of course, this already existed in the form of the popular
language, but it was isolated from the basic lexicon by the barriers
that culture, the language of cultivated society, class, and even
geography created. The language of the country differed radically
from that of the city. The language of the Ukraine, like that of the
distant provinces, had no access to the capital. The vernacular could
not penetrate the normalized language of intellectuals.

Now all these barriers came crashing down. The capital was
flooded with peasants and demobilized soldiers come with their

jargons and dialects from all corners of Russia. And these simple people felt themselves masters of the country, masters of the street and of the language. Under the influence of the new conditions and ideas, they were caught up in an irresistible current of linguistic creation, one at odds with the literary language. Because correct or overly sophisticated speech indicated an affiliation to the old ruling classes, the established linguistic norms became odious, socially suspect. The vernacular intruded everywhere, permeated everything, including the literature. Mayakovsky welcomed this change with great enthusiasm in his 1926 article "How Are Verses to Be Made?" To him, this new, popular language was like life itself and should stimulate literary creation:

> The Revolution cast the rugged idiom of the millions out on to the streets; the slang of the outer suburbs flowed across the avenues in the city center; the enervated burbling of the intelligentsia with their vocabulary of castrated words like "ideal," "principles of justice," "the divine origin," "the transcendental countenance of Christ and Antichrist" — all this kind of talk, once mouthed in restaurants, has been wiped out. A new element of language has been liberated. How is it to be made poetical? The old rules with their "moons" and "Junes" and Alexandrines are useless. How is popular speech to be introduced into poetry, and how is poetry to be extracted from popular speech? . . . Give the new language full rights of citizenship at once: the shout instead of the lilt, the thunder of the drum instead of the lullaby.[1]

To these lines one can contrast the purist verses of Symbolist poetess Zinaida Hippius who, on the eve of the revolution, had watched with horror as common words invaded verse, transforming the literary language and poetic style:

> *So many words with muddy hems*
> *That dared not enter . . . But now*
> *In humdrum flood they rush in*
> *Through the broken door!*

---

1. Translation by Alex Miller in *Mayakovsky*, vol. 3 (Moscow: Raduga Publishers, 1987), pp. 181–182.

*Rush in, kicking, covered with dust . . .*
*Street fighters cackling . . .*

The appraisals of these two poets conflict. But the fact is indisputable: the language of the street has won; it isn't just cluttering up the literary language, it is starting to define new literary forms. No barrier, no covering force, can stem this linguistic tide. Moreover, some of Russian literature's most interesting and important works in the revolutionary period and the twenties would be based on a broad assimilation of this new language: Blok's "The Twelve," Zoshchenko's stories, Babel's prose. The words are foul, dirty, incorrect, but they played a positive role in the emergence of new forms. They turned literature toward the living language in all its variety, insofar as it could assimilate this idiom. The literary successes that resulted were a function of this incorrectness, of the effect of this dense, unwonted language on the writer's ear. Literature after October, in a sense, made a new leap. And though certain writers and poets who cut themselves off from the new language also created beautiful works, they were like something stillborn, buried in the past, museum objects.

But it's not the strictly literary evolution that interests us as much as the language's popular and spontaneous element. This mass speech is distinguished primarily by its crudeness. This also is connected to the social upheaval that occurred in Russian life and in the Russian language.

Marina Tsvetayeva, in a 1917 essay, "October by Train," describes a journey to Moscow at the time of the uprising. In her car was a sailor who had stormed the Winter Palace.

> About this sailor. A stream of foul words. Others keep quiet (a Bolshevik!). Finally I, meekly: "Why do you swear like that? Can it really give you pleasure?"
> Sailor: "But comrade, I'm not swearing, that's the way I talk."
> The soldiers roar with laughter. . . .
> This same sailor, by an open window, at Orel, in a very tender voice: "What wonderful air!"

Two extremes live cheek by jowl in the Russian language: crudeness and tenderness. The sailor doesn't recognize his swearing as such, it is the standard accompaniment to his habitual speech. Obviously, he hasn't just learned to swear, swearing is part of his linguistic milieu. Before, he swore among his friends or in any case among his own. Now he swears at the top of his lungs for the whole car to hear, unperturbed by the presence of a young lady of the nobility, which Marina Tsvetayeva then was. Before, he wouldn't have dared make a sound, he would have kept quiet all the way to Moscow; now he is preening and crowing because he has the full power to say anything he wants, any way he wants. The language of the people has finally acquired its rights. And this means chiefly swearing and crudeness. Hence the coarsening of the Soviet language apparent even today.

When the critics reproached Zoshchenko for gratuitous crudeness, he objected: "Ordinarily they think that I twist the 'glorious Russian language,' that for a joke I use words in ways life never intended, that I purposely write in broken Russian to make fun of the esteemed public. This is not true. I twist almost nothing. I write in the language that the street now speaks" ("Letters to the Reader").

The street, of course, spoke in a broken language. But this coarseness and incorrectness produced a mass of new words that went unrecognized by dictionaries. Crude words corresponding to the spirit of the street; sometimes very apt and exact, sometimes word monsters.

The rapprochement between the language of the intelligentsia and that of the people was facilitated by the crude, simplified Soviet way of life that forced one to adapt to any language whatsoever. In the early 1930s, Zoshchenko published a letter from a reader who confessed to speaking one language at home, in her intellectual milieu, and another language entirely with her friends at vocational school. At home she spoke about her "friends" whereas at school she referred to them, vulgarly, as "the girls." If a boy accosted her, she would naturally say, "Shame on you!" But at school, it was: "Get away from me or I'll smash your face!" This cultivated young girl was divided between two languages. And, of course, the life, the mores, and the language were constantly pushing her toward popular speech. Unconsciously, young people today and even intellectuals of my generation address each other the way common people used to (by adding the suffix -*ka*): Mashka! Lenka! Yulka! Andryushka! . . . And this does not signify contempt but, on the contrary, warmth and intimacy.

This phenomenon is not purely the result of external pressure. An inner need emerged, to be simpler and cruder in one's language than one was in reality. The intelligentsia turned toward the people and tried to adopt the "simple life." Just as sometimes happens when a cultivated woman marries a simple man: she begins, almost without noticing, to use his vernacular. Metaphorically speaking, the Russian intelligentsia had married a muzhik.

But let's go back to the language of the governmental elite, to that of the muzhik seated on high. On the one hand, his head is full of the artificial language made up of abstract formulas, and on the other, the natural, crude, and semiliterate language he has known from childhood, which now bursts forth like some suddenly liberated principle of popular Russian speech. What is the result?

Khrushchev's memoirs are highly interesting from the point of view of the language.[2] His reaction, for instance, to the occupation of the Baltic countries in 1940, after the pact with Hitler:

> Now about Lithuania, Latvia, Estonia. This was already later, the appropriate measures had already been taken. And I, so to speak, in the details, aside from the newspapers, or, so to speak, on the basis of conversations I had had, that is, when I came to Moscow, with Stalin, that is. Well, these conversations were . . . they were also of that nature . . . so to speak, joyous because we, that is, now had the opportunity, because these Lithuanians, Latvians, Estonians would again, that is, be part of the Soviet State, that is. Well, in the first place, it's the expansion of territory and . . . the increase in the population of the Soviet Union. That is, and also the reinforcement of the State of the Soviet Union, that is . . .

2. *Translator's note:* Near the end of his life, Khrushchev dictated his memoirs, and copies of the tapes were sent to the West by a relative. These became *Khrushchev Remembers,* translated into English by Strobe Talbott and published by Little, Brown (Boston) in 1970. In 1971 Progress Publishers (Moscow) translated Talbott's English version back into Russian, but only top Soviet officials had access to this strictly limited edition. In 1989, the popular Soviet weekly *Ogonyok* (circulation three million plus) began running excerpts in the original Russian (from the original, unedited tapes) courtesy of Khrushchev's son Sergei.

What does this mean, not literally but stylistically? It means that many Soviet leaders cannot put a thought into words because they are illiterate, crude, and primitive. When these leaders give speeches on the radio or television, it offends the ears of any educated Soviet person.

The reaction to the crudeness and boorishness of the elite is best conveyed by a not altogether proper anecdote about Khrushchev who, preparing to appear before the U.S. Congress, had written a speech and given it to his aides to check. They read it and reported back: "Nikita Sergeyevich, it's perfect. Just one minor stylistic change: 'kick ass' is two words."

## THE BUREAUCRATIZATION OF THE LANGUAGE

The bureaucratic language, though a product of the Party apparatus, was never confined to it and has become a part of popular speech. Soviet life at this point is so regulated by the State and its ideology that bureaucratic clichés and euphemisms permeate the society from top to bottom. Blok pointed this out in "The Twelve," written two months after the October Revolution, in the language of the street, in the popular idiom. But already this idiom contains words from on high, borrowed from the bureaucratic lexicon, from the language of political meetings and the press, words that before would have been unthinkable in this illiterate street milieu; now they sound perfectly in keeping with the Soviet language.

Petka, one of the poem's heroes, commits a murder. He kills his beloved Katya; tortured with remorse, he turns to his comrades. They console him, first with crude jokes, then with some of the new stock political phrases:

> *Hey, Peter, shut your trap!*
> *Are you a woman or*
> *are you a man, to pour*
> *your heart out like a tap?*
> *Hold your head up*
> *and take a grip!*[3]

3. Translation by Jon Stallworthy and Peter France in *The Twelve and Other Poems* by Alexander Blok (New York: Oxford University Press, 1970), p. 153.

The last line echoes the countless Party declarations calling on the working class to keep its grip on society, on the factories and the plants. But here this propagandistic jargon has gone beyond the economic and political bounds to be used in everyday life.

Also in "The Twelve," we hear prostitutes talking among themselves, far removed from politics, but still affected by this new language brought by the revolution. Their linguistic model is the slogan inscribed on red banners — "All Power to the Constituent Assembly" — and hoisted into the sky, on the wind, hung throughout the city. The streets are full of these slogans, of these bureaucratic words that people don't understand but have seized on anyway to characterize the everyday atmosphere of the times. The prostitutes talk about a "session," "discussion," "motion," but carry their own "political resolution": to charge clients according to the number of hours worked, on a basis of equality, of democracy, and on that of the new lexicon:

> *The wind rejoices,*
> *mischievous and spry,*
> *ballooning dresses*
> *and skittling passers-by.*
> *It buffets with a shower*
> *of snow the banner-cloth:* ALL POWER
> TO THE CONSTITUENT ASSEMBLY,
> *and carries voices.*
>
> *. . . Us girls had a session . . .*
> *. . . in there on the right . . .*
> *. . . had a discussion . . .*
> *. . . carried a motion:*
> *ten for a time, twenty-five for the night . . .*
> *and not a rouble less*
> *from anybody . . . Coming up . . . ?*[4]

But this is just the beginning. As Soviet civilization becomes more entrenched, so will this language. And it will become increasingly bureaucratized as the bureaucracy becomes more and more of a force in society.

4. Translation by Stallworthy and France in *op. cit.,* p. 143.

This language has two essential aspects. First, it is estranged from normal human discourse. It is a word divorced from its original meaning. It is an emasculated language in which words do not denote things but symbols or conventions, accepted by the State but often without any relation to reality. Second, it is an extremely standardized language, its norm or basis being the handful of stock words and locutions most often used in Party propaganda and political agitation. It is a very constant and very limited vocabulary that tolerates no synonyms. The normalized language in Soviet society is that of the clichés that abound in the Party press and are received as the actual basis of the system. Take, for instance, this slogan: "The Soviet people unanimously support the resolutions of the Twenty-fifth Party Congress." This is an alienated language, because nobody remembers or has any real idea what was decided at the Twenty-fifth Congress, but this is also a standardized language that must confine itself to words that have been approved, such as "Party Congress," "Soviet," "unanimously," "people," "support" . . .

However impoverished, absurd, and cut off from life, this bureaucratic language carries a lot of weight in Soviet society. In Mayakovsky's *The Bedbug,* it's not a Party bureaucrat but Prisypkin, a simple worker until very recently, who announces at his wedding: "I want to get married in an organized way." And later: "I declare this wedding open . . ." as if he were at a Party meeting.

The bureaucratization of the language occurs at all levels, if with different, sometimes contradictory aims. Two examples:

The first, from Zoshchenko's story "The Honest Citizen" (1923), is a denunciation sent to the militia by the most pedestrian, most illiterate of Soviet types.

"Being, of course, on the level, I declare that apartment No. 10 is suspicious as regards moonshine which, most probably, is being concocted by citizen Guseva who, what besides that, charges workers through the nose.

". . . And also, as an honest citizen, I declare that that girl Varka Petrova is suspicious and loose. And that when I goes up to Varka, she turns squeamish.

"You can arrest or do whatsoever you sees fit with the above-mentioned persons.

"For now, I also declare that this here statement has been checked by me, since I'm on the level and down with the opium of the people, even though I've been fired, owing to a reduction in staff, for the truth . . ."

Here you have popular speech, in all its unaffected crudeness, peppered with officialese. Why? Solely so that the authorities will listen to and believe the informer.

But this verbal demagoguery can also be used to positive ends, to convey the most human emotions, as in this second example, from a story by Alla Ktorvaya of the new emigration. A maid is speaking to a top Party official:

"So, you think that if I'm illiterate that means I don't know anything. No, Comrade Commander, I don't know any less than you do! You think, so Lenin died, so now there's no one to stick up for us illiterates. Sure, Lenin died, but Leninisma lives! Tell you the truth, I used to think that Leninisma was Lenin's wife."

The meaning of these official locutions is immaterial, it's their formal aspect that counts. Even without understanding the words, the people know which language to use with a superior, and not to stint. Because the bureaucratic lexicon and phraseology are all-powerful in the new society.

A personal experience with verbal demagoguery: In the early fifties at Moscow University, a colleague and close friend asked me to be on the jury at the defense of a thesis he had supervised. The thesis, written by a Vietnamese, was on Mayakovsky. It was well done, but its Western-educated author had relied heavily on Hegel, quoting him throughout, and given a positive assessment of Russian Futurism. Both were crimes from the point of view of Soviet ideology. Naturally, I gave the thesis a favorable review. But the academic council questioned these two points. It was then that I had to resort to verbal demagoguery. "Comrades!" I said. "This is the first thesis written by a Vietnamese" — this was during the Vietnam War — "and not just on anyone, but on the premier poet of the Russian Revolution, on Vladimir Mayakovsky! Wouldn't it be a political mistake for the academic council not to approve it?"

These few words worked like magic. The thesis, with all its criminal inclusions, was unanimously approved. It wasn't so much the logic that did the trick as the incantatory power of the official language.

The most standardized language of all is that of the press. A Soviet newspaper doesn't only inform readers, it preaches to them, infused with the spirit of Party policy and the slogans forever being dinned into the mass consciousness. Using the same stock words over and over again is a cardinal rule of the journalist's trade: the slightest deviation from the norm is viewed as a political mistake, as a crime.

In 1937, Partizdat (the Party publishing house) brought out a collection of articles about the unmasking of "enemies of the people," of "wreckers" and "spies"; one entry was devoted to enemy methods in the press. Evidently, one reporter had taken the liberty of calling Germany "a highly industrialized nation." For this he was accused of being a Nazi sympathizer working for German intelligence. Another journalist, in an article attacking Hitler, made the mistake of quoting one of the Führer's speeches. This quote was interpreted as an aggression, as pro-Hitler propaganda. To quote an enemy in the press was unacceptable, even when accompanied by criticism. This was what was known as "giving the floor to the enemy." Misprints were another sin:

> Misprints have multiplied over the last two or three years. And most of these misprints differ from previous ones in that they twist the phrase in an anti-Soviet spirit. . . . The usual technique with misprints is to change or omit one or two letters so that the phrase takes on a counterrevolutionary meaning. For instance: "covert" instead of "overt," "fair warring" instead of "fair warning," and so on. Often the "not" is intentionally dropped so as to grossly distort the sense.
>
> The enemy resorts to all these devices and disguises wherever vigilance is slack. Sometimes he changes whole words: "socialism" is replaced by "capitalism"; the "Spanish" turn into "fascists"; "enemies of the people" into "friends of the people"; the "theoretical level" into the "terrorist level," and so on.

This vigilance leads to the standardization of the language, especially that of the press. It is a language of clichés through which nothing filters.

And as the Soviet State grows, so does the extraordinary pompousness of the official lexicon. If in the beginning peasants were known as "peasants," in the 1930s they became "collective farmers," and since the Second World War they have been called — in the press, on the radio, and even in verse — "grain-growers," a still more solemn appellation.

Another example: When the Arlequin cinema in Paris began showing exclusively Soviet films, it was renamed the Kosmos because this sounds impressive and official. Arlequin was too frivolous for the Soviet language, laboring under a sense of its own dignity and superiority to all other languages, including Russian.

The pompous style of the Soviet press also has to do with the fact that Soviet man is, officially if not in his own eyes, the most important person on earth, living in the greatest country in the world. Thus one cannot say that he rides a camel since the word "camel" is too crude, too ludicrous; he must ride a "desertgoing vessel." And if he finds himself on a steamboat, it must be known as a "liner." Surrounded by these grandiloquent words, he inhabits a make-believe world or, in any case, one that looks down on reality. The language doesn't so much reflect reality as replace it.

The abusive language of the press plays the same role, only aiming in another direction: to blacken the enemy or anyone who thinks or lives differently. Lenin himself pioneered this language long before the revolution, tarring his ideological adversaries with labels that doubled as stinging political accusations. One eyewitness, Lenin's onetime associate Nikolai Valentinov, wrote in *Meetings with Lenin*:

> Lenin could hypnotize the crowd with words; he beat his comrades over the head with his rhetoric to make them relinquish one idea or another. Instead of long explanations, a single word could provoke, as in the experiments of Professor Pavlov, "conditioned reflexes." In 1903 and the beginning of 1904, the word was "Akimovism"; in subsequent years it was: "likvidator," "otzovist,"

"Machist," "social-patriot," and so on.[5] The only way to save oneself from the mesmerism of these clichés was to go far away from Lenin, to sever the connection.

These labels proliferated in the Soviet language. Leaders of Western states and parties were "capitalist sharks," "agents of imperialism," "fascists" (including those who merely disagreed with Soviet policy), "double-dyed reactionaries," "traitors to the working class." Prosperous peasants were "kulaks," while the poor peasants who refused to join collective farms were "subkulaks." Intellectuals who expressed some doubt or showed compassion for people were "rotten," "spineless," "petit bourgeois." Trotsky was "Judas-Trotsky." Anyone arrested on political charges was an "enemy of the people"; anyone who had his own opinion was an "ideological saboteur." A misused word, a letter of protest or a displeasing literary work equaled "ideological sabotage."

This terminology is meant to arouse fear and disgust in the people vis-à-vis anyone out of favor with the Soviet power. And like the solemn, pompous language of the bureaucracy, these derogatory labels influence Soviet citizens and society. They prompt the same conditioned reflexes, and at times the Soviet man has utterly false notions of the world and even of himself.

I remember one incident in a Moscow bakery in 1949 or 1950. Bread was being rationed, two kilos to a person. When one man — maybe he'd come in from the country — wanted to buy three kilos, the cashier balked. And he started screaming: "So, we're living in America, are we? It's only in America they won't sell you more than two kilos!" What struck me then was that nobody smiled. Either they all took this man's statement at face value or they pretended to. Not that the Soviet press literally wrote such things. This outpouring was less a function of ideology than of language,

5. *Translator's note:* V. P. Akimov (1872–1921) was a Menshevik and leader of the economist movement. The likvidators were a Menshevik group (1907–1912); they demanded that the illegal revolutionary party be liquidated. Otzovists (Recallers), a Bolshevik group (1908–1909), demanded that Social Democrats be recalled from the Duma. Ernst Mach (1838–1916) was an Austrian physicist who pioneered empirical criticism. Social patriots was a pejorative term applied to Social Democrats who supported their own "bourgeois" governments (Russian, German, etc.) during the First World War.

which constantly associated "America" with the words "unemployment," "poverty," "slavery" . . .

Or here's another incident, which I learned about from a history
teacher at a school for adults in Moscow. At an exam, in the early
sixties, a young man drew the question: "Who made up the coalition of the Great Powers in the Second World War?" He said
nothing. The examiner, thinking he didn't understand the word
"coalition," rephrased the question: "Which countries were our
allies in the last war?" The young man was still silent. The examiner persisted: "In the war against Hitler's Germany, whose side
was America on, ours or Hitler's?" Then came the calm reply:
"Hitler's."

This young man hadn't gone through the war and couldn't remember it, but from the papers and the radio he knew about
"American fascists" and "American warmongers."

The crudeness of this abuse directed at the adversary does not
mean, however, that the language of the Soviet press is crude. On
the contrary, it has been cleansed of everything but the stock
phrases and strictly established forms to which even the harshest
political attacks are confined. Which makes for an odd duality in
the Soviet language. In day-to-day life, people express themselves
extremely crudely, as do their leaders, away from the public arena.
But this natural speech has little bearing on the official language,
which has always been forced to maintain a certain purism, especially under Stalin. Beginning in the thirties, many good and recognized Soviet writers were attacked for using vulgar words, popular
expressions, dialects, and bits of slang. They were accused of ruin-
ing, of fouling the great Russian language, though theirs was the
language the Russians actually spoke. Typically, the first salvos
against Solzhenitsyn's *One Day in the Life of Ivan Denisovich* (1962)
were fired at the language. Too crude, they claimed, though everyone knows what sort of language is used in a labor camp.

This defense of the language's purism has to do with the fact that
the Soviet press is afraid of colloquial speech and oriented, directly
or indirectly, toward the official, strictly standardized language of
the bureaucracy. A language hypocritical in its purism, since its
principal aim is to hide the truth.

Hence the plethora of euphemisms. In a Russian salon of the last century, so as not to say "She's pregnant," one said, "This lady is in a delicate condition"; similarly, in Soviet political parlance, a prison is an "isolator," a concentration camp is a "corrective labor colony," and Soviet prisoners must refer to themselves as "convicts." Why? What's the difference? Before, one said "prisoners," but after the revelations about Stalin's camps, the word was too odious. So to get rid of all the prisoners, they renamed them convicts. And to call oneself a convict was to acknowledge that one had been judged according to the law.

It's impossible to guess what word will be replaced by a euphemism next. After the revolution, the word and idea of a "priest" disappeared from official usage. In life as in literature, it was replaced by the vulgar word *pop*. But what to use in official documents? Priest? Impossible, since this suggests something sacred. Thus an official phrase was coined: "servant of the cult."

When the anti-Western and anti-Semitic campaign was launched in the late 1940s, the press began referring to Jews as "cosmopolitans." Or, in the more pejorative form, as "homeless cosmopolitans." Everyone knew who was meant, but the word "Jews" was never articulated; the euphemism "cosmopolitan" replaced the unmentionable but implied "Jew." The Soviet Union is still waging war against "world Zionism," a term as amorphous and terrifying as its brother "world imperialism."

The official Soviet language likes vague, indeterminate phrases: "certain circles in the West," "certain agents in foreign intelligence," "certain drawbacks yet to be overcome," "certain collective farmers who have not fulfilled the plan," "certain writers," "certain critics" . . . But exactly which ones isn't made clear. This formula, in the press, sounds nebulous and threatening. It may refer to something insignificant ("certain drawbacks") or very serious. "Certain" could mean anyone; it is a cloud hanging over anything unpleasant or inconvenient to the power.

Thus the Soviet language dissembles and mystifies, trying all the while to persuade itself that it is right. Moreover, it insists on its own interpretation of many foreign terms such as "democracy," "humanism," "human rights," or "constitution": "The whole world knows that genuine democracy exists only in the Soviet Union." Real humanism is proletarian humanism, as opposed to bourgeois, abstract humanism. Given this, genuine humanism is mass executions, while genuine democracy is dictatorship. "Imperialists" are those we attack, while "fascists" are liberals shouting about justice . . .

The language is used not only as a substitute for reality, but as a substitute for language. The language as a means of communication among people has been turned into a system of incantations supposed to remake the world. Which is why it is so difficult for Westerners to have a dialogue with the Soviet press or State.

Even a Soviet citizen who wants to understand is hard put to parse this murky language. True, he's helped by having had a lot of practice: he knows that words signify other than what they mean, perhaps even the opposite. But what they are hiding, what specific facts, is hard to guess.

The American journalist Hedrick Smith, who spent three years in the USSR, gives a good idea of the Soviet press and the language it uses to address the people in his book *The Russians* (1977). Here is Smith's account of the Soviet press report of Khrushchev's death:

> When the man who had ruled Russia for most of a decade died, the Soviet press was struck dumb. For 36 hours, we waited for a word about Khrushchev. Finally, there appeared a tiny item at the very bottom right-hand corner of the front page of *Pravda* and *Izvestia* . . . one solitary sentence announcing the death of "pensioner Nikita Sergeyevich Khrushchev," squashed beneath a fat harvest report and a profile of the visiting King of Afghanistan.[6]

Yet Soviet journalists, especially those in prominent positions, conduct themselves with aplomb. "We do not fear criticism," Aleksandr Chakovsky (editor-in-chief of *Literaturnaya Gazeta*) loudly declared while receiving some American correspondents. This large, imposing man, whose "I" is as overblown as his girth, expounded on Soviet life with ostentatious sincerity, and couldn't stop saying: "I'll tell you honestly" or "Let me give you an exhaustive answer to that question."

Indeed, these protestations of sincerity and promises to answer any question became as much of a stereotype as expressions like "the

6. Hedrick Smith, *The Russians* (New York: Ballantine Books, 1977), p. 490.

whole world knows" implying a blatant lie or deception. But some Soviet citizens are able to decipher the press, to read between the lines. After Stalin's death, a friend of mine left for the Caucasus. There she received a telegram from her mother: "Return immediately." Back in Moscow, she learned that Beria had been shot and disturbances were expected in the Caucasus. Why had her mother sent the telegram? She had read a long article on "friendship between peoples" and concluded that in the Caucasus they were already drawing knives.

This reading between the lines can produce positive results, but it can also lead to error. When the papers talk about unemployment in America, most readers take this to mean that there is no such thing. Such is the reverse effect of the official language. Some readers, giving in to this language, imagine hunger throughout America (as we saw in the bakery episode). Others decide that everybody in America is rich. Hence the drama of émigrés who go to the West expecting to find paradise on earth. And still others are scared to leave, believing that in the West there is nothing but poverty and crime.

All this comes from the fact that the official language is unreliable and opaque, giving rise to myths and to fantastic rumors. Such as the hearsay that the Soviet Union had never launched a single satellite into space, or a rocket to the moon, that this was only propaganda. This denial of the most obvious facts indicates that people have stopped trusting the language. The more solemn the announcement of a victory, the less believable it is.

## THE POPULAR WORDSMITH

If the official language has made deep inroads on popular speech, it has not taken it over or exhausted it. The living, colloquial language, far richer and more interesting, continues to exist, not apart from but in constant contact and exchange with this official idiom.

By "popular wordsmith" I do not only mean an inventor of new words. Many existing words were suddenly on the move, turning up in odd places, out of context, loaded with a new emphasis and emotional content. The oldest words — some of them forgotten and now revived — as well as the most common ones sounded in a new way.

The current official form of address in the USSR is *tovarishch* (comrade) or *grazhdanin* (citizen). These terms replaced the pre-revolutionary *gospodin/gospoda* (sir/gentlemen) and were intended to underline the idea of democratic and, later, socialist equality. Meanwhile "sir," stripped of its civility, assumed an ironic, threatening tone. To call someone "sir" was to express one's distrust, to suspect connections with the old order, to insult; in forty years, I never heard the word used in a positive sense. It signified "gentlemen capitalists," or gentlemen of old ("landowners" and "tsarist generals"), or "enemies of the people"; sometimes it was said that these "gentlemen" of the left and right wanted to overthrow the Soviet power and that they had miscalculated.

When I grew up, I was naturally "citizen" or "comrade," terms which, however, are not semantic equivalents. "Citizen" is more severe, more distant, and one must be able to grasp these subtleties. In the street, anyone may address a stranger as "citizen" or "comrade"; both are equally polite and nondenominational, their nuances having been erased by usage. If one asks a passerby, "Citizen, can you tell me where such and such a street is?" or "Comrade, can you tell me where such and such a street is?" the meaning is virtually the same. But if a militiaman were to stop me for crossing the street in the wrong place or because he wanted to check my identity, he would say: "Stop, citizen!" or "Your papers, citizen!" He would never say "comrade!" As for me, I would say "Comrade militiaman," never "Citizen militiaman." If I did, he might think I'd just come out of prison or camp. But the fact that I say "Comrade militiaman" when he says "Citizen!" conveys the relationship between the rank and file and the power. Even if the power treats you coldly as a "citizen," you must respond in a warm, comradely way and say "comrade!" By the same token, if I am speaking at some official meeting or scientific conference, or simply saying hello to my colleagues, I say: "Comrades." "Citizen" here would be stylistically impossible. But if I am arrested, if I am on trial, I must say: "Citizen investigator!" or "Citizen judges!" This indicates that I have ceased to be a comrade to all Soviet people. And also that between the technical synonyms "citizen" and "comrade" there exists a complex and subtle hierarchy that every Soviet person senses unconsciously.

The subtleties increase when addressing a woman. At work or at a meeting, I can say: "Comrade Timofeyev considers that Socialist Realism is such and such, but Comrade Trifonova and Comrade Semyonova disagree . . ." On the street, however, I would feel uncomfortable addressing a woman as "comrade." If I were to say, "Comrade, can you tell me where such and such a street is?" it would sound slightly absurd. Either too "Party," or too familiar, too playful. Because what sort of "comrade" is she to me? Besides, "comrade" is a masculine noun and thus sounds odd when used to address a woman. True, there is the other official term: *grazhdanka* (citizeness). But this word, because of the specificity of the Russian language (the feminine suffix *-ka*), seems less respectful than "citizen." What to do? I say: *grazhdanochka* (good citizeness). These affectionate diminutives, typical of Russian, lend the official term greater warmth and politeness.

Originally, "citizen" and "comrade" were full of fervor and exultation. But their different historical origins took them different ways. "Citizen" was introduced into general usage by the revolution of February 1917, after the fall of the autocracy. It derived from the events and language of the French Revolution and evoked La République (and its motto, "Liberty, Equality, Fraternity"). If we refer not just to the documents, but to the historical novels devoted to this period in France — such as Victor Hugo's *Ninety-three* or Anatole France's *The Gods Are Athirst* — we hear the lyricism of this new official term: "Citizens." More than a century later, it was articulated on the streets of Petrograd with no less exultation, as attested to by "Revolution (A Poet's Chronicle)" (April 1917), Mayakovsky's first response to the February Revolution:

> *Citizens!*
> *Today topples your thousand-year-old Before.*
> *Today the foundations of worlds are revised.*
> *Today,*
> *to the very last coat-button, you're*
> *to start remodeling everyone's lives.*
>
> *Citizens! . . .*[7]

7. Translation by Dorian Rottenberg in *Mayakovsky*, vol. 1 (Moscow: Raduga Publishers, 1985), p. 69.

The word "citizens" here sounds like a revelation in the language and in human relations. One imagines that after February, people of all different classes threw their arms around each other on the streets of Petrograd and shed tears of joy: Finally we are citizens and not the loyal subjects of His Imperial Majesty! But this enthusiasm didn't last long. The October Revolution turned the republic into a "democratic dictatorship," which in reality led to the absence of all freedom and democracy, under the sign of still greater equality and fraternity. The word "citizens" was thus legitimized by the Soviet power, but then quickly assumed the cold, formal character of an acquisition from the past. As a complement to "citizen," as an expression of this new stage of history and new socialist life, the term "comrade" was introduced.

The word had two sources: First, narrow Party confines, where the term had long been used and implied mutual confidence. Second, old popular Russian usage, in which it signified a friend, contemporary, acolyte, or collaborator. Hence the old Russian proverbs and sayings: "The goose is no comrade to the pig"; "The servant is no comrade to the barin"; "Ivan is no comrade to Maria"; "The pope is no comrade to the devil"; and so on. The word suggested a closeness and equality of relations. It was fairly widely used, though never on a mass scale: "comrades" were two or three people with close ties; the word did not apply to anyone on the outside or to anyone one didn't know. But after October, the word became applicable to everyone in the sense of fellow citizens, colleagues, friends. And for certain people, as Blok said, it was a "marvelous word." A word full of promises and one rooted in the Russian language. In his 1918 poem "The Scythians," Blok used this word to signify a new, universal fraternity where men would no longer be enemies. Addressing himself to the West, Blok wrote:

> *Come to us — from your battlefield nightmares*
> *into our peaceful arms! While there's*
> *still time, hammer your swords into ploughshares,*
> *friends, comrades! We shall be brothers!*[8]

8. Translation by Stallworthy and France in *op. cit.*, p. 163.

If the word "comrade" became so widely and organically accepted in the new revolutionary life of the people, it is because it had a warmer sound — more friendly, more brotherly — than "citizen." "Comrade" evoked notions of the Soviet people and, ultimately, all of humanity as one big family. Which is why the word sounded so marvelous at first, and simple, tied as it was to the popular language like something new and yet age-old. Humanity, with this word, would bar enmity's way. "Comrades" in the language of socialism could be compared to "brothers" in that of Christianity.

But over the years even "comrade" lost its original meaning; it became formal and devoid of all emotion. It also began to sound hypocritical and blasphemous since, in reality, no comradeship emerged. "Comrades" was only what the new masters wanted the slaves to call them, in recognition of the fact that this new slavery was the best and fairest system of human relations in the world. The boss became the "comrade boss," and the commander the "comrade commander," though they weren't comrades at all, and thus this word took on a false ring in people's consciousness. At a certain stage in the development of Soviet society, there was a reaction against it. Though "comrade" is still commonly used today, its value has depreciated; some people or groups try to avoid it, or give it an opposite, inimical meaning.

At a meeting, I once heard a religious man contrast the terms "comrade" and "brother":

"We are brothers in Christ! All men are brothers in Christ! But who are we in Antichrist? We are comrades!"

Fortunately, Russian is sufficiently rich and inventive not to confine people to the official terms "comrade" and "citizen" in addressing one another. There is also what one might call the language of kindred relations. The Russian people and language still retain traces of the old, patriarchal family, which included the entire people and, by extension, everyone on earth. On the street a simple man will often address an older man he doesn't know as *otets* (father) or *papasha* (daddy); a contemporary as *brat* (brother), *bratets*, or *bratok* (variations of "brother"); a younger man as *synok* (little son) or *vnychek* (little grandson); and a much older man as *dedushka* (little grandfather) or, more familiarly, *ded.* In addressing a woman he doesn't know, he might say: *mats* (mother) or *mamasha* (mommy); *sestritsa* (sister) or *sestryonka* (little sister); *dochka* (little daughter); *babushka* (granny) or, more crudely, *babka*.

All these words, more than their official counterparts, speak to the heart. Incidentally, when the war with Germany broke out and Soviet troops began being defeated, Stalin, in his first radio address, appealed to the people as "brothers and sisters" which, coming from the Party's leader, sounded very odd. But under pressure, Stalin knew he had to appeal to the big family, that neither "citizens" nor even "comrades," but only "brothers and sisters" could save him. This style in State speeches didn't last long, however, since the Soviet regime is far removed from man and remembers its "brothers and sisters" only in extremis.

This familial aspect inherent in the language is a relic of Old Russia that the Soviet language not only adopted but expanded. As if the people, weary of official relations, longed to return to the familial idiom, whose terms they revived and infused with new meaning and emotion. As a member of cultivated society and living in Moscow, where everything is fairly standardized, I felt this acutely when, on the street, instead of "citizen," I was suddenly "daddy" or "brother" or "little grandfather" or "little son." (This happened quite often for the simple reason that I started wearing a beard rather young.) Here it wasn't the observance of hierarchy that mattered, but the desire to imbue the language with greater warmth, with familiarity or intimacy.

Another familial form of address is *zemlyak* (fellow countryman) or *zemlyachok*. It once signified a kinship by locality. Now the locality in this word has disappeared. I once heard a Russian muzhik address a Kirghiz as his fellow countryman. Here the term conveys nothing but the friendly disposition of one man toward another, usually a stranger. Similarly, one may address a passerby as *droug* (friend) or *druzhishche* (old fellow).

In the end, one observes a curious linguistic paradox. Schematically, one could say that the words "citizen" and "comrade," supposed to unite the people, actually divided them. And that it is the language, sidestepping the rules, that attempts to fill this void, this cold alienation, and searches for new forms of human contact.

I remember that during the war — I was very young — an older soldier called out to me with the words: "Hello, war!" "War" was a sign of kinship with many men united by a common fate. "War" sounded warm and friendly, it meant: "We can trust each other, we're members of the same family, children of the same fate, we understand each other." At the same time there was something terrifying, a bitter irony: "You are war, little boy, and so am I, an old man, there's nothing but war around us and no end in sight . . ." Here, in this one word, cheerful support and encouragement shone through: "Steady, war! Because you are war! I've gone through the whole war and I'm okay, war!"

In the mid-sixties — when I was no longer Comrade Sinyavsky but "citizen the accused" and "citizen prisoner" — I found myself in an utterly new and astonishing surround, that of Soviet camp. Linguistically astonishing, for one, since gathered together in this limited space was the entire Soviet Union. People of all classes, creeds, and nationalities, of all ages and all fates. A Georgian addressed me as *katso* (friend). A former priest asked me: "Where have you come from, slave of God?" A former thief said mockingly: "So, *pakhan* (smalltime godfather), how's it going?" There were all sorts of stand-ins for the terms "citizen" and "comrade." A young Russian approached me and said, "Gospodin Sinyavsky"; a Ukrainian, "Pan Sinyavsky"; a Latvian, "Mister Sinyavsky." To say "comrade" or "citizen" would have sounded indecent, since those were official words scorned by prisoners. A few years later, I was standing in a crowd of other prisoners when a man came running up to me from headquarters. He was one of those ex–police officers who had worked for the Germans during the war and now, as prisoners, worked for the camp authorities. "Comrade Sinyavsky!" he yelled. "The boss wants you!" This "Comrade Sinyavsky" sounded so incredible and so comical I burst out laughing and the whole crowd with me. When the poor man tried to correct himself with "Citizen Sinyavsky! The boss wants you!" the crowd laughed even harder. If a boss could say "citizen" to a prisoner and vice versa, this was unacceptable among prisoners, whose relations were assumed to be equal and brotherly. The word "comrade" was doubly taboo. The bosses themselves, since Stalin's time, had forbidden prisoners from using this word with respect to free Soviet people, since they were enemies of the people, not comrades. If by mistake or habit a new prisoner called the prison doctor "Comrade Doctor," the instantaneous reply was: "I'm no comrade to you." Also, the word "comrade" had become repugnant to prisoners, since it was associated with the Communist Party and the Soviet regime.

Consequently, the word "sir" was revived in camps and among the dissident intelligentsia. But this was more than simply the reinstatement of a prerevolutionary civility. Now it was said as if to distinguish a new fraternity, a proud reference to the human dignity of everyone in it. If one takes the entire history of Soviet society — from the beginning of the revolution to the present day — one sees that the word "sir" has come full circle. Initially humiliated, destroyed, it went on to recover its dignity and even triumphed over "citizen" and "comrade." But this is not a repetition, it is an ascending spiral. "Gentlemen," in its current usage, is opposed to "comrades" and yet refers back to it; it implies greater friendship, greater comradeship. On high, the "comrades" are, in fact, our masters — or "gentlemen," as they used to say. But we, here, are "gentlemen" and in fact, among ourselves, comrades.

In one's own milieu, one can say "gentlemen" or *bratsi* (brothers); or, like soldiers, *rebyata* or *khloptsi* (boys); or *muzhiki* (even with refined intellectuals). But one no longer says "comrades" or "citizens": these words are too dead for the living language.

One last example. The day I arrived in camp, I was approached by an old man with a wild, bushy beard. He was, as I later learned, a Pentacostalist. "Man! Man!" he said. "Here's something you need!" And he handed me a homemade pen: this was the greatest gift he could offer me, a man. Evidently he had heard that I was a writer and had decided to give me this pen as a token of his esteem. His present amazed me, but his words even more so: "Man!" No one had ever called me that before. I had been called many things, but this was the first time I had ever heard the word "man" used in this way. Suddenly it dawned on me that all these synonyms, all these names we use in conversation, in living communication, are only pale copies of the word "man"; assuming, of course, it is not an empty term, but a logos full of tragicomic intonations, love, and sorrow, even if before you — a strange "man" — stands another strange "man." The Pentecostalist's "Man" included everyone, from Adam to each one of us. He had resurrected the word in its original sense. This could not have been done, I suppose, without the experience of Soviet history, without that of the camps and prisons, without that of the loss of all denominations . . .

For its multiplicity of synonyms, Russian is one of the first languages in the world, perhaps even the first, the richest. This is due, notably, to the fact that a great many foreign words from various countries and peoples entered the language at each stage of its development; they took root and, beside indigenous words, began to live a Russian life. This led to an immense diversity of synonyms, but also to hybrids of meanings and styles. At certain junctures in Soviet history, this process was accelerated, words combined and multiplied in a chaotic flood. In reality, this did not always equal good; the civil war, for instance, saw a proliferation of synonyms concerning mass executions and summary justice. Here colloquial speech exhibited a cynical wit and ingenuity while shyly avoiding any overt references to executions or death, or else conveying this as something simple, prosaic, easy, and even funny. Thus, instead of the verb *rasstrelyat'* (to shoot), one uses *razmenyat'* (to break), *spisat' v raskhod* (to write off, in other words, to cross off the list), *shlyopnut'* (to spank), or *otpravit' k Dukhoninu* (to send to Dukhonin[9]).

In 1921, Maksimilian Voloshin wrote "Terminology," a poem composed entirely of new synonyms for execution and torture. Even the title has a tragifarcical ring, grotesque or nightmarish. This is not a word game but an attempt to present real events through the prism of language: men are turning into beasts for whom the business of murder has become a daily, if not pleasant affair.

> *"They took aim,"*
> *"Put him up against a wall,"*
> *"Wrote him off"* —
> *Thus the nuances of daily life and speech*
> *Have changed from year to year.*
> *"To clap," "to wreck,"*

9. Dukhonin was a general brutally murdered by mutinous soldiers in 1917. As one of the first acts of summary justice, it staggered the imagination: simple soldiers had up and killed their commander in chief. Also, the name Dukhonin is associated with the word *dukh* (spirit): to kill is to expel the spirit and send it to heaven, to the Holy Spirit. A.S.

*"To send to be spanked,"*
*"To send to Dukhonin at headquarters,"*
*"To break"* —
*You can't put it*
*More succinctly or scathingly than that*
*Our bloody beating . . .*

Voloshin ends with the thought that this terminology will leave its mark, will resurface not just in the language, but in reality.

*We'll all be standing on the deadline,*
*All lolling on lice-infested litters,*
*All split open by bullets in the back of the head*
*And by bayonets in the groin.*

At the same time, the development and use of synonyms in colloquial Russian speech often attests to an astounding creative energy. An ability to understand and call things by their names which I would not hesitate to compare to poetic art, to artistic creation. Except that here the artist is the people, even if they are not always conscious of this artistry, even if they are only talking.

One evening in the late 1950s, I happened to be at Moscow's Savelovskaya Station — a small and unpresentable place, fouled, chaotic, and meant for the rabble, the "draftees," laborers, and tramps conscripted to work in Russia's great north, near Vorkuta — with a French friend, a Slavist. We were going to Pereslavl-Zalessky, a small town, a sliver of ancient Russia. Late at night, our train was announced. But to get into our car was impossible. A crowd — armed with sacks, trunks, crying children, and appalling language — was taking the train by storm. We stood on the platform, waiting for the passions to subside. A little gnome of a man skittered past, disheveled, ragged, and also resigned to not getting on the train. Spinning around and indicating the crowd, the hurly-burly, the people crushing each other so as to sit down first, he exclaimed: *"Shalman!"* But with such emotion, such despair, and at the same time a sort of deadly delight: *"Shalman!"*

Naturally, my French Slavist said: "What? What did you say?!" A fine connoisseur of the Russian language, he wanted to pin down every rare or unfamiliar word. By way of explanation, the gnome blurted out: *"Bardak!"* Again the Slavist expressed his puzzlement. But the little man, unaware he was talking to a foreigner, only said, *"Kolkhoz!"* and disappeared into the fray.

This all happened in the space of about ten seconds. These three words were meant to sum up the situation, each new word, from the speaker's point of view, amplifying on the one before. Borrowed from different registers, they all mean the same thing to a Russian. *Shalman* is thieves' slang for a den or, as they say, *malina* (literally a "raspberry," figuratively "to be in clover"): this is their retreat, their refuge. A place to unwind, to drink, to sing songs, to meet women and lead the fast life between forays. As regards Savelov-skaya Station, *shalman* meant chaos, merry and yet menacing, since many of those getting on the train were thieves.

*Bardak* is the equivalent of a brothel. But in Russian it sounds both cruder and more encompassing, an allusion to anything disorderly or slapdash. One can say: This isn't a factory, it's a *bardak;* this isn't a country, it's a *bardak.*

Finally, *kolkhoz* is a perfectly official Soviet term designating a social and economic organization, the collective farm where the Russian peasantry lives. But in this case, it signifies ruin, negligence, disorder.

Interestingly, this series of synonyms follows a progression, an ascending order: *Shalman! Bardak! Kolkhoz!* Each new word is more exact and more execrable than the one before. And the last word, *kolkhoz,* explains the meaning of the first two.

Meanwhile, this phrase sounds like a poetic definition, like an artistic formula, composed of a babel and blending of different jargons. This is the Soviet language in its living expression. Its colorfulness is in the juxtaposition of disparate lexical and stylistic sequences, the horrible and the beautiful merged in a model of the marvelous grotesque.

## THE NEW FOLKLORE

Out of this mix came the three principal genres of Soviet folklore: the chastushka, the thieves' or camp song, and the anecdote.

Russian folklore, in decline around the turn of the century, was suddenly infused with new life by Soviet power, which unwittingly suggested new forms by prohibiting the freedoms of thought and speech.

These three genres of the new folklore — chastushka, camp song, and anecdote — though also acting in tandem, can be arranged in historical order. The first, having appeared before the revolution, flourished during the first years of Soviet power. It's no accident that Blok's "The Twelve" is made up of chastushkas.

These short couplets were sung by young factory workers and peasants. Born in the suburbs, they made their way to the country, where they replaced the old Russian song, long, drawn-out, and lyrical. By their style and construction, these couplets are good for a day, distinctive in their daring, crudeness, and mischief.

> My darling's like a calf
> Except for one thing:
> My calf eats slops,
> My darling doesn't!

But full of spirit and verve, they take in everything the life and language have to offer. The peasant girl sings:

> Don't curse me, Mama,
> For going to the library,
> I'm not killing time,
> I'm keeping up with politics.

In the twenties and thirties, the Soviet power used the chastushka as mass folklore, even commissioning poets to compose new, Soviet chastushkas. But since folklore is an organic creation and cannot be made to order, anti-Soviet chastushkas also appeared: protests in the same Soviet language, except that here the words tended to mean what they actually meant. Take the official term *myasozagotovka* (meat procurement), in fact the surrender of cattle or meat to the State for almost nothing. Or the State bonds that all Soviet citizens had to buy annually in the form of an additional tax. There was also a chastushka about the ruin of the countryside in the early thirties, but composed entirely of the official language:

> All the wheat goes abroad,
> The oats go to cooperation,

> *The women go to meat procurement,*
> *The girls go to bonds.*

There are some astonishing chastushkas, epitomizing one or another period of Soviet history. For instance, the war and postwar
years. Here, in four poetically impeccable verses, objective and
devoid of emotion, the entire Soviet way of life is expressed:

> *The girls love lieutenants,*
> *The women love drivers.*
> *The girls love for money,*
> *The women love for wood.*

But despite their modern language, these quatrains refer to the
past. As do the thieves' songs — the second echelon of Soviet
folklore. The most current and most promising genre is the third,
the anecdote.

The Soviet Russia of today — and that of recent decades —
abounds in anecdotes, oral ways around the bans on the written and
printed word. What does this spoken word do? In a broad sense, it
goes beyond the language's border, beyond that which is received
by society as the norm.

Hence the division of contemporary anecdotes into two categories: the obscene and the anti-Soviet. Both are inspired by a desire to
go over the line drawn by Soviet censors, to express the essence of
Soviet life and language.

Leaving the ribald anecdotes (which would divert us into general
linguistics) aside, I will focus on the anti-Soviet variety. Noting,
however, that this qualifier was invented by the Soviet power. In
fact, these anecdotes are the ultimate development of the Soviet
language. Their spice is in the word, but taken to its truly comic
extreme.

Thus, Lenin's centenary gave rise to slews of anecdotes pushing to
absurdity the idea of a nationwide celebration. They all began with
the ostensible fact that every enterprise would have to produce some
sort of commemorative item: a perfume called Lenin Scent, or a bed
for three inspired by the motto "Lenin Is with Us" — a formula that
corresponded exactly to innumerable official slogans.

Another anecdote, tied to the mass exodus of Jews from the

Soviet Union, said that in Leningrad there was only one Jew left and her name was Aurora Kreiser (the Russian word *kreiser* — cruiser — comes from the German and sounds Jewish). Every Soviet person knows from childhood that the October Revolution began with a salvo from the cruiser *Aurora,* the signal to storm the Winter Palace. The *Aurora* is a sacred relic shown to tourists, remembered on the radio and in the press, celebrated in poetry and in prose. And suddenly this stock word is exploded with the transformation of the cruiser *Aurora* into a Jewish girl named Aurora Kreiser.

All of Soviet history could be told through anecdotes. For the anecdote is always immediate, coming hot on the heels of events. Even in the cruelest times, the anecdote persevered. Better yet, it flourished precisely because it was prohibited and flouted this prohibition. In the USSR, people were followed, sometimes imprisoned, for telling anecdotes; under Stalin, they could cost ten years in camp. But the harshest measure only abetted new anecdotes about their would-be decimation. Take the one about the lecturer who gave a talk on the successes of communism, then asked: "Are there any questions?" The Jew Rabinovich stood up and said: "That's all fine. But I have one question: Where can I get some butter?" A year later, the same lecturer was back and winding up another talk: "Are there any questions?" Another Jew, Haimovich, stood up and said: "I won't ask you where the butter is. What I want to know is, where's Rabinovich?"

The same goes for anecdotes: they are ineradicable. Given no freedom of speech, no freedom of the press, people take to the anecdote the way a duck takes to water. Thus it has become the leading folklore genre, the constant companion of Soviet life, with great influence over the modern language. But despite its belonging to the opposition, the anecdote is neither marginal nor alien to Soviet civilization. It is the natural fruit and adornment. Linguistically, it is the product of the official Soviet cliché which, when translated into colloquial speech, sounds absolutely ludicrous.

It's no accident that many anecdotes revolve not around an event but around a word. In the political anecdote, that word is the official stock phrase.

Question: What is democratic centralism? (The Communist Party is founded on the principle of "democratic centralism." This is obviously pure scholasticism, but such is the cliché.) Answer: Democratic centralism is when everyone individually is "against" and everyone together votes "for."

Question: "So, Rabinovich, is it true? Have you gone into the Party?" Rabinovich looks warily at the sole of his shoe and says: "Why? Does it smell of shit?"

Many anecdotes hinge on the materialization of metaphors hidden in the language. A figurative expression is taken literally, materially, exposing the illogic, the absurdity. The dead word, the cliché, comes back to life through its materialization.

Sometimes an anecdote can seem trivial, insignificant. Taken separately, every anecdote certainly is a negligible grain. But taken en masse, they attest to the people's vast and fertile linguistic creativity. These grains and their new shoots keep the Soviet language from ossifying and express its vitality. The hero of the anecdote is the word: the word-hero. If, purely speculatively, one were to imagine that Soviet civilization had disappeared, its traces would be found in the anecdote's word-hero.

# 8

## Hopes and Alternatives

I HAVE TRIED here to consider Soviet civilization as a whole, in its classical form, minus deviations from the norm. This normal, classical Soviet civilization could exist, in principle, for a very long time. It reached its zenith under Stalin, notably after the Second World War. Since Stalin's death, it has gone into a decline, one which, however, does not necessarily herald the demise of this system. The first signs of decomposition were evident with the emergence of the "dissidents."

The term "dissident" signifies objector, renegade, dissenter, heretic, heterodox, in conflict with the official doctrine. Specifically, Soviet dissidents are people who, since the latter half of the fifties, have contradicted the Soviet State and its ideology. They are a perfectly organic, natural phenomenon; not products of "ideological sabotage" or "bourgeois influence," as the Soviet State would have had one believe. Dissidents are not class enemies or elements alien to Soviet society, but the children of this system now in decay.

Therefore, the word does not apply to opponents of the Soviet power or past critics: the Whites or the remains of the old intelligentsia. Pasternak, Mandelshtam, and Akhmatova were not dissidents, though they were heretics, heterodox voices in Soviet literature. With their nonconformism they anticipated dissidence and paved its way. But they were tied to the past, to prerevolutionary traditions in Russian culture. The dissidents are a new phenomenon, exclusively the result of Soviet reality.

## DISSIDENTS: WHO ARE THEY
## AND WHERE DO THEY COME FROM?

The dissidents appeared forty years and more after the October Revolution. The West's sudden interest in them has to do with the fact that they are Soviet people, raised in Soviet society and yet in conflict with it. This is their superiority, for the West, over the first and second waves of Russian emigration. The old, White emigration began just after the revolution. It possessed a quantitative and qualitative advantage over this new dissident wave. In the early twenties, some cities in Europe — Berlin, Paris, Prague — became preserves of Russian culture. As if the Russian elite had replanted itself beyond the borders of Soviet Russia.

Nevertheless, the West remained relatively indifferent to this oppositional wave. Partly because the Western liberal intelligentsia was infatuated with the revolutionary ideas and ferment in Russia. After the First World War, Soviet Russia struck many as the only source of something new, of hope for social justice. The West very often refused to listen to the first emigration, which found itself intellectually marooned. Stories of atrocities committed by the Cheka fell on deaf ears. This distrust was bolstered by the fact that the Whites had an obvious interest in seeing the prerevolutionary order in Russia restored. The Western intellectual elite reasoned: Yes, these people have suffered, one can sympathize, they have lost the power, their land, their possessions. But they are all former landowners, former capitalists, victims of the revolution who therefore hate it. They are Russia's past, its doomed past, incompatible with the Soviet power and so without a future. Their only goal is to bring back their past.

The dissidents are Soviet people of recent formation who go beyond the framework of class or political concepts. They are the Soviet intelligentsia, raised under the Soviet power, with no social roots in the past.

How did this come to pass? Why did yesterday's members of the Komsomol — the Young Communist League — turn into today's dissidents? When did the era of Soviet dissidence begin?

In my view, the dissident movement in Russia began in 1956, when Khrushchev, at the Twentieth Party Congress, read his historic speech about the mistakes made during Stalin's personality cult. People knew about these "mistakes," these crimes, before Khrushchev chose to talk about them — and knew much more than he chose to say. Thus for many, the importance of his speech was not the information it contained, but the fact that the government had confessed to committing crimes against humanity, against its own people, and even against the Soviet power and the Party. The obvious conclusion here was that the State-Party system was vicious if it had not only allowed but also committed all these crimes to which it was now confessing.

But the Soviet leaders would not and could not go that far. They asserted, against all logic, that despite these crimes, the Party and State policy was correct. Stalin had erred, but not the Party, which was leading the country to a radiant future, to communism.

This extreme inconsistency in the official revelations prompted the emergence of the dissidents. The crimes confessed by the State were so real, so monstrous, and the State's explanation so naive and so stupid, it came down to pure sophistry, to verbal sleight of hand in the form of one flimsy phrase: "the personality cult of Comrade Stalin." The cause of it all. But now this cult was finished and everything was fine.

This explanation and the very term "personality cult" contradicted all the laws of Marxism, according to which no one man, no matter how great, plays any sort of independent role in history; economic forces, the masses, and class interests decide everything. So then, whose class interests did Stalin's cult represent? And how could Stalin have steered history all by himself? Every Soviet citizen learns, from childhood, to mock those bourgeois historians who ascribe everything to the will of individuals: tsars, commanders, heroes. Soviet historians used to love to tell the story about the scholar who claimed the reason for Napoleon's fall was that he had a cold during the Battle of Waterloo, a cold that caused him to lose and changed the whole course of European history. And now this "cold" was being palmed off as an explanation for the personality cult of Stalin who, they said, had a bad character, a character that changed the whole course of Soviet history.

This was unbearable to listen to not just for Marxists, but for anyone with any sense. Millions of Soviet people had been murdered and all because of Stalin's personality cult, tolerated by the Party despite the laws of Marxism-Leninism by which it nevertheless continued to be guided.

But if the State persisted in its refusal to answer questions, individuals began asking those subversive questions of themselves and those around them: Where was the Party looking when Stalin was in power? Where was the guarantee that Stalinism — created and backed by the Party — wouldn't repeat itself? The people who asked themselves these questions and who answered in their own way can already be called, in part, dissidents.

Thus one can say that dissidents first appeared in 1956. Again, not because the Twentieth Congress opened their eyes, but because it didn't provide a single serious explanation for Stalinism or any serious guarantee that this would not happen again. People were supposed to listen to this news and then go quietly home without giving it any thought, trusting in the Party as before. But many people could no longer blindly believe and not think. Dissidence is thus an intellectual movement first, a process of independent and courageous reflection on the mysteries of the history and system of the Soviet State.

In his memoirs, Vladimer Bukovsky describes his reaction to the Twentieth Congress:

> What were these advanced ideas if they had produced Stalin? What was the Party if it, having promoted Stalin, was incapable of stopping him? The Party was either scared or didn't know — isn't it all the same thing? . . .
>
> At the same time, there was a lot of talk about democracy inside the Party, but to us it was unconvincing. Why should this democracy be limited to the Party. What about everyone else? Weren't they people too? We don't elect the Party, it elects itself. And now the same people who had produced Stalin, who had supported him, meant to reestablish a higher justice by means of internal democracy? The same scoundrels who had lied to us for thirty years about Stalin would now lie to us about Party democracy. Who could believe them?

This typifies the exchanges between novice dissidents, or one dissident's internal monologue. If these crimes were committed in our name (the name of all Soviet people), with our indirect or

passive support, how can we now be silent and not think? The
intelligentsia is compelled by nature to interpret life, to criticize, to
develop individual and social consciousness. Thus, the intellectual
task — the necessity of understanding all that had happened — was
combined with the sense of moral duty that makes a person think
independently.

This moral aspect is extremely important in dissidence. It's not
by chance that dissidents have been referred to as the "moral resistance." Or as one writer put it with such style: "The dissidents save
the honor of the population of a vast empire. They prove that not
everyone in it is rotten, they protect the heritage of spiritual
values."

To save the honor of one's people, or simply of man, is a moral
duty of the intellectual. But what does it mean, to "save the
honor"? One example: When Soviet forces occupied Czechoslovakia
in August 1968, seven Soviet dissidents went out into Red Square
with posters of protest. Did they really think they could stop the
tanks or change Soviet policy? Of course not. They knew they
would be arrested in a matter of minutes, that their demonstration
might even go unnoticed, that the handful of passersby wouldn't
necessarily understand what was happening. In practical terms, it
was a senseless undertaking. But this was a symbolic and moral
gesture, not just in defense of Czechoslovakia, but in defense of the
honor of the Soviet people, about whom one could no longer
say that they unanimously supported the Party and government
policy.

The activity and person of academician Andrei Sakharov, the
self-appointed conscience of the Soviet intelligentsia, illustrate the
role of the moral imperative in dissidence. One should note that in
him, these moral principles preceded all dissidence. In his memoirs,
Khrushchev alludes to the fact that Sakharov asked him not to go
ahead with tests of the hydrogen bomb. Sakharov's moral position
obviously conflicted with Soviet policy, and the conversation went
nowhere. But it's interesting that Khrushchev, though he disagreed
with Sakharov, called him a "moral crystal."

This example shows why the dissidents did not become a political
movement and why the political aspect of their activity and consciousness is restrained: they have no selfish interests nor do they

aspire to power; their means are peaceful, mainly intellectual and moral. In this they differ significantly from the Russian revolutionaries of the past. If they create a revolution, it is only at the level of ideas and social concepts.

This is also linked to the fact that Soviet history is a lesson in the dangers of policy becoming an end in itself: the blood and cruelty of revolution, which is where too much faith in the system can lead. Marxist-Leninists set out to remake the world. But this aim became repugnant to those who, from experience, knew its cost. Thus, among the dissidents, it is not deeds but words that matter most. Here they return to the time-honored occupations of the intelligentsia: thinking, speaking, and writing.

This formulation by the Russian religious philosopher Lev Shestov, at the beginning of the twentieth century (in *The Apotheosis of Groundlessness*), could apply to them: "Man begins to think, to really think, only when he has satisfied himself that there is nothing to do." This "nothing to do" implies those hopeless situations in which man finds himself, or sometimes entire generations. Several generations of the Soviet intelligentsia remained for too long in thrall to the State, mechanically doing as they were told. This only led to an impasse, a situation in which there was nothing to do but to start thinking and trying to explain what happened.

These are not abstract speculations. This marriage of thought and moral imperative can make dissidents even more ideological than their adversaries in the State system. A man in camp told me about his interrogation, and how the KGB investigator kept telling him that if he didn't get carried away with his ideas, he could carve out a wonderful career for himself, marry the girl of his dreams, buy a nice apartment, furniture, and so on. But this young man, still an ardent Komsomol member and dreaming of communism with a human face, was outraged by the old colonel's words and said: "If everyone thinks only about their own career and material prosperity, how are we going to build genuine communism?" The colonel spat back angrily: "And I thought you were smart! You're an idiot!" He had long since stopped believing in any communism, so that in fact the young dissident was a far more devout Communist than this representative of State power.

This was the classic refrain with respect to dissidents: "What didn't they have? A nice salary! An apartment! Could have lived like normal people, like everyone! But no! . . ."

That's the problem. Dissidents, unlike normal Soviet people, have interests that go beyond their own person: intellectual, creative, spiritual, or simply moral needs.

But other factors, too, stimulated the dissidents and helped them become established.

First, there was the revival of the various traditions of Russia's intelligentsia and literature, the most important being those of truth, humanism, and the need to live for something higher than one's own parochial concerns. At his trial, when Pavel Litvinov, grandson of a renowned diplomat, raised to be a Communist, was asked who had influenced him, he said: "The Russian classics." The judge was amazed: "How? In what way? Can the Russian classics really teach dissidence?" Yes. Providing one reads Chekov, Nekrasov, Tolstoy, Korolenko not just with one's eyes but with one's heart and receives these books as spiritual sustenance.

In addition, there were some traditions of twentieth-century Russian literature and even, oddly enough, of Soviet literature that influenced the dissidents. Paradoxically, many young Soviet people arrived at dissidence via Mayakovsky, via the revolution's officially recognized poet. In the early sixties in Moscow, young people began gathering by Mayakovsky's statue to read poems and argue about everything under the sun. For some, the statue on Mayakovsky Square became a baptism of fire, even the execution place of unofficial Russian poetry. Others waited there for the plainclothes agents they knew were coming. Thus Mayakovsky was transformed from standard-bearer of the revolution and the Soviet State into — for certain people at least — a symbol of opposition.

Why were dissident youth so drawn to Mayakovsky? His charm lay, first of all, in his rebelliousness, his nonconformism, his refusal to compromise, his utter lack of anything "bourgeois" or "establishment." Even his early nihilism and his desire to shock the stolid authorities now played a positive role in the forming of independent thinkers. Through Mayakovsky, they learned to abandon the stereotypes instilled by family or school and to look at reality with a fresh, unbiased eye.

Mayakovsky also represented access to new art, new poetry. For

Soviet schoolchildren and students, especially in the forties and early fifties during "Zhdanovism,"[1] all of modernism was banned, while innocent French impressionists were considered dangerous criminals. Mayakovsky was the only chink through which to glimpse that forbidden world of leftist art, the only way to transgress the law of what all the textbooks called "realism."

Schoolchildren and college students who wanted to know this forbidden world began with Mayakovsky and ended with Pasternak, Mandelshtam, and Tsvetayeva. Or they became passionate about Picasso, Braque, Chagall . . . Mayakovsky was often the catalyst for a more professional perception of art.

Soviet samizdat — the underground system of publishing — started with poetry, with the recopying or retyping of unavailable or forbidden verses. Four great Russian poets—Pasternak, Mandelshtam, Tsvetayeva, and Akhmatova — thus helped create dissidence. It's not by chance that today they are the most widely read, most respected writers among the Soviet intelligentsia.

It all started with the poetry lovers, mostly students, who retyped these verses for friends and friends of friends and acquaintances. They had their work cut out for them in the sense that they were rebuilding the bridges and restoring the severed connections between the two eras and the two cultures. Between the "silver age" and Soviet modernity.

Soviet civilization had cut the cord of cultural continuity: for at least forty years, it burned down everything that was original, everything that didn't square with its standards. These four poets became the idols of Soviet youth because they had gone through this scorched zone, this scorched earth of Soviet civilization, and had sown the green shoots now coming up in the new era.

The dream and prophecy of Maksimilian Voloshin, himself barred from literature after the revolution, had come true: "It is more honorable to be learned by heart, to be secretly, furtively recopied, to be not a book, but a copybook in one's own lifetime." Because a book is censored by the State, whereas a copybook remains independent and transmits the true voice of the author.

1. *Translator's note:* "Zhdanovism" stands for Communist Party control over culture at its most repressive, in connection with the notorious 1946 speech of Politburo member Andrei Zhdanov attacking Mikhail Zoshchenko and Anna Akhmatova.

Initially, samizdat was simply an attempt to get around the Soviet censor and connect with Russia's cultural past, an alternative literature that competed very successfully with the official one. The indestructible force of samizdat was in its complete spontaneity, its ungovernability, its mass nature. Anyone who wanted to could be self-published (the meaning of the word *samizdat*). Anyone could retype his own manuscript or someone else's and give the copy to a third person who, if he liked it, would retype it and pass it on to a fourth. Samizdat ran on the energy not of writers or publishers, but of readers.

A song written in the 1960s by Aleksandr Galich evokes the enthusiasm with which these readers tackled their work ("Erika" is a brand of typewriter):

> *"Erika" turns out four copies.*
> *Just like that!*
> *And that's plenty!*

Such is the fate of samizdat, bound to Russia's creative process and literary traditions. It goes beyond dissidence since it embraces everything that could not be printed, including many works from the past. But without samizdat, dissidence, whose only weapon is the word, could not have existed. Through the word and samizdat, dissidents rediscovered their true ancestors and free literary creation.

Yet dissidence is not, overall, a fact of literature, it is a fact of life. Everyone comes to it in his own way, proceeding from his own problems. For one person, the stumbling block may be the Jewish question, even if he isn't a Jew. One Russian girl I knew converted on the day of her entrance exams at the institute when she suddenly realized that the examiners were giving her excellent marks only because she was Russian, while the Jewish students, clearly brighter, all received bad marks.

For another person, this school of life may be the army. For a third, work in the country or the provinces. But it was the Soviet camps and prisons that exercised the strongest influence. Primarily through the prisoners themselves, amnestied or rehabilitated after Stalin's death. These were people of another generation, mostly old men, returning home after long terms to tell their own and other

people's stories, life experience that the young intelligentsia greedily consumed. In every house, these returnees appeared, heroes of
the day and the most desirable guests. Very often these were old
Communists or distinguished people once devoted to the Soviet
power. But time in camp had forced them to change, to reconsider
their ideals. Even if they couldn't be an active ideological force,
they served as a touchstone for Soviet dissidents. Their bitter irony
came out in their parodic name for the post-Stalin period: "the late
Réhabilitance" (by analogy with the early or late Renaissance). The
"Réhabilitance" was "late" in the sense that it was usually posthumous or only at the end of these unfortunates' lives. But even their
hard experience had the advantage of pushing the younger generation into action. These older people were coming back from camp,
to which they had been sent for no real offense, while the younger
ones were about to be sent off: it is in this context that a sort of
nostalgia for camp emerged. "Can I consider myself a man, an
honest intellectual, if I've never been in prison? Can I judge life if I
myself have never been through life's chief experience, that of
prison?"

It's not by chance that in dissident literature and samizdat,
memoirs about camps and prisons past and present occupy a central
place: Varlam Shalamov's *Kolyma Tales* (1980), Solzhenitsyn's
*The Gulag Archipelago* (1973–1975), Evgeniya Ginzburg's *Journey
into the Whirlwind* and *Within the Whirlwind* (both 1967), Anatoly
Marchenko's *My Testimony* (1967), and so on. The subject is not
exhausted, it remains interesting and current, at least in dissident circles, because it touches on an essential element in the life
of the individual and in the history of Soviet Russia: Soviet civilization as seen by its victims.

Morally, the experience of camp and prison becomes decisive, as
if it were the ultimate test of the dissident. He must not break,
must not repent, but assume the full responsibility for his words
and actions. He must confirm his dissidence with his behavior at the
trial, then in camp. There is a kind of camp ethic: if a dissident
breaks, he is no longer a dissident. This is what happened in the
1970s to Ivan Dzyuba, to Father Dmitry Dudko, and to the dissident leaders Pyotr Yakir and Viktor Krasin, who all pleaded guilty
and repented publicly. It is to this, to confession and repentance,

that the system of coercion devotes all its energy. One might think, what difference does it make legally whether or not the criminal confesses, since this changes nothing in the corpus delicti? But for the State, this changes everything; the principle, however, applies only to dissidents and prisoners of conscience — in other words, to those who are persecuted for their opinions, ideas, and words. Confessions and repentance are not demanded of thieves, murderers, delinquents, or embezzlers. For them, the State limits itself to the corpus deliciti. But dissidents are required to confess. In many cases, the person guilty of a serious crime gets off with a light sentence only because he confessed; whereas the person guilty of almost nothing is severely punished only because he refused to confess.

From a legal point of view, this is ridiculous. But this corresponds to the nature of the State and to that of dissidence. The State, as we have discussed, is more of a Church. And this Church, like that of the Middle Ages, aspires to control the souls, minds, and words of its subjects. It considers them coreligionists and punishes them harshly, like heretics, for any deviation from the form and letter of its religion. The Soviet heretic is pressed for one purpose: so that he will confess his sins. So that at least formally, in words, he will renounce his heretical ways. To do this, the KGB has developed a system of threats and promises, bribery and blackmail. One example: "Say you're guilty, and tomorrow we'll send you home. Don't say you're guilty, and we'll send you to camp which, given the state of your health, could kill you." More recently, the KGB has changed its tactics and assumed, at least outwardly, a more benign stance. But the basic tenet remains: there is only one true religion, State Communist. All the rest is heresy.

This belief is the basis for the use of psychiatric hospitals to "treat" dissidents. If a person persists in his nonconformist views, this means he is either an enemy or mentally abnormal. An ordinary citizen is considered normal when he agrees with the State on everything. To describe those who disagree, there are medical terms: "justice complex" or "criticism complex" or "personality hypertrophy" . . .

Rejection of the Soviet stereotype is considered a sign of mental abnormality. But the real sickness is in the society, with its stereotypes. To lock up nonconformists in psychiatric hospitals is to demonstrate, ad absurdum, its own mental deficiency, its own psychic sclerosis.

But this also says something about the nature of dissidence. It cannot renounce itself, its own conscience. Hence the sacred importance attached to the legal confession. A researcher, Boris Shragin, once wisely remarked that dissidents are people who have lost all sense of guilt before the Soviet State and the Party, and who therefore do not see themselves as guilty. Whereas any normal Soviet person always feels an actual or potential sense of guilt before the State.

This is not to say that dissidents have no sense of guilt whatsoever. It is their sense of guilt before the people, before history and their own conscience, that incites them to dissidence. Guilt not before the State, but for the State; they are ashamed of what happened and of what continues to happen, ashamed of themselves or of their fathers, who were silent for so long. From this sense of guilt, typical of the Russian intelligentsia, comes the consciousness of one's own responsibility, the will to speak the truth and to think for oneself. By refusing to acknowledge guilt before the State, the individual ceases to be a loyal subject and becomes simply a person, an independent person. And this has had enormous resonance in the sociohistorical existence of Soviet Russia. All the big political trials in the USSR were accompanied by confessions from the defendants. It had become a ritual, with the "enemies of the people" calling themselves just that. The dissidents broke this evil tradition and proved that people were people and not some abstract design divided into "friends of the people" (Bolsheviks) and "enemies of the people" (everyone else, even the people themselves).

Another major factor in the evolution of dissidence was the West. After Stalin's death, Soviet Russia ceased to be as isolated, as closed as it had been before. The iron curtain didn't disappear, but it became more transparent, more permeable. Large numbers of foreign tourists appeared; all sorts of meetings, contacts, and festivals were organized. Some say dissidence began with the youth festival in Moscow in 1957, the first mass exposure to Westerners. Little by little, the psychological barriers between Russia and the West began to crumble. Under Stalin, all foreigners were spies and enemies to be assiduously avoided. Acquaintance with a foreigner often ended in arrest. But now it turned out that foreigners were also people, that the West was not hell. Books arrived from there and manuscripts were sent out, returning in book form. Dissidents openly appealed to Western democracy, unafraid of playing into the hands of "world imperialism." And for its part, the West was fairly receptive to the voices coming from Russia. Its dialogue with dissidents proved more lively and interesting than that with the Soviet State under Brezhnev. This was a breach in the Soviet system and ideology. With the help of the dissidents, Soviet camps and Soviet "human rights" became the property of the West and subject to public debate. Subject to *glasnost*![2]

Soviet dissidents often address their statements and documents to the West because this is the only way to make them public, and thus the only guarantee against a return to Stalinism. Thanks to *glasnost* (openness), a person unable to change the regime and secure democratic freedoms can at least say what he thinks about this regime.

Soviet dissidence assumes many forms and aspects, and these are constantly evolving and changing. One joke definition has it that dissidents are not those who fight the Soviet power, but those whom the Soviet power fights. The Soviet power, of course, fights all ideological deviations. But among the various forms of dissidence, the cement, the nucleus, the connecting link, was the movement to defend human rights and democratic freedoms; or to make public the numerous violations of these rights in the Soviet Union. All people — writers, workers, believers, ethnic minorities, rightists, leftists — have an interest in seeing the most elementary of these rights respected, especially freedom of speech and freedom of conscience.

This struggle can strike members of the Western intelligentsia (particularly those of the left) as elementary, banal. Some ask why the dissidents don't fight for workers' economic rights instead of only for their own freedom, that of the intelligentsia. For the West, the right of free speech is so natural as to seem secondary or self-evident, like the air one breathes without thinking. But a dying

2. Here *glasnost* refers to the demand of the first dissident demonstration in December 1965. Later, Mikhail Gorbachev borrowed this term, evidently from the dissidents. A.S.

man does not take this air for granted and inhales it hungrily. For it is the basis of life. Just as freedom of speech is the basis of thought in evolution.

Most dissidents are intellectuals who value freedom of expression above all else. This is natural and even necessary given that their principal task has been to try to make sense of events and to put these thoughts into words. But it is on freedom of speech that the fate of other freedoms depends. One cannot defend workers' economic rights when it is prohibited even to talk about them.

On the other hand, in the Russian milieu of a nationalistic and authoritarian tendency, one sometimes hears it said that "human rights" are not the essential thing as compared to religious or spiritual needs. That may be true. But human rights are the minimum without which spiritual needs cannot develop or declare themselves.

Here we touch on a question of principle, a phenomenon that sparked the human rights movement. This movement fights not for "class interests." Not for land. Not for the tsar. Not for material privileges. Not even for democracy. It fights for the individual. After a hiatus of fifty years, the Soviet man suddenly discovered that he was a person, not an impersonal sociopolitical category. And he dared to speak out, not in a class voice or a Party voice, but in his own human voice. Dissidence reintroduced into Soviet civilization the notion of the individual.

## THE NATIONALITIES QUESTION

One of the most critical and controversial issues now facing Soviet civilization is the nationalities question. I see four basic reasons for its extraordinary complexity.

The first is the empire: the Russian Empire as it evolved over centuries and was inherited by the new system, and then the Soviet Empire — built on the ruins of the old empire — a larger and mightier power. Today it is unique in the world for the expanse of its territory and the number of its nationalities.

The second reason, oddly enough, is internationalism combined with great-power chauvinism. Internationalism, as we know, is the cornerstone of Communist ideology and policy, and is the opposite of great-power chauvinism. Given internationalist principles, the nationalist contradictions only seem more pronounced.

The third reason is the national revival that, in the twentieth century, has touched numerous peoples and led them to fight for national independence.

Finally, the fourth is the numbness and erosion of the Communist ideology in the Soviet Union, which needs a replacement and finds none. So, as a new stage of the empire's expansion, an openly nationalistic doctrine is advanced, and it comes into conflict with the national consciousness of other peoples. Thus the future of Soviet civilization largely rests on the nationalities question.

According to official Marxist, then Soviet dogma, internecine war and national discrimination are rooted in societies founded on class contradictions: the oppression and enslavement of certain nationalities by others are the result of a more general social oppression. This is why the nationalities question was never stressed by Marxists, who considered it a social question of secondary, indirect importance. With the destruction of classes and social oppression, all national conflicts would resolve themselves and disappear, making way for the equality and fraternity of workers of all countries, for a socialist concord of nations. This seemed axiomatic.

The Russian Empire, as compared to other empires and colonial powers, had the advantage of being able to annex other peoples and lands without leaving the continent. It thus expanded, rarely encountering serious obstacles. With a few minor exceptions, it assimilated neighboring lands, which were not considered colonies at all, but an integral part of the state, of a single, indivisible Russia.

In this expansion, the Russians have always had not only a military and economic advantage, but a numerical one, which allowed them to annex small, mostly backward peoples, such as those of Siberia. Poland was an exception in the sense of its cultural development and, for this reason, caused the Russian tsars many difficulties, with its desire for national independence.

Russian rule never took the form of a cynical oppression: the conquered peoples were generally not considered slaves or inferior races, but subjects of the Russian state entitled to "full civil rights." When Catherine II introduced serfdom in the Ukraine, this was considered a magnanimous act that gave Ukrainian peasants the same rights as Russian peasants. In the ideal (only), all loyal subjects were equal for the Russian emperor, regardless of nationality, unless they became "traitors" (i.e., refused to submit). This policy, this state psychology, and even this terminology still exist. When the USSR annexed the Baltic states in 1940, Latvians, Lithuanians, and Estonians who were disgruntled, or thought to be, were shot or deported en masse as "traitors to the Motherland," when it was they who refused to betray their motherland.

Thus the Russian Empire maintained relative stability. Which is not to say that it wasn't rent by national contradictions, created primarily by Russian great-power chauvinism, about which one can glean some sense from *Book of Memories* written by the Grand Duke Aleksandr Mikhailovich in emigration and published in 1933. A humorous and wistful reminiscence about his youth and upbringing, it is set in 1885. The place is an official course of education for members of the imperial family, future or potential tsars of Russia, in a spirit of strict patriotism. Called on to stand at the state's helm, they were thus required to distinguish themselves for the purity and precision of their conception of Russian history and politics, instilled in them by proven teachers and by the Orthodox Church:

> My spirit was burdened by a strange surplus of hatred. . . . It isn't my fault if I hated the Jews, the Poles, the Swedes, the Germans, the English, and the French. I blame the Orthodox Church and the doctrine of official patriotism drummed into me during twelve years of study for having rendered me incapable of feeling amicably toward these nationalities, which had done me no harm personally.
>
> . . . Every day my religious teacher would tell me stories about the sufferings of Christ. He corrupted my childish imagination and managed to make me see a murderer and torturer in every Jew. My timid attempts to invoke the Sermon on the Mount were impatiently dismissed: "Yes, Christ taught us to love our enemies," Father Georgy Titov would say, "but this mustn't alter our sense of the Jews."
>
> ". . . The All-Russian Emperor may not distinguish between his subjects who are Jewish and those who are not," was the response of Nicholas I to a report from the Russian hierarchs advocating that the rights of Jews be restricted. "He looks after his loyal subjects and punishes the traitors. Any other criterion for him is inadmissible." Unfortunately for Russia, my grandfather's ability to "think like a

tsar" was not inherited by his successors. . . . I had to make great
efforts to overcome the xenophobia sown in my soul by my professors of Russian history. . . . My "enemies" were everywhere. The
official notion of patriotism demanded that I always keep alive in my
heart the flame of "sacred hatred" for one and all.

This does not mean, of course, that every Russian school and the
Orthodox Church taught only this to generations of Russians. But
this example of official education shows what great-power xenophobia is. Both Russian society and the intelligentsia (especially the
revolutionary milieu) ultimately responded to nationalism and
xenophobia, to the doctrine of the Great and Indivisible Russia,
with a revival of the International.

When the Bolsheviks came to power, after the collapse of the
empire, they had to rephrase the nationalities question, which now
seemed far less simple than it had before the revolution. They
realized that the class struggle had not resolved everything. That
the freed peoples were in no rush, or else had no desire, to embrace
Soviet Russia; that under the flags of different countries, parties,
and armies, a system of national states was beginning to take shape
around the edges of the old empire. Thus the pieces of this crum-
bling country would have to be picked up all over again — under
the flag of a single, centralized power — by military, diplomatic,
and ideological means.

The restoration and expansion of the empire, renamed the Soviet
Union, was carried out in the same two fundamental stages that
characterized the treatment of the nationalities question. The first
stage was Leninist and internationalist. The second was Stalinist
and chauvinistic. These stages are not divided by strict historical or
even ideological borders: the principles of Leninist internationalism
continued to operate after Lenin's death, just as the Stalinist
chauvinistic tendencies are still in effect today. These two ap-
proaches to national politics, however, remain distinct in Soviet
history and in the psychology of the Soviet man.

The first stage of restoring the Soviet Empire was carried out
under the banner of the Communist International, a Lenin-inspired
revival of the international socialist fraternity of workers, which
called for freedom and equal rights for all nationalities, including

the right to self-determination. By themselves, these ideas are grand and noble. Freedom, peace, and the fraternity of all peoples on earth, the old dream of humanity's best spirits. Which is why the aims of the International seemed so compelling when the First World War revealed all the horror that could arise from strife between nations and from chauvinistic claims. Partisans of the old Single and Indivisible Russia had nothing to match these beautiful notions. This earned the Bolsheviks the relative sympathy and support of small nationalities as well as the goodwill of the leftist Western intelligentsia, of workers, and of colonial and semicolonial peoples.

But these internationalist ideas concealed a series of unforeseen dangers, most of which emerged only later. Despite their theoretical equality, the nations that made up the former Russian Empire were not equal politically, territorially, economically, or culturally. The Russian tsars, too, had tried to maintain a formal equality, at least in the ideal. In "Felitsa," his ode to Catherine the Great, in 1784, Gavril Derzhavin depicts the Russian Empire as the ideal kingdom, as a sort of "international" gathered round the Russian throne. He dreams of seeing all other peoples submit to Catherine, to her great and good protection. For Catherine is "celestial clemency incarnate"; she tends to the happiness of all her subjects regardless of their nationality and, if they obey, grants them freedom and autonomy. Derzhavin dreams of American Indians and other primitive peoples flocking to this universal, internationalist empire where the empress is all benevolence:

> Freedom I give you to think,
> To understand that I value you,
> Not as slaves, but as subjects . . .

This, of course, is just pseudo-internationalism and pseudo-freedom of nationalities living under the wing of a great empire. But if the empire wants to preserve itself, it must profess a relative "internationalism." It must pretend that all the enslaved peoples have come to it voluntarily.

Machiavelli, master analyst of the despotic state (and greatly admired by Stalin), wrote in *The Prince:* "No matter what country the Romans occupied, they always did so at the natives' request."

This illusion of an association desired by the natives has long been maintained, foisted on some indigenous peoples for centuries on end: "You wanted this, you asked for our fraternal aid. We only did you the great favor." Thus, "internationalism" goes far back in world history, to the time of the great empires, sometimes serving as justification for imperialism. Machiavelli's brilliant formula is universal, as valid for the Roman Empire as for Soviet troops going into Afghanistan at the summons of the Afghan people and government. In other words, at the natives' requests.

Not that Soviet Communist internationalism was always a fraud or a means of restoring the old Russian Empire. The continued annexation of new territories proceeded from the idea of world revolution and a single, universal, socialist state. In fact, this was imperialism of a new type, aimed not at one nation's predominance over others, but at a pan-national fraternity under socialism's wing.

Many tsarist officers, partisans of Great Russia, faithfully served the Soviet power because they saw in it the only real chance of reestablishing the Russian Empire. Later, after the civil war, certain representatives and ideologues of the Whites joined the Soviet power they had fought, again out of hope for Great Russia. For them, the Bolsheviks' internationalism was just a form — temporary, transitional, tactical — of great power. But for the Bolsheviks, at the start of Soviet history, it was hardly that: for genuine Communists, internationalism was (and remains) not a form but the only possible solution to the nationalities question.

The true revolutionary of Marxist formation does not accord his national affiliation an essential role. He lives and breathes the higher, universal idea of all humanity's liberation. He is ready to take part in the liberation of any people, ready for any revolution, since for him the international duty outweighs the national.

But the desire for a nonnational consciousness was only one of the manifestations or possibilities of the International. Curiously, in some circles it promoted an upsurge of national sentiment. This affected many peoples — including the Russians. The International was apparently meant to abolish Russian nationalism and to propose for the unification of nations means other than those advanced by the old empire, which was founded on Great Russian chauvinism. On the other hand, the revolution had raised the prestige of Russia in its own eyes and in the eyes of the world. By overthrowing the old regime, the nation had, it seemed, taken revenge for the rout of its fleet by the Japanese at Tsushima in 1905; for its defeat in the war against Germany; for its secular poverty and ignorance. At the same time, the nation had been robbed of almost all its national past, its religion, its traditions, and even its name "Russia." In exchange, it had been given a sense of national strength and vast, worldwide prospects. And Russian national sentiment assumed with the revolution and the International a messianic character; for many the Party hymn, "The International," was virtually the Russian hymn. This was one precondition for the degeneration of internationalism into great-power nationalism. But in the twenties, the International played a different role: one of its missions was to restore among the small peoples of the USSR their confidence in the Russian center and in unification within the framework of an integral State. This is why the Bolsheviks broke with Russia's past, cursing all the tsarist wars of conquest, cursing this Great Empire, this "prison of the peoples": now it had to be replaced by a voluntary union of national republics.

The principle of free consent is stressed by a point in the Party program about the right of nations to self-determination and even separation. This point is still part of the Soviet constitution, though long since a mere formality. Lithuania's efforts to become independent have not met with any support from the powers that be in Moscow. At first, however, it wasn't quite this way. Lenin himself insisted on the real right of national republics to independent status:

> As internationalists, it is our duty, first, to fight with energy against the vestiges (sometimes unconscious) of Great Russia imperialism and chauvinism in "Russian" Communists; second, to make concessions on the relatively minor nationalities question (for an internationalist, the question of state borders is of second-rate, if not tenth-rate importance). Other questions are the important ones: the basic interests of the proletarian dictatorship . . . the leading role of the proletariat with regard to the peasantry; far less important is the question of whether the Ukraine will or will not be a separate state. We must not be surprised — or frightened — even by the

prospect of Ukrainian workers and peasants trying out various systems and over the course of several years, let's say, merging with the RSFSR, then separating from it in an autonomous Soviet Socialist Republic of the Ukraine. . . .

To try to resolve this question in advance once and for all, "firmly" and "irrevocably," would be proof of narrow-mindedness or simply stupidity.

Lenin may seem uncommonly generous and tolerant in his interpretation of the nationalities question. But this is not really the case. Lenin is ready to make any concession as to the status of the Ukraine on one condition only: that it maintain the dictatorship of the proletariat, thus that of the Party apparatus and its leaders, who must be internationalists — in other words, loyal to Soviet Russia. And should they decide to build their Ukraine on other, non-Communist principles, they would become "bourgeois nationalists," which Lenin condemned.

Even so, Lenin showed great flexibility on the nationalities question and great faith in local and national Party cadres, precisely because he was a confirmed internationalist. He warned Communists of the majority nationality against the danger of Great Russia chauvinism, and demanded that they show the greatest tolerance vis-à-vis minority nationalities.

Lenin was well aware — and said as much in his articles and speeches — that if one didn't make some concessions to the small nations, they would become hubs of discontent and resistance. One would then have to revert to the old great-power practice, which Lenin, as an internationalist, did not want to do. This is why he so fought the Great Russia spirit sometimes exhibited by other Communists, whether or not they were Russian.

Given his cast of mind, the scope of his activities, his penchant for centralized power, Lenin was in fact a great-powerist, not a federalist. But he tolerated concessions to federalism in a bid to create a new, internationalist empire. These measures in no way threatened unification; if anything they reinforced it, at the same time making the Soviet Union into a sort of ideal model of the future Communist order, the prototype of a universal International. Lenin wanted this prototype to be beautiful so that the whole world would aspire to such harmony.

In one sense, however, this spelled the end of national cultures and the peoples' originality. Stalin's decree that these cultures be "national in form and socialist in content" did not depart from Lenin's policy; it, too, expressed the idea of proletarian internationalism.

Some may judge this formula acceptable. "Socialist in content" implies that they are united in the essential thing, united in one's being, united at a higher level: that of equal rights, fraternity, and mutual love. At the same time, "national in form" supposes a diversity and richness within this unity.

But if one applies this classic formula to historical reality, a horrible sight is revealed: the national principle is pure form, while the content, stripped of all allusions to nationality, conforms to a single, socialist standard. Practically speaking, this means that one can and one must glorify communism and the Party of Lenin and Stalin in Ukrainian, in Georgian, in French, in English, in Chuvash, or in any other language.

Language aside, the word "form" ("national form") implies and sanctions certain ethnographic details such as the lyrical evocation of one's native soil — "Ah, my Daghestan!" "Ah, my beautiful Kamchatka!" — or the national costume or folklore. Hence the many music and dance ensembles — from the Ukraine, Georgia, and so on — that journey to Moscow to demonstrate their devotion to communism and their gratitude for their national independence. The entire International is reduced to decoration, a perfectly natural result of Lenin's nationalities policy: the basis of everything is the "dictatorship of the proletariat," but sing and dance all you like around this dictatorship.

The old Russian Empire afforded the small nationalities and their cultures more latitude; they preserved not only the form, but the content: their way of life, their religion, their folklore, their economic system.

The twentieth century has streamlined many civilizations. What happened in Soviet civilization was somewhat different. It wasn't enough to just civilize, say, the peoples of Siberia: they also liquidated the shamans, the repositories of the pagan religion and the folklore — a folklore that happened to be among the world's most extraordinary and only very partially collected. In exchange, these peoples were given the right to study and to assume any position: engineer, professor, secretary of the Party's regional committee. In terms of career opportunities, they won. Any Yakut may, given the desire and the will, equal any Russian. He can read Pushkin in Yakut. But when I asked a Yakut, a professor of philology and a top Party official locally, if one could still find a shaman from whom to collect the Yakut folklore, he started to cry. Not because he was attached to his pagan past or to the shamans, but because his people had lost its nationality.

Thus, Leninist internationalism, in granting privileges to the small nations, precipitated, perhaps unintentionally, their elimination. And this internationalism naturally turned into great-power chauvinism, derived from the International as a theory of world supremacy which in practice was a totalitarian Communist dictatorship.

If the International began by proclaiming the equality and fraternity of all nations, its obligation to create a State based on a centralized power and a Communist dictatorship led to a great-power policy. But this was a spontaneous evolution, so much so that the transition from an internationalist extreme to a nationalist extreme was barely noticeable.

A good illustration of this is found in Mayakovsky's "To Our Young Generation" (1927). An honest and consistent revolutionary-internationalist, he welcomes this fraternity, this model of worldwide communism. He is also glad that every people may preserve its national identity. But he worries that these nations and republics will be isolated from each other by language: they lack a unifying principle. He proposes that they align themselves on the Russian language and on Moscow as the political center of the world fraternity of workers:

> *Young comrades,*
>
>     *keep eyes on Moscow,*
>
>         *train ears*
>
> *to Russian consonants, vowels.*[3]

3. Translation by Dorian Rottenberg in *Mayakovsky*, vol. 1 (Moscow: Raduga Publishers, 1985), p. 204.

Mayakovsky then explains why Russian is so important. It is not that the Russian people is superior to other nations. And it is not because he, Mayakovsky, is a Russian. He is even ready, as a true internationalist, to renounce his nationality. No, the important thing is something else:

> *Why,*
> > *were I a black*
> > > *whom old age hoars,*
> *still,*
> > *eager and uncomplaining,*
> *I'd sit*
> > *and learn Russian*
> > > *if only because*
> *it*
> > *was spoken*
> > > *by Lenin.*[4]

This priority given to Russian and to Moscow is ascribed solely to the fact that Moscow and Russia have become the center of the world International. After October, Russian would become the language of internationalism.

In a poem for children, Mayakovsky wrote, half joking, half serious: "The Earth, as we know, begins from the Kremlin." Later, under Stalin, it was said that the Russian people was "first among equals." If not for this "first" among "equals," the world International would have collapsed. Just as communism would have collapsed had it not been for the "dictatorship of the proletariat." Thus the idea of a "dictatorship of the proletariat," the dictatorship of one party, naturally led to the dictatorship of one nation, the dictatorship of Moscow.

In short, to make the International materialize, one had to resort to a great-power policy.

The historian and philosopher Fedotov noted that the Party became "more and more Russified" after Lenin's death. In the mid-twenties, a purge began among the top Party ranks against the "Judaification of the cadres." By 1927, the most visible Jewish

4. Translation by Rottenberg in *op. cit.*, p. 204.

leaders had been expelled from the Politburo, and later from the Central Committee. This campaign, of course, was not explicitly anti-Semitic. At first, it was linked to a general changing of Party cadres. A "new class," to quote Milovan Djilas, was taking shape: its core was no longer the revolutionary elite, but the conservative mediocrity, the man of the masses; and its composition — Russians and some Ukrainians — naturally reflected the national majority. The Jews and the Latvians who had played such a notable role during the first years of the revolution now, in the 1930s, left the stage.

In 1934, the heroic rescue of the *Chelyuskin* crew prompted Stalin to solemnly reintroduce the forgotten word *Rodina* (Motherland).[5] The word was a surprise since all official ideology until then had supposed that the actions and emotions of the Soviet man were determined by love for the revolution and for communism, by a feeling of fraternity and solidarity with the workers of the world, not by love for one's own country or national roots. Notions of the Motherland and patriotism smacked of the prerevolutionary past, of tsarist Russia.

It was no accident that this patriotic outpouring came in 1934, the year collectivization — the dispossession of the kulaks and enslavement of the countryside — was completed. The people had been deprived of their land, deprived of their national peasant organization. In exchange, the State played on the patriotic feelings of the people, presented as the greatest, the mightiest, and the happiest in the world. This tawdry sham of an ideology was meant to compensate for the irreparable national losses.

Henceforth, one would no longer march under the banner of the International, but under that of the Motherland. The word corresponds more exactly to the primitive mentality of the new class, with its thirst for a master, its slavish ways, and, at the same time, its reborn sense of dignity.

In 1937, the 125th anniversary of the Russians' battle — under Mikhail Kutuzov — against Napoleon at Borodino was celebrated

---

5. *Translator's note:* On a trial run from Murmansk to Vladivostok via the North Sea, the *Chelyuskin* was crippled by ice. The pilots who set down on the floes to save the ship's crew became the first Heroes of the Soviet Union.

with great pomp and saluted by the press in pieces whose style was as inflated as the language.

"In 1812, the soldiers of the Russian Army, despite their being serfs, showed the entire world the might of the great Russian people, who rose up as one against the foreign invaders. . . . The people shall revere this supreme patriotic feat for centuries to come!" (*Vechernyaya Moskva*).

Nothing extraordinary in this, one may say. Russia did ultimately defeat Napoleon. And the Russian soldiers did exhibit fantastic bravery even though they were, for the most part, former peasant serfs. The novelty and oddity are elsewhere: in the fact that class contradictions and dignity ceded to national sentiment. Setting aside all consideration of serfdom, of landownership, of the tsarist yoke — thus setting aside all Marxist-Leninist conceptions of history — the Russian people still turns out to be the greatest and the mightiest. Which is to say that in history, it is not class factors that prevail but national factors. That the Russian people is primordially stronger and better than all others. At this same point, in violation of all revolutionary-proletarian traditions, *Pravda* praised Field Marshal Kutuzov and published his portrait festooned with tsarist medals. This was the first time since the revolution that a tsarist general had been considered fit to "live eternally in the hearts of workers." Until then, this fate had been reserved for the great revolutionaries or rebels, like Spartacus, Stenka Razin, and Emelyan Pugachev. And now, suddenly, some tsarist generals — always deemed enemies of the workers and terrible reactionaries — acquired dignity in the eyes of the "Soviet man" and the "Soviet people." The internationalist "class principles" beat a hasty retreat before the grandeur of heroes, become symbols of Russian and Soviet great power.

Russian great-power nationalism and chauvinism reached their zenith in the late 1940s and early 1950s, in connection with the extraordinary resurgence of the USSR's military and political might after the rout of Germany and the annexations in Eastern Europe. All these conquered and dependent countries now had to be kept in check. Everything pointed toward chauvinism: the Soviet Union's aggressive policy, the cold war with the West, the abrupt increase in anti-Western sentiment. Propaganda's job was to present yesterday's allies — the British and the Americans — as accomplices of fascism. Having seized half of Europe, the ruling power had to prevent the European air from infiltrating the Russian metropolis. It was also necessary to compensate ideologically and psychologically for the terrible losses incurred during the war and camouflage with extravagant phraseology the low standard of living, the poverty especially obvious to officers and soldiers returning home from Europe. Thus the patriotic hysteria began, the limitless self-glorification.

Many accuse Stalin of having replaced internationalism with great-power chauvinism. He indeed lent a hand and led the country on a nationalistic course. He was a Russo-centrist. Svetlana writes: "All his life, my father had a strong and profound love for Russia. I do not know another Georgian who could have so forgotten his own national traits and had such a strong love for everything Russian."

In my view, the matter is more complicated. Lenin also loved Russia, and yet he opposed great-power chauvinism, one of his criticisms of Stalin.

Personality perhaps explains why Stalin, not being sufficiently Russified and remembering his Georgian past all too well, tried to rid himself of his nationality. First, as an internationalist who must minimize his origins. And then, as absolute ruler of a vast empire who, in this role, did not want to present himself as a Georgian.

Stalin did not want to be a Georgian tsar in Russia, but a Russian tsar, emperor of all Rus. Hence his taste for quoting the classics and old Russian proverbs, which he proffered in a tone of great wisdom. But he avoided Georgian sayings; his accent was enough.

He was not dissembling. Stalin sincerely felt that he served the interests of the entire empire and, notably, of Russia, as the majority nation, that he did not have the right to favor Georgia. They say that one historian, in an effort to insinuate himself into Stalin's good graces, wrote a paper claiming that Peter the Great was actually the illegitimate son of the Georgian ambassador to Moscow, the tsarevich Vakhtang. Stalin's written comment was: "A great man belongs to that country which he serves."

Stalin, of course, could not sever all connections with internationalism: this would have been a gross violation of Marxism as well as bad for the government of the empire and for contacts with sister nations and Communist parties around the world. But he emphasized a more centralized power, backed by the Party bureaucracy and Russian chauvinism. The thirties saw an intensive Russification of peripheral regions and the repression of local nationalism, which led to terrible reprisals against objectionable peoples. After the war, Stalin reportedly said that he would willingly have deported the Ukrainians — as less than devoted to Moscow and the Soviet power — except that unfortunately there were too many, so one couldn't treat them like the Crimean Tatars.

The international fraternity was not a success: peoples generally do not like to live in friendship, especially under one state roof, and especially when that state is a dictatorship, a centralized power. For socialism is not only the equality and fraternity of workers and not only the edification it has achieved. It is also a yoke, an ideological uniform, an alienation of labor, and in some measure an alienation of national affiliation. Even if this oppression is not exercised by the Russian people but by an anonymous State power that embraces everyone, it still remains tied to Moscow, to the Russian power. And it's pointless to argue that Russians suffer as much if not more than others, since the national minorities have a counterargument: the Russians made their own bed, let them lie in it! The Kazakh whose livestock has been confiscated by a collective farm is not comforted by the fact that the Russian peasant has also been robbed; for him, collective farms are a Russian invention. Even Lenin's policy in the early twenties of granting privileges to peripheral nationalities did not produce the desired results. Given a dictatorship, a person still wants freedom, especially national freedom.

Ultimately, as Fedotov noted in the 1920s, "the international patriotism of the Bolshevik party, as it decomposes, is giving rise to nationalisms — Great Russian nationalism and that of minorities — whose struggle is sapping the Party today, and tomorrow will place the question of Russia's unity in sharp and ominous relief."

Meanwhile, hope of a world revolution and of uprisings in various countries in Europe faded. A new policy of military occupations had to be put in place. Hence the Soviet Union signed the nonaggression pact with Hitler. And planted forced socialism, under threat of its bayonets, in every country it managed to occupy. The shift from the idea of revolution to that of military occupations naturally led to chauvinism.

Finally, another cause of Great Russian chauvinism lies in the closed nature of the Soviet State. A process which, curiously, began under the banner of the International and flourished thanks to it. In *Europe and the Spirit of the East* (1938), the German philosopher Walter Schubart, opponent of Bolshevism but passionate Russophile, called this

> a strange irony of history: international Marxism, which recognizes no national boundaries, is severely isolating Russia from all other peoples. Despite its manifest intentions, it is reviving national sentiment and spreading it among strata it never touched before. It is separating Russia from the rest of the world with a great Chinese wall. Russia has never been so given to itself as it is today.

One cannot develop internationalism in a closed state; it assumes that peoples are in constant contact, learning to know and to respect one another. But the Soviet State has been afraid to open its borders. The people, if you will, stew in their own juice and choose nationalism as the only meaning to their existence. They have the falsest ideas of foreign countries. Could it be otherwise? Aside from the propaganda, the isolation from the non-Soviet world plays a big part. The anecdote about the Frenchman telling his transportation problems to a Russian is indicative: "In the morning when I go to work," the Frenchman says, "I take the Metro since there's too much traffic and no place to park. On the weekends, I drive to the country. For vacations, I go abroad by plane." The Russian replies: "I do almost the same thing. I take the Metro to work. On Sundays, I take the electric train out to my dacha. But when I go abroad? I usually go in a tank."

Such a closed world naturally fuels all sorts of fears and phobias. And also a sense of superiority, sometimes based on an unconscious sense of inferiority. This is a phenomenon well known to psychiatrists which one observes on the scale of Soviet civilization.

Chauvinism, however, engenders the reciprocal hatred of other nations vis-à-vis Russia and the Russian people. The examples I will give here are decidedly extreme cases that should not be generalized but that do give one an idea of what the "friendship of peoples" entails and where it can lead: to a notoriously unjust expression of national intolerance. To illustrate the complexity of the problem and the difficulty different nationalities have understanding one another, I will quote discussions with some of my non-Russian friends. We were bound by a mutual empathy in that I was not a proponent of a single, indivisible Russia and felt that every nation should be free and independent, if not separate. But I also hoped that then there would be no shadow of xenophobia between us and that there would remain the possibility of cultural or simply human contact across the borders that would separate us in that utopian future. I wanted to believe that then the Russians would not be a bugbear for these peoples, that they might even inspire trust and understanding. All this went by the board.

My first conversation was with a Balt intellecutally influenced by Western Europe. He told me about the horrors committed by the Soviet Chekists against his people, about the barbarism of the Russification, about the obscenities scrawled on the old houses and the tombs of his ancestors by simple Russians come to live in his native city.

I tried to explain that much the same thing was happening in Russia, that the Russians desecrated their own temples and tombs, and that this wasn't entirely their fault but also that of Soviet ideology. He objected with reason: "Desecrate your own tombs all you like. But why did you have to come to us?" I said: "We didn't. The Soviet State occupied you. The Russian people have nothing to do with it." He said: "If that's the case, then they should try not to act just like the Soviet State."

I had only one argument left: "You know Russian culture, you love Russisan literature. Imagine as a kind of utopia that you were an independent nation — part of Western Europe, free of the Soviet threat — and that the passions had cooled. What good words could you say then to Russia and to its culture?"

And he said: "Not to know and to forget!"

My second conversation was with a Ukrainian nationalist, a modern intellectual. I expressed the hope that the independent Ukraine he dreamed of would still retain some spiritual ties to Russia. After all, I said, there are things that we share.

Him (with irony): "For example? What do we share?"

Me (as gently as I can): "We have a common cradle: Kievan Rus, out of which the Ukraine and Russia came."

Him: "Russia has nothing to do with Kiev."

Me: "Fine. Then take Kiev. That's not the point."

Him (interrupting): "Thank you very much for giving us our Kiev!"

Me: "But in the distant past, it's still Kievan Rus that produced Russian culture, which then migrated north. The Kievan epic songs were written in the Russian north."

Him: "You do not come from Kievan Rus!"

Me: "From where then?"

Him: "From the Mordvinian swamps!"

The irony is that this talk took place in Mordovia, in the camp where we were both prisoners. But I realized that he was thinking of the Finnish tribes that, before the formation of Russia, inhabited the northern territories of the future Muscovy.

Me: "But that's not serious! Russian culture, the culture of Muscovite Rus, is a great and complex culture and could not have come solely from some Finnish tribes."

Him (with a sarcastic laugh): "And you say you're not a chauvinist! But you don't want to be descended from the Mordvinian or Finnish tribes! You scorn them! They are too insignificant for you! You want to come from Kiev!"

I didn't take offense. Because the member of a majority nation cannot take offense at the member of a badly treated minority nation. His unfairness and intolerance were thus pardonable. I changed the subject, to Gogol, who can be considered as much a Ukrainian writer as a Russian one, and who revealed the Ukraine to Russian literature and to the entire world.

My interlocutor snapped: "You can have that Gogol, that traitor to himself! We don't need him!"

For him, Gogol had betrayed the Ukraine because he wrote in Russian. I tried to explain that, for precisely that reason, Gogol was able to make the Ukraine accessible to the universal consciousness, to readers around the world. That if, in the first half of the nineteenth century, he had written in Ukrainian, he would have remained a provincial writer and the Ukraine would have remained unknown. My logic and my philology had no effect. Gogol was a traitor because he wrote in Russian. Because he left the Ukraine for St. Petersburg and wrote about Russia instead of the Ukraine. In other words, he went over to the enemy side.

My third and last conversation was with a Moslem. He did not like Russians, which is understandable: he knew the old legends about the conquest of the Caucasus and had suffered himself. Deported as a child, he had watched his mother, grandfather, and little brothers die in a freight car during the transport. I naturally shared his sorrow, but I still tried to explain that Russians aren't that bad, that they are also men, not beasts. And that besides the Koran, there is also the Gospel, which contains the moral commandments of Christianity. Then I discovered that he made no distinction between Russians, Bolsheviks, Christians, and Europeans. I tried to make him see that Bolsheviks and Christians had nothing in common. But he insisted they were one and the same: conquerors, liars, murderers, violators . . . What about the Gospel? For him, this was not an argument. Christians do not adhere to the Gospel, whereas Moslems do adhere to the Koran and live by the truth. The Gospel for Christians-Russians-Bolsheviks-Europeans serves only to deceive. I pointed out that many peoples have committed atrocities. The Turks for instance, though Muhammadans, used to torture people by impaling them. He didn't believe me. He said that it was all a lie, because Muhammadans could not commit cruel or immoral acts, that this had been concocted by those dogs the Christians-Bolsheviks-Europeans-Russians to disguise their own cruelty. For him, the ideal system, the ideal state, was the Arabian Caliphate. He even idealized the Tatar-Mongol invasion of Russia: a handful of noble knights who, without any cruelty, for the sake of justice, conquered the immense Rus, cowardly and bestial. It's too bad they didn't conquer Europe . . . I couldn't believe my ears. But this was a very honest, kind, and intelligent man. It's just that Russia, which, for him, combined Christianity, Bolshevism, and Europe, had inflicted too much suffering on his little people . . .

This is why it's so difficult to build a veritable International on earth.

## We Are Russians!

The national character, any notion of the "popular soul" and its psychology, is a mystery that goes far back into the past and would require endless research. Thus, I will try to outline only a few tendencies of the Russian national character. With the proviso that these can be contradictory, divergent, or mutually exclusive, and that combined, they may add up to a bizarre picture. Given the difficulty of arranging this material in strict categories, let's consider the following a tentative sketch.

I would define the first Russian national quality as patriotism, however tattered the word may be in its Soviet usage. All people love their country. But for Russians, this can mean a mystical devotion to something vast, vague, even inexplicable. To "poor Russia," which one loves for its indigence, its humility. Or to "great and mighty Rus." And the old motto "For the Faith, the Tsar, and the Country!" can be translated into other slogans: "For the Power of the Soviets," "For the World Revolution!" or "For the Party, for the Cause of Lenin and Stalin!" But consciously or not, these are always based on the patriotic idea. Its symbols change, but it remains, ineradicable, without a truly rational foundation. Stalin knew what he was doing when he pushed the button marked "patriotism," even if he reduced it to its simplest, most vulgar denominator.

Russian patriotism cannot be equated, most of the time, with nationalism, though it fairly often engenders this and feeds off it. Still, the two notions are distinct. Blok, for instance, worshipped Russia but was not a nationalist. The Motherland for Russians is at times such a supraindividual and supranational principle that it becomes a sort of religious feeling. The State exploits this feeling, but it goes beyond all material idols, which change while the essence remains. And as with the religious consciousness, Russian patriotism often verges on messianism. Russia carries, or should carry, the world a higher idea.

If patriotism turns Russians into one big family, these familial relations are far from ideal and unusually frought with painful discord and civil strife. Friendships between Russians often end in fights over different interpretations of the concept of Motherland.

Another national trait is what I would call the Russian "shape-lessness." I do not see this as necessarily bad, but the Russian national character strikes me as somewhat amorphous, not com-pletely formed. In 1917, soon after the October Revolution, Vla-dimir Korolenko wrote in his journal: "Yes, the Russian soul has no skeleton. The soul, too, must have a skeleton so as not to bend under any pressure, so as to be steady and strong in action and in opposition. And we do not have this, or we have too little of it."

By skeleton, Korolenko means the moral imperative that compels a man to have the courage of his convictions and not to let himself be influenced. Ivan Bunin, in *The Well of Days* (1933), in his journal of the same period, made a similar observation: "The Russian peo-ple is terribly mercurial, or 'unsteady,' as they said in the old days. The people has said about itself: 'From us as from wood, one makes both cudgel and icon' depending on the circumstances and on who treats the wood: Saint Sergius of Radonezh or Emelyan Pugachev."

It is not by chance that so many foreigners took part in treating this wood: Varangians, Greeks, Tatars, Poles, Germans. And one must say that these intrusions did produce brilliant results at times in the cultural domain.

Yet another aspect of the Russian national character is what Dostoyevsky and other writers after him called the "universal com-passion" of the Russian soul. In his celebrated speech on Pushkin, in 1880, Dostoyevsky presented the poet as the prophetic figure who most fully expressed the "spirit of the Russian people," whose essence is the attraction "to universality and to all humanity." "To be a real Russian, to be entirely Russian, means ultimately to be the brother of all men, to be *pan-human*, if you will." These hyperbolic and overly rhapsodic remarks are in the spirit of the Russian mes-sianism toward which Dostoyevsky inclined. "Universal compas-sion" better describes the Russian culture than the Russian man and his mores. And yet one observes, even in the ways of simple people, a relative tolerance toward other nationalities. The Russian people is European, for all its Asian traits. Possibly this *relative* national tolerance was favored by the circumstances of history, which forced the Russian to live together, for better or worse, with the many tribes that populated Russia. This multinational diversity accus-tomed him to a breadth of vision, to close and sometimes friendly contacts with other nationalities. And even if one is far from the pan-human here, it is possible that this relative openness of the Russian soul helps to avoid too fierce an enmity toward others. The Russian people, in some measure, play the role of a buffer that the State uses to oppress other nationalities. Thus, despite their hostility toward Russians as the symbol and physical force of a great-power empire, these other nations may also see in them not only the inflexible exponents of the dominant nation, but ordinary people, with the usual human failings as well as the ability to understand the misfortunes of others.

But here one must add a contradictory peculiarity, the last in our composite of the Russian soul: the insularity, the satisfaction from the fact of being Russian (and thus good). And, conversely, the suspiciousness of other peoples, the intolerance, even xenophobia. Notions such as *svoy* (one's own) and *chuzhoy* (alien), *nashi* (ours) and *ne nashi* (not ours), are profoundly ingrained in the Russian psychology. This must go back to the patriarchal and familial structure, in which relations hinged on kinship. Is he from our clan? From our village? From our province? In short, Is he one of ours? Certain small peoples in the Caucasus refer to themselves nationally by names that, translated literally, mean "like us" or "our people."

Old Russian tales contain some amusing locutions on this score: "Then the not-ours came running" means "Then the devils came running." "Ours" can mean only Russians. Whereas the German spirit is alien, inhuman. The Russian word for Germans (*nemtsy*) has the same root as the word dumb (*nemy*): the Germans are those who can't speak Russian, "nonpersons," sometimes evil spirits. "Tatars" are those who come from Tartar, from Hell. But we Russians, we are bright, we are good, we are Orthodox, we are Slavs.

Of course, the roots have been forgotten in the Soviet usage of these words. But the distinction between ours and not ours persists, if in a more diffuse, less precise form. The old form, however, keeps resurfacing. The day before yesterday, ours were the Russians (or the boys from our village). Yesterday, ours were the Reds. Today, ours are the Soviet people. Tomorrow, ours could be the Whites or the any-old-colors. The nuances tied to a specific historical period are not that important. It's the principle that counts: ours or not ours.

This instinct runs very deep, and the Soviet power uses it for all it's worth; the distinction between ours and not ours is part of the psychology and the official language. When interrogating a dissident at the KGB, they often begin by saying: "You're not one of ours!" Then, to push him to repent: "But you're one of ours, aren't you? Answer! Are you, or aren't you?" One wants to ask: "Why do I have to be one or the other?" But that is forbidden. Because humanity is divided into ours and not ours. And this is rooted deep in the subconscious in the form of that disjunctive question: "Russian or non-Russian?"

Hedrick Smith writes in *The Russians:* "They are confident of Mother Russia as rock and refuge. It rarely seems to dawn on Russians, except for dissidents, that their land may be unvirtuous or guilty of moral transgressions. Their sense of moral innocence is . . . unshaken."[6]

But how does the distinction between ours and not ours reconcile with the universal compassion of the Russian soul, with the Russian's ability to be the universal man? It doesn't reconcile, of course, and the Russian national consciousness oscillates between acceptance of all nations — or almost all — (internationalism, universalism) and rejection of anyone who isn't Russian (xenophobia).

Xenophobia is one extreme and does not define Russian nationalism as a whole. But it still exists, which is why the offended nations sometimes consider that all Russians are xenophobes. One example: "Russian literature . . . has never had a good word for the peoples oppressed by the Russian power, the great writers have never lifted a finger to defend them." So says V. Zhabotinsky. This is unfair. There was Mikhail Lermontov who, during the war in the Caucasus, described the mountain-dwellers with profound respect; there was Lev Tolstoy with his *Hadji Murad;* there was Korolenko, who defended the Moslems . . .

I suggest that xenophobia in Russians is usually linked to a sense of their own poverty, misery, inferiority. This is the source of the contradiction: we Russians are the best because we have it the worst. But added to this is envy, a feeling that the revolution and the Soviet power stimulated by fanning the flames of the class

6. Hedrick Smith, *The Russians* (New York: Ballantine Books, 1977), pp. 414–415.

struggle. Now this class hostility suddenly assumed the form of hostility between nations, an explosion of hatred for rich countries, precisely because they are rich when we are poor. When Soviet forces invaded Czechoslovakia, there were people who said: "And right they were to do it! What didn't those Czechs have. They lived better than us Russians. And they still wanted more!"

This is class envy translated into national language. The Russian people, incidentally, have always thought of the nobility and the intelligentsia as foreigners. The differences in dress, language, comportment, designated them as "not ours." The barin was the man who came from somewhere else. In other words, class hostility again assumed a national form. One observes something similar in Soviet society when simple people treat an intellectual like a foreigner. But added to the envy is an idea of equality: if a person stands out, this means he's not one of us. Russian intellectuals have been known to be taken for Jews solely because they wore glasses or read a lot.

Given social equality and uniformity of life, the least suggestion of individuality is taken as an indication of nationality. A peasant says to a young Russian: "What are you, a Jew? Letting your beard grow like that!"

This sounds comical, since not so long ago all Russian peasants wore beards while the man who was clean-shaven was taken for a foreigner (a barin). Now it's the reverse: all Russians shave, and the man with a beard is "not ours."

The notion of ours versus not ours has become especially prevalent under the Soviet power. Years were devoted to ferreting out, diagnosing, and destroying the class enemy, branded as not ours. And when they finished with him, the national enemy appeared. Interestingly, the first signs of State anti-Semitism cropped up soon after they had liquidated the last class enemies, the kulaks, or prosperous peasants. The State itself converted class hatred into hostility between nationalities. Then came the "national class enemy": the Jew. Shortly after the Second Word War, the Jewish question became the critical issue it remains to this day. The Russians harbor numerous prejudices against the Jews, which are perhaps best expressed by the poet Boris Slutsky, who fought in the war:

*Jews don't sow grain.*
*Jews trade in shops.*
*Jews go bald sooner.*
*Jews steal more.*

*Jews are shrewd people,*
*But they make bad soldiers:*
*Ivan fights in the trenches,*
*Abraham holds down the co-op.*

In short, everything would be fine if it weren't for the Jews, suddenly become a sort of foreign body in the USSR. Even a Jew who was more Russian than the Russians carried something hostile to Russia and to the Russian people. He was an alien — and a hidden one at that — who must be rooted out. Thus the idea of the class struggle ended in anti-Semitism at all levels, from the top echelons of power down to ordinary, everyday life.

Some consider that the Jews brought this wave of anti-Semitism on themselves because they made the revolution. Bunin put it very simply in *The Well of Days:* "The 'left' blames the old regime for the revolution's 'excesses,' the Black Hundreds blame the Jews. But the people, they are innocent! What's more, they will pin everything on someone else: on a neighbor or the Jews. 'What have I done? I've done the same thing Ilya has. All this, it's the Jews who made us do it.' "

The Jews in the USSR are a bone in the craw, the new "class enemy" who must be liquidated. Why? Perhaps partly because the Jews have played the role of the Russian nobility in Soviet history. After the revolution, they occupied many posts in literature, in art, and in science. But it's absurd to want to get even with them for their having assumed this positive role of the intelligentsia.

Unlike many Russians who made careers in the Party or the administration, the Jews had no choice but to study, to educate themselves, and finally to form the intelligentsia that replaced the old, noble one. This filled the Russians with hatred — the sort of hatred plebeians feel for those who are more cultivated: this is the Russian's inferiority complex vis-à-vis the Jews.

The most unhappy people — the Russian People — want to find a non-Russian culprit. The logic is this: It can't be that we Russians are so bad as to have established the Soviet power and created the ruthless Communist State. We didn't do it; somebody else did. Then the rumors start: Russia is being run by foreigners, but since there are no foreigners, this must mean the Jews. Though Jews have long since been expelled from all positions of authority and from the government, whose policy at times has been openly anti-Semitic, still, in the mind of the Russian people it is the Jews who are in power. By way of explanation, one hears: "But how could a Russian government so oppress the Russian people? This is obviously not 'our' people, it's 'others.' " And who are these "others" mixed in with the Russian people? The Jews, of course. The Politburo is all Jews. The KGB too. Foreigners pretending to be "ours."

Russian anti-Semitism, I suggest, is not only hatred for Jews but the desire to cast off one's own sin, to externalize it as something "foreign" that has infiltrated "our" life. Plus the usual Soviet spy mania, the eternal search for the "saboteur," the "enemy."

In the early 1950s I had a conversation with a senior Party official anxious to prove, on the basis of Marxism-Leninism, that all Jews were traitors. He claimed that the Jews were the bourgeoisie, which had always engaged in commerce and was now selling the Soviet Union to the Americans. And all enemies of the people are Jews. In his view, Jews had replaced the class enemy. Destroy the last class enemy, and prosperity will reign.

### A GLIMPSE AT THE FUTURE

Now let's try to glimpse this empire's future from the angle of the nationalities question. It strikes me as rather somber. Either the empire will continue to swallow new countries, or it will disintegrate. Or both: one does not exclude the other. If independent states are emerging in Africa, why not in Georgia, Armenia, the Ukraine? There are no eternal empires; sooner or later, the Soviet Empire must disintegrate. This will be terrible for the Russians living in remoter regions; they will be slaughtered. And to assure the survival of the Russians within their own national borders, we may see Marxist ideology supplanted by Russian fascism. It is already in evidence: a grass-roots movement exists, as do several types of Russian fascism.

The first type is national bolshevism, the core of the Soviet State, for which Marxism and internationalism are only demagoguery. Its real idea is a great-power policy with the unhappy and mighty Russian people as its head.

The second type is outright fascism that has dispensed with all Marxist phraseology in favor of a direct appeal to the Russian people. It affirms itself by denouncing as principal adversaries the Jews (the internal enemy) and the West (the external enemy), alias an international Jewry. This fascism argues that the Jews want to rule the world. To this end, they first — as a provocation — invented Christ and Christianity, which they palmed off on Western Europe. Consequently, after the glory of Greco-Roman antiquity, Europe plunged into the gloom of the Middle Ages. And when, thanks to the Renaissance, it began to free itself from these chains, when national forces and states finally awoke, the Jews, in place of Christ, palmed another bomb off on Europe: Marx and his socialism.

The main enemies of this type of fascism are thus Christ and Marx. But if people must have a religion, then let them return to the cult of pagan national gods. The slogan is at the ready: "There is no other God besides Thor, and Hitler is his prophet." Thor corresponds to Perun in Russo-Slavic paganism. Of course, the cults of Thor, Perun, or Wotan are essentially decorative and refer to national sources free of all Judeo-European culture. This strain of fascism is unlikely to develop in Russia, if only because Russians are not of a pure race. The blood in their veins is a mixture: Tatar, Finnish, and many others. The Russian physiognomy does not square with the Aryan. For the unity of the nation, one must look for a broader definition.

Hence the third type of fascism: Russian Orthodox fascism. Its ideologues say the Russians are the Orthodox; whoever is not Orthodox is not Russian. Their ideal of a government is theocracy, or power of the church in place of that of the state. Their watchword: "Orthodoxy for the whole world!" One of their theoreticians, the dissident Gennady Shimanov, writes:

> The Soviet power is pregnant with theocracy. . . . The Soviet power is predestined to become the instrument of the creation on earth of the THOUSAND-YEAR KINGDOM, which has never existed before in world history, but which, according to the Scripture (if

you believe it), must come. . . . Such an absolute power has never existed before. . . . The monarchic regime treats society's dominant moods almost liberally. . . . And it is only now, with the formation of the Soviet State, that it has become possible for a PARTY, as absolute ruler unchallenged by any rival . . . to be guided not by something vague, like our former Sovereigns, but by a PROGRAM for the construction of a genuinely Christian society. . . . Assuming that the Communist Party must imminently transform itself into an ORTHODOX PARTY OF THE SOVIET UNION, we will then have a truly IDEAL STATE. . . . The Russian Revolution has UNIVERSAL implications and thus with time its fruits should be scattered throughout the world. After the Great October, it's a matter of ORTHODOXY FOR THE WHOLE WORLD, hence its Russification. The idea of the coming ORTHODOX THEOCRACY is the only creative idea we have today.

This may seem like gibberish, and no danger to the West, unlike communism. Certainly for the moment. But these ideas threaten Orthodoxy as much as they do the Christian religion, since they strive to turn religion into a leading party, an instrument of violence. The Soviet State is itself built like a church (where God is not). But the next stage would be to transform the Orthodox Church into a State founded on the structure of the Soviet Church. In other words, to leave everything the way it is, only having replaced the Red star with a cross. I don't know how feasible this is, but the attempt to unite Orthodoxy to a nationalistic State strikes me as extremely dangerous. Dangerous first of all for Orthodoxy and for Christianity, which, given this alliance with the State, with nationalism, with politics, could only lose. To marry the cross to the Red flag would be a disservice to the cross.

# Afterword: Can a Pyramid Be Converted into a Parthenon?

SOVIET CIVILIZATION is built of huge, heavy blocks. It is well suited to crushing human freedom, not to nourishing or stimulating it. Overall, it resembles an Egyptian pyramid constructed of mammoth pieces of stone, painstakingly fitted together, lapped, and polished. A mass of dead stone, an impressive monumentality dedicated to our once grandiose goals, now unattainable, for the usable space within is infinitesimal. Inside, a mummy: Lenin's. Outside, a windswept desert: sand. Such is the image.

These are the sorts of "stones" — metaphysical symbols of Soviet civilization — I have tried to reproduce in this book, a sort of a sketch, mentally breaking up the represented object to reveal different angles and cross sections. But how to extract these stones separately without damaging the whole? In fact, can they be extracted?

The revolution, for instance, which in a distant past rolled in so easily and then rolled away. Later on, it served as a colorful slogan for other achievements, other "revolutions" from above, counting on the enthusiasm of the masses. (Collectivization under Stalin, *perestroika* under Gorbachev: these are "revolutions from above" meant to be supported from below.) But this same revolution engendered a power unprecedented for the pressure it exerts on society and the people, a power from which there is no deliverance.

The utopian idea that, despite Marxism, is at the base of the pyramid is also immovable: ideology determines politics, politics determines economics.

Lenin remains to this day an unshakable authority. If one rejects him, what will be left of the Soviet power, of the "dictatorship of

the proletariat," of Soviet civilization? Yet Stalin came from Lenin.
In putting the accent on "unlimited violence," Lenin created the
Party bureaucracy, which he then tried to combat with bureaucratic
measures.

It might seem that we could easily dispense with Stalin, something we've been trying to do for over thirty years. His cruelty
doesn't suit socialism. We will attenuate the cruelty. But the criticism itself of Stalin, which has intensified recently in the Soviet
press, reveals the permanent role he played and continues to play in
the socialist State system and in the people's consciousness.

And what to do with the "new man" who, standing up to his
full height, displays heroism, slavish obedience, and blind self-
satisfaction simultaneously? As for the Soviet way of life and the
Soviet language, they are the transposition of general principles into
everyday life.

Today, we are seeing a renewal of a relatively ongoing phenomenon: Mikhail Gorbachev's *perestroika* (restructuring). Relatively ongoing because Khrushchev, with his "thaw," feared it would turn
into a real "spring" and, after consulting the Party apparatus, decided to "freeze" it. In his memoirs, published post facto, he writes
(referring to himself and the entire leadership): "We went ahead
with the thaw . . . and were consciously apprehensive about it. . . .
We restrained it, to some degree, so as to prevent it from causing a
flood."

Gorbachev seems to have gone farther. (Seems, because no one
knows anything. The information is nil, almost what it was under
Stalin. Maybe Gorbachev is wrestling with Boris Ligachev. Perhaps
they've agreed that one will brake while the other pushes *perestroika*.
The State power, as before and always, is shrouded in impenetrable
secrecy.) In any case, this is the first time Soviet civilization has
been put to the test of freedom. Will it stand up to it? Will it pass
this exam? a white-lipped intelligentsia inquires. For now, Gorbachev's only support is this intelligentsia, which welcomed and
took part in the verbal *perestroika* (the only kind so far), while the
Party bureaucracy resisted furiously and the people showed nothing
but indifference and passivity.

Consequently, a certain portion of the press has started using a
living language. For the first time, the press is interesting to read;

as they say in the USSR: "Today, the reading is more interesting than life." Given the changes in the language, one might think that the principles of this civilization were about to give way. This, of course, is an illusion. But it's worth noting to what extent, in the minds of contemporaries, this whole iron structure hinges on the word, on the official phrase.

The law of *glasnost* (openness) has its effect: "Don't feed us, but at least let us say that there's nothing to eat," the intelligentsia declares. And even the people are beginning to get out of hand: "Who the hell needs this *perestroika* when there's still nothing to eat!" The eternal divergence between the intelligentsia and the people: the one needs freedom, the other demands bread.

Slowly but surely, cities are winning back their original names. No one wants to live in a city once rechristened in honor of some hack or notorious criminal. The city of Ustinov has taken back its given name of Izhevsk (what a triumph!); the city Brezhnev is again Naberezhniye Chelny; the city Andropov is now Rybinsk; the city Mariupol as well as Leningrad University have rid themselves of that hateful yoke Zhdanov, bitter enemy and oppressor of Russian culture.

But if one takes this a little further, how should one deal with Leningrad? With Ulyanovsk (Simbirsk)? With Kalinin (Tver)? With Kaliningrad (Königsberg)? With Gorky (Nizhny Novgorod)? . . . This list alone makes one's head spin. The city of Togliatti found a nice solution: the old, illiterate peasants simply said Telyatev (thinking of calves: *telyata*).

It's gotten to the point where people are even carping about the formula "Power to the Soviets" (from which the Soviet Union was formed, with its entire system of political and linguistic ramifications). Where is it, they ask, this famous soviet power and what role does it play in our lives? Where are the soviets (or councils)? What and whom do they counsel?

At the same time, new stock words are turning up and dictating to life (forging the language): *perestroika,* or restructuring (to which Stalin already resorted); *glasnost* (instead of ordinary freedom of speech); "democratization" (that of the dictatorship). Everything has to be translated from one language into another. What can "socialist pluralism" mean? Heterodoxy within the bounds of orthodoxy? And what can they do with the "Soviet man" and "Soviet civilization"? Or perhaps this entire book has been about fictions, about what never existed.

And yet this time of *perestroika* has opened something up, something in the country has changed for the better. More specifically, many chronic diseases long kept secret are now better seen. Suddenly, it comes out that the Party, here and there, has turned into a terrarium, that the bureaucratic forces are threatening to become a banditocracy, that the Soviet Union almost across the board is a backward country. What don't they write about these days in the Soviet press! It's a storm of suicidal confessions. This tempest attests, first of all, to the mighty conservatism of a society which, for all its flapping about *perestroika,* never gets off the ground. Besides the bureaucracy, the country is weighted down by its huge army, by the KGB, by the necessity of retaining in the "socialist concord" the various republics and sister nations, by the inertia of the masses who, deprived of their own initiative for so long, have unlearned it . . .

I am far from thinking that *glasnost* and *perestroika* are only a smokescreen put up by a deft hand so as to deceive the Russian people and the West about impending "liberating reforms." I am glad of the *glasnost* proclaimed by "General Dissident" Gorbachev, who has transposed certain of Sakharov's ideas into the Party idiom. Nevertheless, it's impossible not to expect that one fine day all this *perestroika* will wheel around and start back along the beaten path to new frosts and stagnations. In the USSR it is easier to take away the fragile "freedoms" than to give them, to instill them.

Academician Tatyana Zaslavskaya, president of the Soviet Sociological Association, warns us of the possible dangers: "Our society has always been characterized by a very high concentration of power. . . . It has always had a strong ruling core, accountable to no one" (*Izvestia,* June 4, 1988).

"Always" means since Lenin. This permanent concentration of power in a few hands promises that attempts to democratize society are predestined to be thwarted by the hierarchy, followed more or less docily by the sprawling bureaucracy.

On the other hand, such attempts to democratize the system are only possible given the vigilant tolerance of courageous top leaders with the guts and the power to introduce "freedom" in measured doses and by means of authority. All of which creates a vicious circle. Democracy is insinuated on orders from the bosses, who are free at any moment to increase or restrict it. Coercion is the condition of this "freedom." Hence the inconsistency and timidity of *perestroika* which, as if frightened of itself, is forever glancing back at its "stagnant past."

For now we have no reason to doubt the sincerity of Mikhail Gorbachev and of his noble efforts and intentions. However, once again, Soviet liberalism and the sovereignty of the Russian people are ultimately contingent on the goodwill of the father-tsar and his loyal courtiers.

Judge for yourself: just like in the old days, it's still follow the leader; when journalists express a daring thought, they cite the highest authority, M. S. Gorbachev, who said it first (and include an appropriate quote). I cannot imagine Western journalists invoking the opinion of Mitterrand, or Bush, or any other president today with such enthusiasm. How long can this infantile game of the great Indian leader go on? As the unforgettable Mark Twain wrote in *A Connecticut Yankee in King Arthur's Court:* "It makes a mighty power, the mightiest conceivable, and then when it by and by gets into selfish hands, as it is always bound to do, it means death to human liberty and paralysis to human thought."

Judging from the current Soviet press, all the Party leaders — between Lenin and Gorbachev — have periodically proved to be, for some reason, of poor quality: villains, cowards, mongrels, half corpses, or unabashed miscreants. Next to Stalin, Brezhnev looks like a small-timer. For the dumbfounded reader, there is reason to despair. As if the entire life, history, and theory of the Soviet State have been in vain, only to man's detriment, a fiasco. The great slogans of Lenin and the October Revolution have yet to be made good. "Power to the Soviets," "Land to the Peasants," "Factories to the Workers": none of this exists. The only thing that survives is the dictatorship, buttressed by the bureaucracy.

In *Izvestia* Zaslavskaya reports:

As far as I know, not one deputy [to the Supreme Soviet — A.S.] in the last twenty-five years [and in the last fifty or sixty years or more?

— A.S.] has shown genuine and radical social initiative, even though he would have risked nothing, even though no action would have been taken against him no matter what his demands. . . . The Soviet . . . in effect rubber-stamps decisions prepackaged by the apparatus. . . .

The reaction (let's call it that) retains its forces. Extraordinarily influential rings of organized crime have been dismantled in this country. These rings united a degenerate element in the commercial sector, operators in the shadow economy, and even a corrupt part of the power apparatus, including the militia and the judiciary. These vast crime rings established a regime of lawlessness in their own territorial "wards." Certain mafias have been exposed and punished. But I suspect there are others in hiding. They can hardly be expected to wait passively: for them, *perestroika* signifies the end of everything. And they will stop at nothing.

To make up for this, people have new hope that now things will go right. The power is finally concentrated in deserving and capable hands. In other words, the one guarantee of freedom, progress, and enlightenment in Russia is, as always, tyranny.

The ancient Egyptian pyramid is with reason considered the most stable architectural form, far more solid and durable than the Parthenon. Where are they today, all those airy columned temples? But the pyramids are still standing! Thus, one may legitimately ask if, in general, a pyramid is amenable to *perestroika,* to restructuring? Especially that tackled with great revolutionary dispatch on orders from above? One could, of course, decorate it with a circular colonnade forming a sort of barbican, cover it with moldings, and put up a Greek portico. But will these foreign forms serve its purposes? Will they adapt to its edges? Won't they spoil the original style and profile?

This transparent allegory is an attempt to explain why, despite all my sympathy for the work of the reconstruction, I share the doubts of many concerning any radical dislocations meant to rejuvenate Soviet civilization in the democratic manner. What's the use of moving this pyramid if it will only crush you?

I will be happy if the reality exceeds my expectations and disproves these sad constructions.

# Postscript: The State of Europe

MANY OF OUR FRIENDS from the Soviet Union come to visit us in Paris — Soviet writers, artists and journalists — and I ask all of them: "Who is running the country? And what's going to happen tomorrow?" For a long time now I have been getting the same answer: "We don't know!"

Just think: this was my country, where for decades nothing happened, where one day was exactly like another, and you could predict the future years and kilometers ahead (turn to the right, and you join the Communist Party, eventually becoming one of the bosses; turn to the left, and they call you a dissident and put you in prison). Suddenly the country doesn't know what will happen next week. Nobody in the world knows.

We, the Russians, are once more in the vanguard, once more the most interesting phenomenon on earth — I would even say as an *artistic* phenomenon: like a novel whose ending none of us knows.

Little was needed to make this happen. First the people were granted a relative freedom of speech. Second the idea of global communism, for the sake of which so many pointless sacrifices had been made, was abolished (or at least forgotten for a while). And the very soil, as a result, proved to be immediately fruitful.

But it is here, too, that we find new dangers growing within the empire at its moment of transformation: the dangers of xenophobia and ethnic conflict. In particular, to judge from the press, I see a new form of Russian nazism gathering strength. I see the seeds of it, for instance, in a work recently published in Moscow by Igor Shafarevich entitled *Russophobia*, in which, developing one of Solzhenitsyn's ideas, the author builds up the myth of the Jews as the original and principal enemy of the Russian people. Igor Shafarevich is a world-class mathematician, a member of the Soviet Academy of Sciences, an honorary member or professor of several European academies and universities. Yet the argument of his book coincides with the theoreticians of German Nazism, from Hitler to Rosenberg (perhaps the coincidence is unconscious, but there are passages which seem like verbatim allusions). The thesis is couched in measured, reflective, academic terms. It can be summarized thus: a small people, that is the Jews (the Russophobes of the title), is waging a centuries-old battle to the death against a large nation (in this case Russia): "Russophobe literature is strongly influenced by Jewish nationalist sentiments," he writes. Among the Russophobes he numbers Galich and Vysotsky, Korzhavin and Amalrik, Grossman and Tarkovsky, Ilf and Petrov, Byalik and Babel. In the past, "the typical representative of this tendency [in this particular instance an anti-German one] was Heine." Similar efforts at domination by representatives of this small nation are found, he explains, in "the influence of Freud as a thinker, the fame of the composer Schönberg, the artist Picasso, the writer Kafka or the poet Brodsky." The aim of this small nation, writes Shafarevich in conclusion, "is the ultimate destruction of the religious and national foundations of our life, and at the same time, given the first opportunity, the ruthlessly purposive subversion of our national destiny, resulting in a new and terminal catastrophe, after which probably nothing will be left of our [i.e. the Russian] people."

I am by no means against the publication of Shafarevich's *Russophobia*, especially in Russia, after so many years of being deprived of the freedom of expression. But I am worried by the silence surrounding the appearance of this book, the absence of any serious discussion of it. The danger of the game Shafarevich is playing lies not so much in his ideas, which are trivial enough, as in the soil on which they are falling.

Anti-Semitic ideas have been taken up in the Soviet Union by both the mob and intellectuals. Two events took place recently in Moscow: an anti-Semitic demonstration by the society known as Pamyat (Memory), which was held in Red Square (and therefore had official permission from the authorities), and an anti-Semitic plenary session of the Union of Writers of the Russian Federation. The demonstration of the mob ended with it singing a song whose opening lines are:

> *Arise, thou mighty nation,*
> *Arise, take up the sword!*
> *Against the Yids' foul domination,*
> *Against that cursed horde*[1]

The speakers at the plenary meeting of Russian intellectuals included the distinguished novelists Valentin Rasputin and Vasily Belov. Rasputin accompanied Gorbachev on his visit to China; Belov went with him to Finland. The meeting ended with the demand that the editor of the literary journal *October* be dismissed for publishing works described as "anti-patriotic and Russophobe."

Nationalism in itself is not a serious threat — it can, on occasion, actually be of value to a nation — until it starts to produce, without any substantive grounds, that venomous by-product: "the enemy." In the past, the Soviet Union had the "class enemy." The struggle against the class enemy grew more and more intense just as all classes were being liquidated until indeed there were no more classes left. And now the Russian nationalists, who call themselves "patriots," have summoned up "Russophobia," a modification of the Leninist-Stalinist idea of "bourgeois encirclement" and "bourgeois penetration." The "Russophobe" is a variant of those terrible Stalinist inventions "enemy of the people" and "ideological saboteur."

All of them are, of course, myths.

But the definition of "Russophobia" has expanded to threatening dimensions. It incorporates the "soul-less" West, poisoned through and through by pornography and drug addiction and longing only to destroy the Russian people, who are the incarnation of mankind's conscience. Then there are the enemies within — the liberals and democrats, the intellectuals, the black-market operators, the dissidents and the Jews. Both the old-style myth of the bourgeois threat and the new version — Russophobia — I find equally repellent, not only for their vulgarity but for the very dangerous undertone of hatred which they contain. After all, if Russia's ills and misfortunes

---

1. Translation by Michael Glenny in *Granta* 30 (Winter 1990), pp. 151–154.

derive from its Western Russophobe enemies and its internal Russophobe enemies, and these enemies want to destroy the soul, the body, and the memory of the nation, of Russian culture and of the entire Russian people, why not put an end to all these "parasites," "cosmopolitans," and "pluralists" at a stroke?

When a multi-national empire disintegrates, or finds itself on the verge of falling apart, the peoples who constitute it develop various forms of nationalism. This has marked the breakup of many great empires. A powerful, militant Russian nationalism is arising to shore up and protect the Soviet Empire. As I see it from here, the Soviet Union at the moment is like a garage full of cans of petrol which are giving off so much vapour that the place is ready to explode. In that volatile atmosphere, the Russian nationalists are playing with matches, and one of the most inflammatory matches is called "Russophobia."

Why do they play with these matches? To bring about a national religious revival? God preserve us from any such thing! And may Christ forgive us for once again linking His name with the urge to launch massacres and pogroms.

# Index